The Promise of Democracy

The Promise of Democracy
Political Agency and Transformation

Fred Dallmayr

Published by State University of New York Press, Albany

© 2010 State University of New York

For information, contact State University of New York Press, Albany, NY www.sunypress.edu

Production by Kelli W. LeRoux
Marketing by Michael Campochiaro

Library of Congress Cataloging-in-Publication Data

Dallmayr, Fred R. (Fred Reinhard), 1928–
    The promise of democracy : political agency and transformation / Fred Dallmayr.
        p. cm.
    Includes bibliographical references and index.
    ISBN 978-1-4384-3039-3 (hardcover : alk. paper)
    1. Democracy.   2. Democracy—Philosophy.   I. Title.

JC423.D278 2010
321.8—dc22   2009021089

10 9 8 7 6 5 4 3 2 1

To all young people willing and eager
to practice democracy

Everything depends on establishing this [civic] love in a republic.

—Montesquieu

Democracy is more than a form of government; it is primarily a mode of associated living, of conjoint communicated experience.

—John Dewey

To understand and judge a society, one has to penetrate its basic structure to the human bond upon which it is built.

—Maurice Merleau-Ponty

Democracy needs to be reconceived as something other than a form of government: as a mode of being that is constituted by bitter experience . . . but is a recurrent possibility as long as the meaning of the political survives.

—Sheldon Wolin

Contents

Appendices

Preface

The modern age is often described as an era of science and industry—and also of democracy. Since the time of the European Enlightenment, societies have been rocked by powerful upheavals, and most prominently by democratic or semi-democratic revolutions. The French thinker Alexis de Tocqueville saw these upheavals as momentous signposts and democracy as a near-providential destiny. Ideologies and ideological movements have sprung up in support of this destiny. During the twentieth century, great wars have been fought to make the world "safe for democracy"; and the end is not in sight. In tandem with this massive upsurge, however, grave doubts have arisen regarding its trajectory. In the view of some, the historical trajectory has come to a halt; for others; democracy finds itself now in deep crisis.

A leading American political philosopher has written a book recently raising the question "Is democracy possible here?" (and providing only a very ambivalent answer). In turn, political theorist Jean Bethke Elshtain has published a stirring text titled *Democracy on Trial*. Focusing mainly on American democracy, Elshtain pinpoints as a central concern the "danger of losing democratic civil society" under the onslaught of rampant fragmentation and self-aggrandizement. Although a properly construed democratic agency, she writes, is "not boundless subjectivist or self-seeking individualism," the worry is that "it has, over time, become so." Once this happens, "the blessings of democratic life that Tocqueville so brilliantly displayed—especially the spirit of equality—give way" and in their place "other more fearful and self-enclosed, more suspicious and cynical habits and dispositions rise to the fore."[1]

Worries of this kind are not fanciful, but are grounded in real-life experience as well as in broader historical considerations. What is at stake is not so much or not only (as is often claimed) the relation between individual liberty and security, but that between liberalism and democracy itself. Apart from its other epithets, modernity is also called the time of the unfolding of human freedom; and as a modern

ix

regime, democracy cannot possibly deny the claims of freedom. But here history enters the scene. Modern liberalism arose in the eighteenth century, well before the rise of democracy; hence, there is a sibling rivalry with the elder frequently trying to trump or erase the other. As it happens, early liberalism typically located individual liberty in a presocial and prepolitical "state of nature," a stratagem that inevitably places political democracy in a subordinate or derivative position. This claim of a presocial or prepolitical status is the source of the rampant "individualism" about which Elshtain complains. In our time, under the aegis of neo-liberalism and *laissez-faire* market ideologies, this hankering for a presocial (Hobbesian) "state of nature" has reached its zenith, with the result of undercutting democracy as a shared political regime. Although hard to believe in a presumably "civil" or civilized period, we now have bands of mercenaries and well-paid "hired guns" providing for "public security and peace" without any public accountability. As someone has observed (and only half in jest): democracy is being "outsourced," or has already been outsourced, to private contractors.

Tired of cumbersome bureaucracies, some well-meaning individualists—including some "postmodern" intellectuals—may find appealing the thought of exiting society and "return to nature." On closer inspection, however, they may want to revise their inclination. Returning to nature here does not mean escaping to an idyllic island. In the vocabulary of Thomas Hobbes—to which modern Western thought remains deeply indebted—the so-called "state of nature" is also a state of incessant warfare, of relentless killing or being killed. In the opinion of the political philosopher mentioned above, we are getting close or have already reached that condition. "American politics," he writes, "is in an appalling state.... We are no longer partners in self-government; our politics are rather a form of war."[2] Well-meaning people, especially devoted democrats, should ponder this fact. For, in unregulated warfare—and departing somewhat from the Hobbesian scenario—killing does not happen in an egalitarian fashion. Typically, killing is being done by the side with superior weapons, superior manpower, and superior financial resources. Thus, in a modern state of nature, warfare (civil or uncivil) tends to pit the powerful against the powerless, the rich against the poor, the ruthless against the cautious. What is equally distributed in this condition—which Hobbes correctly described as "nasty, solitary, and brutish"—is only the pervasive sense of fear or what today we prefer to all "terror." Those enamored with the "downsizing" of politics and the project of "privatizing" everything in sight should note well the end point of their project: the unleashed condition of mayhem and fear, with everyone trying to terrorize everyone else.

Have things gone too far already? Maybe so. But this only means that particularly dedicated efforts have to be made to change course and to champion resolutely a "return to the political": in the sense of a return to a well-ordered regime or *polis* committed to justice and ethical well-being. In our time, this has to be a return to democracy—or rather the anticipation of a possible, although not presently actual, democratic regime. As another political theorist has recently remarked: "We could take the perfect storm threatening democracy as an occasion—an instigation—to reinvent boat(s) more worthy of journeys to the democratic promise."[3] It is in this spirit that this volume takes the present dismal condition as an "instigation" to pursue another possibility or potentiality: the largely untapped "promise of democracy" or what Jacques Derrida has called "democracy to come." To be able to move in this direction, however, a radical change or transformation (perhaps a *Kehre*) has to happen: a change from rampant self-interest and fragmentation in the direction of a more generous and other-directed disposition, a disposition sensitive to the needs of others and of society as a whole (as well as societies around the world). This disposition has traditionally been called attentiveness to the "common good" where everyone can participate in the "goodness" (not the fear or mayhem) of a shared public life.

In charting a course in this direction, this book is inspired by a number of great philosophers or thinkers both in the past and the present. A distant, although pervasive, influence is Aristotle's conception of politics as a sustained *praxis*, as an ethical engagement ideally approximating friendship. In modern times, a major instigation or provocation for me has been Montesquieu's *The Spirit of Laws*. As will be remembered, Montesquieu portrayed democracy not as a machine or a Hobbesian artifact but rather as a political regime sustained by a distinct spirit or ethical disposition: the "love of democracy," which is a "love of equality"—where the latter does not mean a quantitative measure but an equality of care and mutual esteem. As one may also recall, Montesquieu defined the central disposition in despotism as "fear"—which speaks volumes about contemporary societies dominated by nothing but fear of terror. Montesquieu's lead was followed, with changed accents, in Hegel's notion of a public *ethos* or *Sittlichkeit* and in de Tocqueville's emphasis on a vibrant civil or associational life. Among later or more recent perspectives, this volume pays particular tribute to American pragmatism, and especially to a philosopher too widely neglected by contemporary political theorists: John Dewey.

Among the great merits of Dewey's work was his emphasis on the needed ethical fiber of democracy, as well as his insistence on keeping thinking and *praxis* closely together, in lieu of the fashionable retreat of philosophy into esoteric abstractions. Another great merit—particularly salient for democratic theory—was Dewey's "holistic" reformulation of political agency in such a way that, in the course of action, both agent and world are simultaneously shaped or transformed.

In my view, it was a great misfortune (approximating an unmitigated disaster) that, in the middle of the twentieth century, Deweyan pragmatism was cavalierly brushed aside in favor of philosophical doctrines massively imported from Europe: especially logical positivism (from Vienna) and analytical philosophy (from England). Basically, this shift signaled a return to some of the more dubious features of modern Western thought: especially Cartesian rationalism with its bifurcations of mind and body, subject and object, thought and practice. From a Deweyan perspective, the development meant the renewed upsurge of (what he called) the "spectator theory of knowledge," manifest in the primacy of logic and epistemology, and the almost complete erasure of ethics and practical politics from sustained philosophical attention.[4] The primacy exacted a cost. To a considerable extent, it accounts for the fact that some of the most egregious political derailments in recent history were rarely noticed in academia and often met only with "deafening silence" on the part of professional philosophers.

The sidelining of pragmatism also had effects in a field presumably preoccupied with politics: political philosophy and political theory. Apart from some efforts to embrace scientific epistemology, political thought tended to become backward-looking and historical or else esoteric, thus shying away from concern with ongoing political affairs—including the deepening malaise of democracy. Favorite preoccupations of political theorists became ancient writers, early liberalism and the "founding fathers"—but not (or rarely) the cultivation of civic dispositions needed in democracy. There were exceptions, to be sure. But even among theorists specifically concerned with contemporary issues, there was a strong tendency to favor an individualistic brand of liberalism, that is, to celebrate private inwardness and disconnected subjectivism—which is another way of leaving politics behind.

This book pays tribute to pragmatism, but not in a doctrinaire or historicist way. As I believe, and as Dewey would surely have agreed, the only way to honor his work is to move beyond it with the changing times. Another figure invoked in the text is a thinker who is rarely suspected of pragmatist affinities: the German philosopher Martin Heidegger. Even more radically than Dewey, Heidegger has been sidelined or expunged by the political theory "establishment." In fact, there is hardly a recent thinker who has been more thoroughly vilified and even demonized by supposedly "liberal" and progressive intellectuals; frequently this is done with the fervent closed-mindedness that the same intellectuals would severely castigate in the case of religious "fundamentalists." (There is also, I am afraid, a liberal fundamentalism.) The condemnation often is based on a deliberate "shunning" or nonreading of Heidegger's work—or else a selective reading of a few (admittedly unfortunate) writings of the period between 1933 and 1935. In this book, I invoke a number of other writings, texts that—in a pragmatic manner—elaborate on the basic meaning of *praxis*, especially the *praxis* of "letting be." At another point I refer to his innovative construal of "humanism" in the sense of connectedness.

As I point out in the introduction, the book moves from Dewey and Heidegger to a number of other political thinkers or philosophers who have been broadly influenced by Heidegger or else by some other recent Continental-European authors; these thinkers include Hannah Arendt, Ernesto Laclau, Chantal Mouffe, and Jacques Derrida. In every instance, an effort is made to explore their closeness to, or distance from, central pragmatic teachings and the contributions their writings can make to the promotion of a viable democracy. From this examination of individual authors the book turns to a discussion of broader themes: first, the idea of a nondomineering "humanism" compatible with democratic self-rule; and next, the relation of democracy to various forms of contemporary religious resurgence, with special attention to Islam. The book concludes with a critical review of the dominant Western model of democracy—liberal proceduralism or minimalism—enlisting for this critique voices from East and West, but especially the teachings of Mahatma Gandhi regarding the need for an ethical and self-limiting *swaraj* (self-rule).

By emphasizing the ethical dimension of democracy I run several risks, especially the risk for either outright rejection or else gross misunderstanding. It has become customary among liberal political theorists—and also some "postmodern" thinkers—to denounce notions like the "good life" or the "common good" as incompatible with individual freedom. Particularly in our time of multiculturalism, it is claimed, the idea of a common good stifles the unfolding of cultural, ethnic, or religious differences. The claim is a complete *non-sequitur*. On the contrary: it is precisely in the context of "deep" pluralism that shared ethical or civil bonds are needed that allow differences to "be" and to unfold into the fullness of their potential. As political theorist William Connolly has rightly remarked, a multicultural or culturally "plural" democracy requires the practice of "receptive generosity"—clearly an ethical virtue—on the part of all participants.[5] But such generosity does not just occur without further ado (as an *a priori* endowment); rather, it needs precisely to be "practiced," that is, nurtured and cultivated over time. And this can only happen in a conducive civil context—the context of an ethical and plural democracy.

This brings into view the importance of education in any present and future democracy. Among political philosophers, no one has highlighted this linkage of democracy and education more eloquently than Dewey—who has not had many successors. The notion of an education in and for democracy is sometimes accused of fostering brainwashing or mind control; but apart from presupposing an a-social mind, the charge only holds for miseducation. As Dewey has shown, democracy does not deal with "finished" agents (endowed by nature with everything needful), but with human beings constantly in the process of formation, of the difficult sorting out of good and ill potentialities. Basically, democracy means that people rule themselves; and if they cannot do this, they will be ruled by others (elites or tyrants). But people are not "by nature" able to rule themselves; hence, self-rule—like any competence—has to be learned and practiced, as part of educational formation. Far from involving brainwashing, educational formation hence aims at something good: the goodness of not wishing to dominate others but to live with others exercising "receptive generosity" in democratic fashion. Seen from this angle, "goodness" does not denote induction into some doctrine, but the willingness and ability to "over-rule" oneself, when needed, in favor of the well-being of others. To this extent, democracy is a form of *orthopraxis* rather than orthodoxy.

Generally speaking, the study presented here aims to underscore the importance of ethical practice and educational formation in democracy—as long as the latter's "promise" is kept alive. Additionally, emphasis is placed on the need to cultivate a proper mode of democratic agency: one that shuns mastery and hyperactivism, as well as passive withdrawal, and thus allows for transformative horizons to emerge. The book was written and is published at an auspicious time when some dark clouds are lifting or at least receding. During the past decade it has appeared to me that the world was drifting steadily into the morass of unlimited violence, blood-lust, and brutality; even in supposedly civilized countries there was an upsurge of unsuspected levels of savagery. But now at last, some rays of hope seem to be breaking into the darkness. Unexpectedly, young hearts and minds are opening themselves again to the call for a good and decent way of life—and hence to the "promise" of democracy.

The usual acknowledgments are in order. As in the past, my thinking has been greatly stimulated and enriched by a number of colleagues and friends. Among them I should mention here, above all, Charles Taylor, William Connolly, Ernesto Laclau, Chantal Mouffe, Bhikhu Parekh, Hwa Yol Jung, Stephen White, and Richard Falk. Many other individuals, of course, have also participated in my ongoing "formation" (*Bildung*). I owe a special thanks again to Cheryl Reed who, with her usual competence and efficiency, has typed and helped correct several versions of the book. My deepest debt of gratitude goes, as always, to my family—my wife Ilse (with whom I recently celebrated our 50th wedding anniversary) and our children Dominique and Philip for being the ever-nurturing soil of my thinking and living.

Fred Dallmayr

1

Introduction

The Promise of Democracy

To present democracy as a "promise" means that it is not presently an actuality or concrete reality. But at the same time, to call it a "promise" does not stamp it a mere whim or empty pipe dream. For, a genuine promise is somehow anchored or latently present in reality: as a possibility or potentiality whose realization may require a long process of maturation and cultivation. Thus, a child may have the promise of becoming a great artist or scientist—but this is not going to happen by itself or without further ado; in fact, it usually requires sustained practice and training. For too long, democracy has been treated either as a readily achieved fact, or else as a hopeless illusion (hopeless because of human viciousness). Little investigation is required to see that presently existing democracies are in large measure travesties, given the enormous abuses and glaring inequalities flourishing in them. As it appears, many so-called liberal democracies hover just an inch over a war-like "state of nature," with slim procedural formalities serving as fig leaves to cover prevailing modes of domination. But it also seems to be a fact of life that millions of people around the world eagerly cling to democracy as a hope or promise to rescue them from their miseries.

To say that millions of people in the world hope for democracy may seem a bold and not fully persuasive claim. As cynics are prone to retort: what people are eagerly striving for are food, shelter, and a decent living—not democracy. However, the retort easily can be rebutted. People striving for food, shelter, and decent living also necessarily strive for a society in which the production and distribution of goods is equitably managed from the people's angle—and this happens (or is meant to happen) precisely in a democracy. Another objection is more difficult to answer because it relies on theological and metaphysical

1

arguments. When we speak of promise in an elevated sense, the objection goes, we usually mean something like the "promised land," the "coming kingdom," the "reign of the Mahdi," or the like—and none of these phrases is a synonym for democracy. In fact, according to some "fundamentalist" theologians, the rule of God and the rule of the people are radically incompatible, such that the latter undermines the former. I cannot fully delve into this issue here (some of it has to be left to the rest of the study)—except to point out: If it is true, as many religions hold, that the "image" of God is implanted in the human heart, then it would seem to follow that, rather than being a pointless appendix, that image is meant to become steadily more manifest in history and approximate society to a promised democracy (which is not at all the opposite of God's kingdom).

Allowing myself to be inspired at least in part by this trajectory, I turn now to several more immediate concerns having to do with democracy as a political regime. First, I discuss the possibility of seeing democracy as an ethical or properly humane form of political life. Next, I turn to detractors of this view, especially to procedural minimalists and rational choice theorists. Finally, I reflect on the promise of democracy in the context of current debates regarding modernity versus postmodernity and against the backdrop of the relentless process of globalization.

Democracy as an Ethical Community

Throughout long stretches of human history, democracy has had a bad press. Philosophers as well as theologians assigned the common people—presumably in charge of democracy—to the low end of a totem pole whose upper reaches were reserved for kings, priests, and sages. Predicated on a fixed or "essentialist" metaphysics, the people were assumed to be base, fickle, and incapable of self-rule—and hence needed to be governed by a qualified elite in the same manner as passion needs to be governed by reason and desire by duty and moral principles. To be sure, different societies exhibited variations of this scheme and different historical contexts allowed for modifications. The most illustrious modification—a kind of fluke of Western history—was the Greek and especially the Athenian *polis*. However, as we know, this "cradle" of Western democracy did not produce a sturdy and long-lasting offspring. Quite apart from being severely limited in its membership, the *polis* was in a way sandwiched between very undemocratic alternatives: the earlier period of tyrants or despots, and the later periods of imperial domination (omitting here the interlude of the Roman Republic). One reason for the short-lived or episodic character of the *polis* may have been the prevalence of a static metaphysics that seemed to foreclose the possibility of genuine transformation (as exemplified by the institution of slavery).

It was not until the period of the early Renaissance that something akin to the Greek *polis* (or the Roman Republic) emerged again in Europe. Particularly in the context of the Italian city-states, the classical spirit of civic autonomy and participatory citizenship resurfaced again in several places; at the same time, learned humanists sought to infuse city life again with some elements of classical (Aristotelian or Stoic) virtues. However, the times were not propitious to this kind of political classicism: soon city-states were overwhelmed by the rise of modern kingdoms or nation-states, while classical learning succumbed to the powerful onslaught of modern rationalism or "enlightened" rationality. The rise of rationalism brought to the fore a radically new worldview or metaphysics. In lieu of the older hierarchical (and qualitatively differentiated) order, modern science favors quantitative measurement, a conception where general laws neutrally govern all parts of the world. In the words of Theodor Adorno, "number" became the modern passkey unlocking the secrets of the universe.[1] Despite the noted radical shift, however, there were at least two important markers of continuity. The first marker was the acceptance of a fixed, static essentialism prevailing outside of human conventions: according to the founders of modern "liberalism," human beings were said to be endowed by "nature" (or nature's God) with certain *a priori* properties, especially liberty and equality. The second, and equally crucial marker was the privilege accorded to reason or rationality (what Descartes called the *cogito* or thinking substance). With this privileging of rationality—presumably shared by all humans—the modern age became saddled with a string of bifurcations or divisions that persist to our time: the divisions between mind and matter, subject and object, thought and practice, duty and sensibility. It is these divisions that Hegel later called "diremptions" (*Entzweiungen*) and that he valiantly strove to overcome through a more "holistic" philosophy.

As one should note, the quantitative and egalitarian character of modern metaphysics did not directly entail an endorsement of democracy. After all, a philosophical conception where all particular elements are equally subject to uniform rules is readily compatible with the kind of enlightened absolutism prevalent during the Age of Enlightenment or else constitutional monarchies constrained by a general rule of law. For enlightened absolutism to give way to democracy a new shift was required, a radically new metaphysics that looks at the world not from the "top down" but from the "bottom up." Basically, what the shift called for was an outlook that may be called a metaphysics of potentiality or possibility: that is, a perspective that treats ordinary people as potentially capable of self-government—*potentially*, which means not by nature or without further ado, but as corollary of a process by which "natural" endowments are translated into practical competences. This process is nothing else but a process of learning and ethical transformation. During the heyday of the Enlightenment only a few voices articulated such a metaphysics of potentiality, but some did it with great verve and insight. Some of the names that can be mentioned in this context are Giambattista Vico, Erasmus, and Johann Gottfried Herder—the latter especially through his idea of a "cultivation toward humanity" (*Emporbildung zur Humanität*). But by far the most famous philosophical pioneer of the time was Gottfried Wilhelm Leibniz. In his metaphysics, Leibniz departed from both the ancient and the modern worldviews: he did not subscribe to a qualitative hierarchy where some elements would for ever be inferior to others; but neither did he subscribe to the modern bifurcations of mind and matter, reason and passion. As seen from his angle, the universe was rather a network—and a steadily expanding network—of interactions and relationships, with each element mirroring and being mirrored in all others, in a complex process of learning and transformation.[2]

Leibniz was not himself a political philosopher; but some of his thoughts could be marshaled in support of democracy—especially if his "relationism" is seen as the antipode to super- and subordination and if transformation is grasped as an ethical or "spiritual" process. Without directly relying on Leibniz, the needed political shift was accomplished with erudition and élan by Montesquieu. As it happens, by the time of Montesquieu, almost all political thinkers had fallen in line with Thomas Hobbes by considering the "polity" or political "state" as nothing but a machine or mechanical artifact constructed with the help of a "contract" reflecting human rationality. Hobbes had consigned whatever ethical inspiration might have been involved in this construction to a private sphere (*forum internum*) with little or no effect on public life. With greater or lesser enthusiasm, most of the "liberal" successors of Hobbes shared the addiction to machines and mechanical procedures. Some relief was provided for a time by a group of Scottish moralists who sought to reconnect social and ethical life—but failed to overturn the Hobbesian paradigm. Viewed against this background, Montesquieu's *The Spirit of Laws* was a revolutionary intellectual event. Instead of being the outgrowth of contractual engineering, political regimes for Montesquieu are animated by a qualitative disposition he called their *esprit général* or *caractère commun*. Whereas the animating spirit or disposition in monarchies, in his view, is "honor" and whereas despotic regimes are pervaded by "fear," the animating well-spring or soul of democratic regimes is a relational kind of virtue: namely, "love of the democracy," which in turn means "love of equality." This spirit or disposition, *The Spirit of Laws* states explicitly, is not a merely cognitive or theoretical virtue or "a consequence of acquired knowledge"; rather, it is "a sensation that may be felt by the meanest as well as the highest person in the state."[3]

"Love of equality" in Montesquieu's work is sometimes taken to be a synonym for egalitarianism—which is far from the mark. In his account, equality does not designate a quantitative or mathematical formula but rather a qualitative, ethical relationship. Moreover, equality is not a static *a priori* essence, but rather a possibility or potentiality requiring nurturing care. Like every other form of love, love of equality demands steady cultivation so that possible dispositions grow into the animating spirit of a regime. This is the reason why Montesquieu puts such emphasis on general education—an aspect ignored by most other Enlightenment philosophers (apart from Rousseau). As he writes in one of the early chapters of his book: It is in a democratic (or republican) regime "that the whole power of education is required"; for love of equality, like every ethical virtue, involves "a self-renunciation which is always arduous and painful." Hence, in a democracy, "everything depends on establishing this love [of equality] in a republic, and to inspire it ought to be the principal business of education; but the surest way of instilling it into children, is for parents to set an example." Wherever this effort is neglected, by contrast, the alternate possibility of corruption and injustice quickly comes to the fore: For, "whenever virtue is banished, ambition invades the heart of those who are capable of receiving it, and avarice possesses the whole community."[4]

As one should note, Montesquieu broke with the Hobbesian model not only by his reliance on *esprit* but also through his conception of "law"—which he construed not as a command from a superior to an inferior but rather as an ethical linkage (in line with Leibnizian relationism). In both his invocation of spirit and his conception of law, Montesquieu earned the strong praise of the German philosopher Hegel. As the latter observed in his introduction to the *Philosophy of Right*, Montesquieu upheld indeed "the true historical view and the genuinely philosophical position, namely, that legislation [or law] both in general and in its particular provisions is to be treated not as something isolated and abstract but rather as an integral moment in a whole, interconnected with all the other features which make up the character of a nation and an epoch." Only when seen in terms of this "holism" or interconnectedness do laws acquire "their true meaning and hence their justification." At a later part of his treatise, Hegel applauds "the depth of Montesquieu's insight in his now famous treatment of the animating principles of forms of government." This insight, he adds, is particularly evident in the discussion of democracy where virtue is extolled as the governing principle, "and rightly so because that regime rests in point of fact on moral sentiment (*Gesinnung*) seen as the purely substantial form in which the rationality of absolute will appears in democracy."[5] As is well known, of course, Hegel's *Philosophy of Right* was not a primer of democracy, but placed its focus on the ethical and legal requisites of constitutional monarchy. Yet, several crucial elements of his perspective, above all the notions of ethical life (*Sittlichkeit*) and moral sentiment (*Gesinnung*), can be recuperated as part of a democratic *ethos*—as I show in chapter 2, "Hegel for Our Time."

By the time of Hegel's treatise, a new democratic (or republican) regime had emerged in America following a prolonged struggle for independence from the British monarchy. The founders of the new regime relied largely on classical examples, but also incorporated important features of Montesquieu's *The Spirit of Laws* into their constitutional design. Innovative both in terms of geographical size and the combination of guiding ideas, the American republic was studied with great attentiveness by observers around the world. By far the most astute and perceptive observer was a traveler from France: Alexis de Tocqueville. Profiled against monarchical France and the largely hierarchical order of the *ancien régime*, de Tocqueville immediately perceived the close connection between democracy and equality. Among all the "novel objects" confronting the visitor, the opening sentence of *Democracy in America* reads, "nothing struck me more forcibly than the general equality of condition among the people." Impressed by the American example and the successive democratic revolutions in Europe at that time, de Tocqueville was tempted to succumb to the lure of historical teleology, stating: "The gradual development of the principle of equality is, therefore, a providential fact. It has all the chief characteristics of such a fact: it is universal, it is lasting, it constantly eludes all human interference, and all events as well as all men contribute to its progress." Happily, a few paragraphs later, he caught himself, turning from teleology to potentiality, speaking of a movement "already so strong that it cannot be stopped" but "not yet so rapid that it cannot be guided." In fact, guidance or pedagogy was central to de Tocqueville's approach. He shunned the idea of people's "natural" (*a priori*) competence for self-rule. In many or most instances, he complained, democracy has actually been "abandoned to its wild instincts, and it has grown up like those children who have no parental guidance, who receive their education in the public streets, and who are acquainted only with the vices and wretchedness of society."[6]

During the nineteenth century, democracy in America grew by leaps and bounds, both in terms of geographical expansion and (more importantly) by deepening its "democratic" quality and removing some earlier autocratic or paternalistic restrictions. This growth of democracy reached important fruits in the domain of scientific and industrial "progress"; but it also led to a steady seasoning of American cultural self-understanding. Some of the important markers of this cultural maturation were Henry George's *Progress and Poverty* (1879), Edward Bellamy's *Locking Backward* (1888), and the so-called American "utopian" movement. However, the high point of cultural and political self-awareness came in the late nineteenth and early twentieth centuries with the emergence of a broad intellectual movement called American "pragmatism." Among this group of gifted scholars and writers John Dewey stands out because of his sustained attention to democracy and democratic theory. In my view, Dewey is a crucial figure in this context because he raised democracy to the level of philosophical transparency (or else lifted philosophical reflection to the demands of modern democracy). Basically, Dewey not only broke with the traditional hierarchical worldview; he also boldly overturned the modern Cartesian or rationalistic metaphysics with its bifurcations of mind and matter, subject and object, thought and practice. Inspired in part by Leibniz's relationism and Hegel's striving for the reconciliation of opposites, Dewey formulated a powerful "holistic" pragmatism that can serve as a passkey to modern democratic politics no longer held hostage by Hobbesian social engineering.

In chapter 3, "Democratic Agency and Experience," I outline Dewey's main contributions in this field. As I show, Dewey in a way "democratized" philosophy by linking it closely with ordinary experience. In a nutshell, philosophizing for him did not mean the rehearsal of perennial ideas stored up in cerebral archives; nor does it permit retreat into the abstract (socially vacuous) realms of pure logic and epistemology—a retreat extremely prominent in modern Western thought. In order to remain humanly salient and fruitful, philosophizing has to remain open and alert to uncharted experiential encounters—without succumbing to the lure of partisan ideologies. In addition to the stress on uncharted "inquiry," Dewey also democratized philosophy by placing it in the reach of ordinary people—although not as a ready-made endowment. His pragmatism was radically opposed to the modern infatuation with *a priori* essences or properties (properties given to people by "nature" or nature's God). Turning against this tenet of early liberalism, Dewey relied on educational nurturing—which turns liberty into a process of potential liberation and equality into a deepening "love of equality." His philosophy is frequently associated with a "progressive" style of education—but the linkage is often misconstrued. The point for him was not to put the student or pupil in the "driver's seat," undercutting the labor of learning—something that would have led back to an essentialist or *a priori* metaphysics. Rather, just like philosophical inquiry itself, pedagogical efforts have to register with the student's background and experiential capacity.

Probably the most important aspect in which Dewey overturned the Hobbesian model was his emphasis on democracy as an ethical fabric requiring cultivation. In contrast to the modern fascination with artifacts and procedures, Dewey sought to uncover the underlying dispositions and motivations, which alone render procedures viable. In this respect, he clearly followed in the footsteps of Montesquieu, and also of Hegel's teachings regarding "ethical life" (*Sittlichkeit*). His repeated statements on this issue are eloquent and justly famous. As he writes in his well-known study *Democracy and Education* (1916): "The devotion of democracy to education is a familiar fact"—but a fact not always fully understood and which needs to be traced to the character of the regime itself: "A democracy is more than a form of government; it is primarily a mode of associated living, a conjoint communicated experience." To this may be added a passage penned in 1939, at the beginning of World War II.

> Democracy is a way of life controlled by a working faith in the possibilities of human nature. Belief in the "common man" is a familiar article of the democratic creed. That belief is without basis and significance save as it means faith in the potentialities of human nature as that nature is exhibited in every human being irrespective of race, color, sex, birth and family, of material or cultural wealth. This faith may be enacted in statutes, but it is only on paper unless it is put in force in the attitudes which human beings display to one another in all the incidents and relations of daily life.[7]

There is another issue where Dewey turned the tables on modern rationalism: the theory of action or agency. Here, in opposition to the engineering "cause-and-effect" model, Dewey proposed the idea of the "unity of the act"—meaning that the effect is not unilaterally produced but that agent and effect co-constitute each other so that (political) agency becomes a midpoint between acting and reacting, doing and suffering.

It is particularly in the latter respect that Dewey's pragmatism links up with European philosophical perspectives in the twentieth century, especially phenomenology and existentialism. As a student of Edmund Husserl (the founder of modern phenomenology), Martin Heidegger often is described as an existential or else "hermeneutical" phenomenologist (a description I accept here). Despite massive apprehensions or prejudices surrounding Heidegger's political engagements, I hold that aspects of his work are crucially important for the development of a viable democratic theory. The main aspect or feature that I highlight in chapter 4, "Agency and Letting-Be," is the notion of action or agency and its relation to experience. Like Dewey, Heidegger radically turned away from the Cartesian or rationalistic worldview. Instead of finding the linchpin of the universe in the *cogito*, the German philosopher inserts human beings into a primary relationship that he terms "being-in-the-world." Again as in the case of Dewey, this change has a profound effect on the conception of agency. Opposing the modern construal of action as the instrumental production of effects, Heidegger portrays the core of action as "fulfilling" (*vollbringen*). What is fulfilled or accomplished in the action is not so much the goal or effect but rather the human quality or humanity of the agent. What in particular discloses this quality is the degree of the agent's openness or receptivity to the claims of others, an openness that transforms action into the midpoint between doing and suffering—something Heidegger calls "letting-be" (*Seinlassen*) and that is far removed from both indifference and manipulative control. As can readily be seen, this kind of "letting-be"—Heidegger also calls it "primordial *praxis*"—is of crucial relevance for democracy provided the latter is seen as a relational practice and not a form of unilateral domination or subjugation. Inspired by "care" (*Sorge*), as I indicate, this primordial *praxis* also can be seen as cornerstone of a democratic *ethos*.

Like Dewey, Heidegger's work has greatly influenced a number of disciples and followers. Having to be very selective, chapter 5, "Action in the Public Realm," focuses on the work of political theorist

Hannah Arendt (who was at least in part Heidegger's student). The affinity with Dewey and Heidegger emerges right away in her approach to theorizing. Like the two philosophers, Arendt was always intent on keeping thought in close touch with experience, and theory with practice; in her own words, her endeavor was to "think what we are doing" or to focus thinking on "what is under foot." What was "under foot" during her lifetime was a series of momentous events: global war, the Holocaust, the Cold War, totalitarianism, the Vietnam war—events on which she commented with astuteness and deep insight. The central focus of her work, however, was on political action in the "public domain," that is, a space where individuals are linked through words and deeds transparent to all. In adopting this focus, Arendt rebelled in her own way against the Hobbesian artifact and against what she called the "central dilemmas facing modern man": the rise of bureaucratic or totalitarian structures, the "alienation" of human beings from the world and each other, and the atrophy of public agency in favor of fabrication.

While applauding the great merits of her work, chapter 5 also draws attention to some downsides, traceable in the main to the persistent influence of modern (Cartesian) metaphysics. Thus, in rigidly separating political action from other modes of activity, her writings obscured the importance of the so-called "social domain"—a domain akin to Hegel's "civil society" and increasingly important in our time of multiculturalism and globalization. Likewise, her portrayal of "action" as individual self-display fell short of the Deweyan "unity of the act" (as well as Heidegger's notion of "fulfillment"). Finally and most importantly, her stress on individual political "greatness" sidelined a crucial teaching of Montesquieu and Dewey: democracy as an ethical community.

Minimalism, Proceduralism, and Rational Choice

The sidelining of democratic ethos, to be sure, is not the result of a particular political theorist: broad intellectual movements during the twentieth century have conspired to render the idea apocryphal. Foremost among these trends is positivism, and especially the transformation of the study of politics into a "science" wedded to the canons of empiricist epistemology. From a positivist angle, politics is simply an empirical process whose various aspects or phases—like opinion data and voting ballots—are amenable to quantitative or statistical measurement. More specifically, in modern democratic systems, governments are seen as complex machines receiving pressures or "inputs" from society and eventually producing "outputs" or policies affecting social life. When approaching this empiricist account, it is good to remember Dewey's distinction between the "idea" and the existing mechanisms and procedures of democracy. As he observed at one point: It is important to "protest against the assumption that . . . the governmental practices which obtain in democratic states: general suffrage, elected representatives, majority rule, and so on are an adequate implementation of the idea or potential of democracy."[8]

To be sure, empirically inclined political scientists have not abandoned the task of providing a theoretical account of democracy. However, seeking to reduce or eliminate qualitative criteria, they have tended to concentrate on observable procedures, bypassing questions of ethical significance. It is for this reason that one speaks in this context of a "minimalist" or "procedural" account of democracy—an account that, in many ways, was prefigured by James Madison with his stress on formal constitutional arrangements (in *Federalist Paper* No. 10). To a large extent, contemporary political science treatments are such a minimalist approach; for purposes here, I select a few examples to convey the flavor. One of the most famous texts spelling out, at least in part, a procedural approach is Robert Dahl's *A Preface to Democratic Theory* (first published in 1956). In the very introduction to his study, Dahl delineates two basic approaches in this field: a "maximizing" theory (either ethical or formally axiomatic) and a "descriptive" or purely "empirical" theory. Traditionally, he notes, the first approach has tended to rely on "internal checks" to restrain governments, such as conscience, attitudes, and ethical dispositions. Pre-revolutionary writers, in particular, had insisted on "moral virtue among citizens as a necessary condition for republican [or democratic] government," a condition that needed to be cultivated through "hortatory religion, sound education, and honest government." On this point, Dahl reminds us, Madison strenuously disagreed, thereby ignoring or playing down "what must have been a common assumption of his time." From Madison's perspective, he writes, "even if internal [ethical] checks might frequently inhibit impulses to tyranny, they may not always do so with all individuals likely to be in a position to tyrannize." Hence, "if tyranny is to be avoided, external [procedural] checks are required, and these checks must be constitutionally prescribed."[9]

Although seemingly Madisonian in outlook, the rest of the study dispels this impression by turning from formal constitutional procedures to social and economic considerations, that is, from constitutional "checks and balances" to the checks and balances operating in society at large. "The Madisonian argument," Dahl states, "exaggerates the importance, in preventing tyranny, of specified checks to governmental officials by other specified governmental officials" and thus "underestimates the importance of the inherent social checks and balances existing in every pluralistic society." But without the latter checks, "it is doubtful that the intragovernmental checks on officials would in fact operate to prevent tyranny." It is at this point that Dahl's own alternative model to both Madisonian and "populist" democracy comes into view: the model of "polyarchy" that operates as an extended network of competing centers of will formation in modern society. In his words: "As distinguished from Madisonianism, the theory of polyarchy focuses primarily not on the constitutional prerequisites but on the social requisites for a democratic order." At this juncture, Dahl makes room for a dimension that presumably undergirds social (and not merely constitutional) checks and balances: the dimension of an "underlying consensus on policy." This consensus, existing "prior to politics, beneath it, enveloping it, restricting it, conditioning it," usually prevails (he says) in a society "among he predominant portion of the politically active members." With this admission, Dahl's polyarchy clearly moves beyond the level of a purely minimalist conception in the direction of a richer, ethical version (reminiscent of Montesquieu and Dewey). However, no indication is given as to how such an "underlying" fabric is to be cultivated and nurtured.[10]

Another prominent text—still more procedural and minimalist in orientation—is Giovanni Sartori's *The Theory of Democracy Revisited* (1987), a sequel to his *Democratic Theory* (1962). Like Dahl's study, Sartori's book distinguishes at the outset between a "prescriptive" or "normative" conception and a "descriptive" or "empirical" conception—but the entire thrust of his argument goes in the empirical direction, confining "prescription" to an axiomatic set of instrumental rules. As he writes, democracy in his conception is basically a design or "project" reflecting an "ongoing human artifact that hinges on a set of ideas and ideals that make [or construct] it." Once that project is implemented, he adds, democracy is "in place" and we can have "an empirical theory of democracy"; but not before: "The artifact 'democracy' has to be conceived and constructed before being observed." As becomes clear in his subsequent reflections, Sartori is not so much opposed to norms or a normative dimension per se, but only to their wholesale infusion into democratic politics. His preference, in this respect, is more for Kantian "regulative" principles or else for Max Weber's "ethics of conscience" (*Gesinnungsethik*), which are restricted primarily to the "internal" or private-individual domain.

Where he draws the line is vis-à-vis a stronger version of public ethics—as reflected in Hegel's "ethical life" (*Sittlichkeit*) and presumably in Dewey's notion of an ethical community. In his words: "To bring morality into politics is akin to playing with fire—as we have only too well rediscovered since Hegel theorized a 'political *ethos*,' or *Sittlichkeit*." Although acknowledging that there may be a "loss of ethics" in politics or a "present-day crisis of democracy," his recommendation is to employ more "minimalist" language and to leave phrases like "political morality, social morality, professional ethics" aside.[11]

What Sartori most strenuously objects to is any association of democracy with friendship or affection—what he derisively calls "demophily." As he asserts polemically: "There is an abyss between *democracy* and *demophily*. Since real-world democracy consists (this is what renders it real) of a democratic machinery, democracy can do without demophily." With this sharp demarcation, what is banished from sight is not only Aristotle's *philia* but also (and more importantly) Montesquieu's insight that democracy, to take hold or roots, has to be cultivated by a "love of democracy" which, in turn, is a "love of equality." For Sartori, this insistence is nothing more than a kind of sentimentalism, which is overcome by modern social engineering and especially by the construction of a "democratic machinery." To be more precise: affection is not entirely shunted aside but rather treated as a "fifth wheel" that does not do any work: "If [democracy] is implemented by demophily, by good motives, so much the better; but the machinery assures demo-benefits even if demo-love is absent—and this is the *security* that the democratic machinery provides, that gives real, not deceptive, existence to actual democracies." Taking his bearings not from Aristotle but rather from Machiavelli, Sartori locates the foundation of "real-life" democracy in "demo-power": "Democracy begins with demo-power and, on that beginning, does not require demophily in order to produce demo-benefits. Demophily is, instead, a sheer possibility." A democratic theory built on political science, in Sartori's view, has to take its stand with actuality or probability rather than possibility. Whereas the connection between demo-power and demo-benefits is "a built-in, highly probable possibility," he concludes, the linkage between demophily and demo-benefits is a highly "improbable possibility," and perhaps even an improbable impossibility.[12]

Although reluctant to probe ethical questions, most proceduralists are hesitant to dismiss public ethics, or the relevance of ethics for politics, altogether. This hesitation is no longer prevalent among devotees of another, increasingly influential perspective called "rational choice theory"—a framework which basically transfers neo-classical economic assumptions to social and political life and, under the aegis of neo-liberalism, is fast emerging as the dominant global ideology. What this model jeopardizes, however, is not only public ethics, but also politics, particularly democratic politics, as such. For, even when seen as a minimally shared regime, democracy is bound to be a burden or hindrance for the ambitions of an a-social or anti-social individualism. No one has articulated this burden more forcefully than William Riker, one of the founders of the model, in his book *Liberalism Against Populism* (1982; where "populism" stands for a Jacobin mode of democracy). As he states at the very outset: "The theory of social choice is a theory about the way the tastes, preferences, or values of individual persons are amalgamated and summarized into the choice of a collective group or society." Because these preferences are not ethically ranked, the primary focus of the theory is on something measurable or quantifiable: the "theory of voting." Like Dahl, Riker distinguishes between a normative or ethical and an empirical or "analytical" conception, while sharpening their edges. "The ideal of democracy," he writes, "is set forth in a normative statement of what we want the natural world of human interaction to yield for us." By contrast, "the theory of social choice is an analytical theory about the way that natural world can [and does] work and what kinds of outputs that world can yield." Hence, "by means of this analytic theory, we can discover whether pursuit of the ideal is promising or futile."[13]

Again like Dahl, but with different consequences, Riker delineates two different genealogies of modern democracy: a "liberal or Madisonian" type and a "populist or Rousseauistic" type. In the liberal (or libertarian) view, he notes, "the function of voting is to control officials, and *nothing* else"—meaning by nothing else: no positive political agendas or programs promoting something like the common good. As he adds, this Madisonian definition "is *logically* complete, and there is nothing to add. Madison said nothing about the quality of popular decision, whether good or bad." By contrast, populists—following Rousseau—desire a more active, participatory role of the people and a politics that creates a "moral and collective body" endowed with "life and will," especially the famous "general will." At this point, Riker endorses whole-heartedly Isaiah Berlin's notion of "negative liberty" and his indictment that "positive liberty, which appears initially innocuous, is the root of tyranny." Riker also alludes to some ideological background—not entirely unaffected by the Cold War. "No government," he asserts, "that has eliminated economic freedom has been able to attain or keep democracy, probably because, when all economic life is absorbed into government, there is no conceivable financial base for opposition." On the other hand, "economic liberty is also an end in itself because capitalism is the driving force for the increased efficiency and technological innovation that has produced in two centuries both a vast increase in the wealth of capitalist nations and a doubling of the average life span of their citizens." Although acknowledging that some may view it as "minimalist," Riker concludes, liberal or Madisonian democracy is "the only kind of democracy actually attainable" and in any case the democracy "we still have in the United States."[14]

Modernity and Postmodernism

As can readily be seen, and as has frequently been noted, extreme *laissez-faire* liberalism is at odds with democracy—even a moderate, constitutionally regulated democracy oriented somehow toward the common good. In line with rational choice assumptions, opposition to democracy is interest-based: the people most vehemently averse to democratic equality are usually those who benefit most directly from minimalist government, that is, people reaping privileges from the prevailing status quo. In common parlance, people of this kind are usually associated with the political "Right." Curiously, however, minimalism is sometimes also favored by people on the opposite side of the spectrum, people with radically "progressive" leanings commonly ranked with the political "Left." Seeing their enemy not only in established elites but in political establishments of any kind—including established democracies—"radicals" of this kind tend to veer toward minimalism as the absolute antidote to public authority. Strongly critical of Rousseau (and sometimes of Hegel as well), the goal favored by such minimalists is not democratic unity or holism, and certainly not a "general will," but rather thorough-going fragmentation or dispersal of interests—to the point that isolated individualism rubs elbows with autocratic elitism. Among recent intellectual trends, the closest affinity with this radical minimalism can be found in versions (but only some versions) of a movement that goes by the summary label of "postmodernism."

Taken literally, the term *postmodernism* seems to denote an outlook that seeks to grapple with and perhaps remedy some of the defects of modernity or the modern age. As previously noted, some leading modern Western thinkers—from Montesquieu to Hegel and Dewey—have charged modernity with harboring some deep rifts or "diremptions" that need to be remedied before their effects become incurably destructive. Thus, in lieu of the isolated Cartesian ego these thinkers have struggled to formulate the notion of a concretely situated self, of a "being-in-the-world"; in place of the separation of thought and action, they have advanced the idea of a practically and experientially nurtured mode of thinking and doing where action is no longer a unilateral project but a complex interaction performed in the "middle voice"; finally, in lieu of the human mastery over nature (rooted in the mind–matter bifurcation), efforts have been made to envisage a subdued, ecologically sane human role in nature. All these and related initiatives might with good reason be termed *postmodern* (which is not the same as anti-modern). Unfortunately, this promising and beneficial kind of postmodernism has from the beginning been contested by another version that does not so much remedy as exacerbate the dilemmas of modernity and, for this reason, might preferably be called "hypermodernism." In this version, the tension between private and public, between internal and external domains becomes rigidified into a hyper-individualism, carrying with it the corollary of a steadily deepening "world-alienation" (Arendt) or "disenchantment" (Weber). In the same manner, the always-difficult relation between self and other selves is twisted into the impossible relation (or nonrelation) between self and absolutely incommensurable others beyond the reach of communication and practical interaction.

As it happens, the intellectual who first popularized the term *postmodern* also was the one who saddled the notion with many of the connotations of "hypermodernism." In his book *The Postmodern Condition* (1979), Jean-François Lyotard zeroed in on certain features that, in his view, characterized the "modern age"—features like universalism, essentialism, holism (or totalism), and historical teleology (captured in "grand narratives")—and then proceeded to demolish them by means of a radical reversal. The upshot was a privileging of particularism, anti-essentialism (or relativism), fragmentation, and local uniqueness. As Lyotard observed in his introduction, the term *modern* is commonly applied to an age where metaphysics and science legitimate themselves through reference to a universal "metadiscourse"; likewise, modern humanities appeal to "some grand narrative such as the dialectics of spirit, the hermeneutics of meaning, the emancipation of the rational or working subject, or the creation of wealth." By contrast, the term *postmodern* means to convey an opposite outlook: a basic skepsis or "incredulity toward metanarratives." What happens as a result of this skepsis, according to Lyotard, is the dismantling of comprehensive knowledge systems and their dispersal into "heterogeneous" discourses or "clouds of narrative language elements." In lieu of holistic schemes, postmodernism tolerates only a "pragmatics of language particles" arranged in many diverse "language games"—a pragmatics giving rise to political institutionalization (if at all) only "in patches—local determinism." Generally speaking, he concludes, postmodern life experience "refines our sensitivity to differences and reinforces our ability to tolerate the incommensurable."[15]

Once universalism is replaced by particularism and interaction by incommensurability, postmodernism can without great difficulty be accommodated to minimalism, including a minimalist conception of democracy. This lure of adjustment was particularly strong in the American context—already saturated with hyper-individualist tendencies. As a result, the meaning of "postmodernism" became highly ambivalent. This ambivalence is particularly evident in the field of political theory or philosophy, most relevant to the issue of democracy. In his *Political Theory and Postmodernism* (1991), political theorist Stephen White distinguishes broadly between "oppositional" and "nonoppositional" strands of postmodernism vis-à-vis "modern" metaphysics, with the oppositional strand largely coinciding with the insistence on rupture or radical reversal. White also notes two prominent questions confronting both strands: what he calls the "responsibility to act" and the "responsibility to otherness." It is precisely with regard to the second question that radical postmodernism can come to grief (or land in "hypermodernism") despite its initial dismissal of modern notions of "subject" or "subjectivity." As he writes: "An *over*emphasis on disruption and impertinence creates for postmodern thinking a momentum that threatens to enervate the sense of responsibility to otherness, by subtly substituting for it an implicit celebration of the impertinent subject who shows his or her virtuosity in deconstructing whatever unity comes along." The result, White adds, is "an ironic one for postmodernism's own self-understanding"—ironic because a movement starting from the deconstruction of the modern subject or agent finds itself suddenly in the throes of an incommensurable, perhaps transcendentally grounded singularity.[16]

Most commonly, derailments of postmodernism are due to intellectual shortcuts: the proclivity to substitute binary reversals for the labor of thinking anew (or "thinking the unthought" of the past). Some of the relevant binaries have been mentioned above: universalism versus particularism, essentialism versus constructivism, measurable versus incommensurable. To these some other binaries need to be added because of their political salience: public–private, positive–negative, presence–absence. The dangers involved in opposing public (or positive) and private (or negative) liberty in a binary fashion have already been alluded to and must always be kept in sight. Equally important, however, is the ontological opposition between positivity and negativity, presence and absence. In an age dominated by positivist science, it is certainly important to remember negativity as the intimate corollary of every positivity, and absence as the corollary of every presence. In his famous lecture, "What is Metaphysics?" (1929), attended by some of the leading German scientists of the time, Heidegger pointed to the dimension of nothingness (*das Nichts*) as the domain modern science does not and cannot know. But of course, for Heidegger, nothingness was not just an empty foil or binary opposition but rather an unmanageable resource able to unleash a stream of possibilities or potentialities.[17]

This view has been applied fruitfully to democratic politics by a number of recent thinkers, most notably the French philosopher Claude Lefort. Positivist accounts of democracy tend to focus (as indicated) on the observable machinery of government together with input and output circuits—all of which are statistically measurable. Without denying the importance of these processes, Lefort juxtaposes two equally important domains: the dimension of overt political behavior, called "politics," and the dimension of the underlying framework or staging site (*mise-en-scène*), termed "polity" or "the political." Concentration on the latter as the constitutive matrix of politics draws attention to trans-empirical aspects: not only the distinction between right and wrong or just and unjust, but (more importantly) between the visible and the invisible, between presence and absence, being and nonbeing. While in traditional political regimes, the constitutive matrix tended to be monopolized by overt rulers or elites, this is no longer possible in modern democracy where the "polity" becomes fluid, elusive, and no longer amenable to static control. In Lefort's words: "Of all the regimes we know, [modern democracy] is the only one to have represented [supreme] power in such a way as to show that power is an *empty place* and to have maintained a gap between the symbolic [or constitutive] and the real." The danger is that, in democracy, the "empty space" is re-occupied by a spurious type of unity called "the nation" or "the People-as-One."[18]

In Lefort's work, an important feature of modern democracy is clearly pinpointed: the fact that nobody in democracy can claim to be the definitive or "essential" embodiment of the regime and that the "polity" hence always exceeds the confines of "politics." Notwithstanding the importance of this insight, the differentiation between the two domains, or between presence and absence, has a tendency to occlude the equally crucial aspect of political agency; in a way, the latter tends to disappear in the "gap" between observable action and constitutive nonaction, or between activity and passivity. A similar deficit of meaningful public action prevails also in the theory of "hegemony" as articulated by political philosophers Ernesto Laclau and Chantal Mouffe. In chapter 6, "Postmodernism and Radical Democracy," I examine some of their salient arguments, by focusing chiefly on their book *Hegemony and Socialist Strategy* (1985). Over long stretches, their study is a critique of traditional Marxism and its "essentializing" treatment of central categories like "class," "class struggle," and "revolution." Adopting a still more radical (loosely postmodern) perspective, the authors proceed to call into question all kinds of sociopolitical essentialism as well as economic determinism, a step that brings into view a welter of antagonisms that cannot be fixed or permanently stabilized.

According to Laclau and Mouffe, "antagonism"—seen as the counterpoint to hegemony—involves not only the conflict between different empirical groups or structures, but also (and more importantly) the tensional relation between presence and absence, between empirical positivity and destabilizing negativity. As in the case of Lefort's "excessive" polity, antagonism here means that, in democracy, a set of rulers cannot erect itself into a permanent regime and that "hegemony" can never be solidified into a closed, fully integrated system. Given this embroilment with negativity, the authors assert, society can never attain "the status of transparency, of full presence," with the result that the "impossible relation" between presence and absence must be seen as "constitutive of the social itself."[19] While applauding the verve and trans-empirical élan of this approach, I conclude my chapter by raising again the Deweyan question of practice or agency (as well as a possible "holistic" bridging of presence and absence).

Without doubt, the most prominent postmodern Continental philosopher is Jacques Derrida. By comparison with both Lefort and Laclau/Mouffe, Derrida has not written extensively on social and political issues; but he has by no means been silent in that field. In chapter 7, "Jacques Derrida's Legacy," I discuss some of Derrida's later texts, which introduced the intriguing or provocative notion of a "democracy to come." I start out by drawing attention to the relation between Derrida and Heidegger. Despite the close affinity between the two thinkers, Derrida's endeavor from the beginning has been to transgress Heidegger's more "holistic" perspective in the direction of a radical trans-empiricism and transcendentalism. Commonly known under the label of "deconstruction," this transgression has tended to transform "being-with-others" into a "nonrelation" with incommensurable "otherness." A corollary of deconstruction is the progressive replacement of (ontological) possibility or potentiality with the notion of an "impossible possibility" or "possible impossibility"—a move prompted by the desire to avoid any kind of teleology or continuity.

As in the case of Lefort's "gap," the move tends to open up an hiatus between "the symbolic and the real" or (here) between ordinary politics and the envisaged "democracy to come"—where the latter refers to an absolute "heterogeneity" and to an "interminable adjournment."[20] Once again—and now with particular urgency—the question emerges how a hiatus which is meant to be utterly unbridgeable can prevent human despair or a slide into a Manichean "two-world" theory. Granted: the envisaged democracy cannot be simply constructed or socially engineered; but, at the same time, it cannot or will not just "come" without further ado. Here the need for a transformative democratic agency emerges, an agency that is as far removed from anthropocentric activism as from pliant passivity. As previously indicated, this agency has to operate in the active–passive or "middle voice" and resemble in some fashion the "primordial *praxis*" of "letting-be" that sustains without appropriation.

Humanism and the Global Promise of Democracy

Having surveyed prominent recent approaches to democracy, I turn to broader themes in an effort to reconnect some of the strands of the preceding discussion. In the course of that discussion, I repeatedly alluded to the possibility of a more "holistic" or holistic–pragmatic perspective as an alternative to minimalist fragmentation. I have also referred to a transformative agency that would bypass the pitfalls of both manipulation or social engineering and passive withdrawal. Clearly, this outlook implies a certain kind of philosophical anthropology, more specifically a conception of humanity or being "human" which shuns both rampant self-aggrandizement or egocentric autonomy and radical self-erasure or surrender to heteronomy. Chapter 8, "Who Are We Now?" reviews a number of alternative construals of "humanism" or what it means to be human, focusing mainly on intellectual developments during the last century. Whereas the first section of the chapter profiles the contours of a basically "subject"-centered or anthropocentric humanism—as upheld by such diverse thinkers as Ernst Cassirer and Jean-Paul Sartre—the second part explores countermoves to this self-confident outlook by recalling the radical "end-of-man" or "end-of-the-subject" rhetoric of early postmodernism and also by paying attention to the postulate of a "humanism of the other" as advanced by Emmanuel Levinas. Pursuing the possibility of a "middle voice" able to support democratic self-rule, the chapter concludes with reflections on the prospect of an "other" humanism, reflections inspired by Adorno's *reductio hominis*, Heidegger's custodial imagery, and Raimon Panikkar's "cosmotheandric" holism.

To a considerable extent, conceptions of an "other" humanism are backed up (or can be backed up) by "religious" beliefs, that is, views regarding the basic relation between humanity, nature, and the divine. In this context, the question that has surfaced in recent times with great vehemence concerns the compatibility of religious faith and democracy: the issue is whether modern democracy can make room for and be reconciled with religion. Chapter 9 explores this issue by focusing on perhaps the most contentious case: the relation between democracy and Islam. The chapter takes its point of departure from the biblical reminder that believers are meant to be "the salt of the earth"—a phrase that militates against both world dominion and world denial, that is, against the dual temptation of either controlling or rejecting worldly society. In its long history, Islam (like Christianity) has been sorely tempted by the lure of worldly power and public domination. Nor is this temptation entirely a matter of the past (witness the upsurge of "political Islam" in our time). Focusing on the concrete example of contemporary Iran, the chapter makes suggestions how Muslims can regain and reinvigorate the "salt" of Islamic faith so that it can recapture the Qur'anic summons for freedom, justice, and service in the world.

Chapter 9 ends with a plea for "multiple modes of democracy" in our world. This global or cosmopolitical perspective is continued in the concluding chapter 10, "Beyond Minimal Democracy: Voices from East and West." The chapter starts out by recapitulating central features, and arguments in favor, of minimalist liberal democracy prominent in the West today. The discussion then shifts to critical assessments of this model, placing the focus first of all on India and especially on Gandhi's teachings. Concentrating on Gandhi's crucial notion of popular "self-rule" or *swaraj*, chapter 10 shows that such self-rule does not involve the power to control or dominate others, but rather the ability of people to rule themselves—an ability predicated on self-restraint, self-transformation, and the cultivation of nonviolence (*ahimsa*) and "truth force" (*satyagraha*). By insisting on the ethical curtailment of self-interest, Gandhian *swaraj* clearly parts company with liberal minimalism—without at the same time endorsing a collec-

tive conformism hostile to social and cultural pluralism. From South
Asia, the chapter turns to the East Asian context and especially to a
perspective called "New Confucianism" represented by such figures
as Tu Weiming, Liu Shu-hsien, and Henry Rosemont Jr. By center-
staging, in a true Confucian spirit, the "relationality" of human life,
these thinkers take a stand against both self-centered individualism
and oppressive collectivism, thus intimating a conception of democracy
broadly compatible with Gandhian *swaraj*. In the end, the chapter re-
invokes critical voices from the West, paying tribute again to American
pragmatism and especially to the work of John Dewey.

In the spirit of Dewey and his openness to East Asian thought, I
want to conclude here by appealing to the work of the great Japanese
philosopher and Zen teacher, Masao Abe. In his writings, Abe has
stressed precisely the political significance of such Zen notions as "self-
emptying" (*sunyata*) and "self-awakening" (*satori*) for a viable mode
of democratic self-rule. What is wrong with existing nation-states and
their leaders, he observes, is that they are ignorant of emptiness and
self-overcoming; instead, states and their rulers take as their guiding
principle "a position of self-affirmation and radical self-assertion"
whereby, in times of crisis, "the position of humankind is overlooked
and destroyed." What is needed, in his view, is neither self-glorification
nor a simple erasure of the self but rather a transformation involving
a "self-awakening of the original self." This change renders feasible
a new ethical and political "cosmology," an ethics of humanity in
which human beings are fully responsible both to each other and to
the larger ecological universe. To conclude with some lines by Masao
Abe, written in the form of a poem:

> We must place humankind within a new cosmology
> Which has extricated itself from anthropocentrism.
> Is not the boundless "expanse of self-awakening,"
> Which gives life to both self and other
> As it sets us the distinction between them—
> Is not this precisely the foundation of a new human society?[21]

2

Hegel For Our Time

Negativity and Democratic Ethos

Some sixty years ago, at the end of the Great War, a Hegel-revival happened in France. In large measure, the revival was triggered by a lecture delivered by the philosopher Jean Hyppolite in Paris on Hegel's *Phenomenology of Spirit* (1807). In his lecture and related studies, Hyppolite managed to rescue Hegel from the tight stranglehold of logicians and epistemologists and render his thought available to ordinary experience—to the experience gathered in what Edmund Husserl, the founder of modern phenomenology, had called the "life-world."[1] At roughly the same time, and partly as a result of Hyppolite's initiative, Maurice Merleau-Ponty turned his attention to Hegel's work, discovering there at least a distant affinity with the more recent phenomenological and existentialist movements. For Merleau-Ponty, the mediating agent between Hegel and the recent movement was Søren Kierkegaard who was the first to use "existence" deliberately in opposition to the later Hegel, the author of the *Logic* and *Encyclopedia*. For Kierkegaard, Merleau-Ponty notes, the late Hegel offered only a "palace of ideas" where all historical struggles are overcome; it was Hegel who had "understood everything except his own historical situation," who had "taken everything into account except his own existence." By contrast, the early *Phenomenology of Spirit* was an account "not only of ideas but of all the areas which reveal the mind at work: customs, economic structures, and legal institutions as well as works of philosophy." Seen in this light, Hegel's 1807 text was "a militant philosophy" and "not as yet a victorious one."[2]

Today, two hundred years after Hegel's *Phenomenology*, another revival may be appropriate. In our time, the revival would have to be directed not only against logicians and flat-footed positivists but also—and more importantly—against champions of a certain Western triumphalism, that is, ideologues celebrating Western liberalism and the liberal state as the completion or "end of history." In this concrete context, what needs to be recovered—in my view—is precisely Hegel as the author of a "militant" and "not yet victorious" philosophy, as the thinker revealing "the mind at work." At the same time, however, revival or recovery cannot amount to a simple repetition of existentialism—especially if existentialism means a focus on private-particular individuality (with Kierkegaard) or on subjective activism (with Jean-Paul Sartre). The effort to retrieve Hegel's thought today hence involves a dual task: first, the need to honor the intrinsic integrity of Hegel's system; and second, the endeavor to renew the inner, unfinished movement of his thought—a movement stamping him (despite his protestations) as the "philo-sopher" or lover, not the victorious proprietor, of wisdom.

In the following, I am faithful to this dual task, by proceeding in three steps. First, I highlight the holistic quality of Hegel's thinking, a quality that, in many ways, still makes him an inspiring mentor for the late modern age. Next, I turn to the unfinished character of his work, and especially to certain "metaphysical" limits or shortfalls—shortfalls having to do mainly with his truncated understanding of both "being" and "negation." Finally, I release his notion of "ethical life" (*Sittlichkeit*) from its confinement in the constitutional state of his time, in order to render it available for cultivation in democratic civil society—and indeed for fostering a civil *ethos* in the emerging global cosmopolis.

Hegel as Mentor of Modern Life

In our time, Hegel can provide valuable guidance both in strictly philosophical debates and in ethical-political discussions concerning modernity and modern life. In the strictly philosophical domain, his work provides an antidote to an arid "logicism" and cult of epistemology that, in large measure, dominate contemporary Western philosophy (especially its "analytical" variant). At the same time, his truth-commitment erects a sheet anchor against a facile skepticism that, by dismissing all knowledge as spurious, lends aid and comfort to private consumerism and self-indulgence. Against both an abstract rationalism and a dismissal of reason, Hegel pits his holistic mode of philosophical inquiry, a mode that—by undercutting the rigid bifurcation of knower and known (subject and object)—portrays reasoning as participation in an ongoing disclosure of truth (or "spirit"). This

"zetetic" (searching) quality of inquiry—not yet reduced to a "dialectical" schema—is most admirably portrayed in the famous 1807
preface to the *Phenomenology of Spirit*. There, following some preliminary remarks, Hegel cuts to the quick of philosophical inquiry,
by locating its mainspring in the ongoing labor of thought. In his
words, pursuit of philosophical inquiry is not confined to the goal or
telos—the ultimate possession of knowledge—but resides crucially in
its "realization" or the effort of "working the matter out." In the same
way, the "result" of philosophizing does not provide the "concrete
whole itself"; rather, the latter comes into view only when outcome
is taken together with its actual unfolding or "becoming" (*Werden*).
Considered apart from becoming, *telos* is only a "lifeless generality,"
and result a mere "corpse" suitable for a postmortem.[3]

In its ensuing arguments, the preface delineates in detail the
actual unfolding and "becoming" of conscious knowledge. Basically, the
process starts from the stage of "substantive" or sensory immediacy,
moves on to the stage of reflection anchored in subjective consciousness, and finally to the stage of the absolute disclosure of spirit and
truth. "In my view," Hegel states in a lapidary formulation, "a view
which the developed exposition alone can justify—everything depends
on grasping and expressing truth not only as [immediate] *substance*
but also as *subject* or *subjectivity*." Substance, in this context, denotes
external reality in itself and prior to inspection; subjectivity, by contrast, refers to reflective consciousness as the reflective negation of
immediacy, and hence to a diremption or alienation between subject
and object, reflection and world. This diremption, in turn, can only
be remedied or overcome through the reconciliation of subject and
world, that is, through the achievement of self-recognition in "otherness"—which, in a way, completes the circular movement. In Hegel's
words: truth emerges finally as "the process of its own becoming, as
the circle which has its purpose both at its end and at its beginning."
The mediated correlation of substance and subjectivity, of beginning
and end, is captured in the Hegelian notion of "spirit," that "most
sublime concept" that, in his view, belongs "uniquely to modernity and
its religion." Seen from this angle, philosophical truth is real (*wirklich*)
alone at the point where "other-being" and "self-being" (*Anderssein* and
Fürsichsein) are reconciled and where spirit hence emerges as "being
in and for itself" (*Anundfürsichsein*). In the words of the preface: "Pure
self-knowledge in the medium of other-being (*Anderssein*), this pure
ether as such is the very soil where knowledge or knowing flourishes
in its universal form. Philosophy begins with the demand that consciousness should dwell in this [ethereal] element"—an element that

attains its completion and transparency only "through the movement of is becoming." The aim of the "phenomenology of spirit" is to set forth "the becoming of knowledge or knowing as such."[4]

In examining the becoming of spirit, Hegel's *Phenomenology* is in a way a modern pilgrim's progress. Basically, it reports the story of the "long and laborious journey" undertaken by consciousness on its way to absolute knowledge or knowing (*Wissen*). This story, in effect, can be grasped as a learning process (*Bildung*) or as the formative experience that consciousness undergoes or makes with itself. In Hegel's words: the task shouldered by his text is to show how "the individual is guided from its pre-reflective standpoint to knowledge" and hence to portray the rise of "general subjectivity as self-conscious spirit in its formation." In a different, more elaborate formulation, the accent is squarely placed on the sustained labor involved in the process of knowing. As the preface states, the study of this process is "the science of the experience (*Erfahrung*) undergone by consciousness"; for consciousness "knows and comprehends nothing but what falls within its experience." As used in this context, "experience" is not just sensation or sensory experience, but rather denotes a transformative movement in which subjectivity initially distances itself from the world and then recoups or recovers itself, as spirit, in and through "other-being." "Experience," we read, "we call that movement in which inexperienced immediacy—be it that of sensation or bare thought—alienates itself in order finally to return to itself out of this alienation (*Entfremdung*)." It is only at this point that knowing reveals itself in its "reality and truth" and as the genuine "patrimony of consciousness."[5]

The transformation sketched here—the sublation (*Aufhebung*) of otherness in spirit—is by no means a smooth progression, but is marked by a wrenching diremption associated with the power of negation or negativity. As Hegel remarks, there is a split within consciousness between subject and world, and this split is their "difference" (*Unterschied*) or the factor of "negativity." In another passage, the split is portrayed as a momentous drama involving self-becoming through self-overcoming. "The act of separating or dividing (*Scheiden*)," we read there, "is the effect of the labor of rational understanding (*Verstand*)—that most miraculous and greatest of all powers, or rather that absolute power." What comes to the fore in this act of dividing, is "the immense power of the negative—which is the energy of [rational] thought, of the pure ego." In a way, this negativity may also be called "death"—which is "the most terrifying thing" and which demands "the greatest strength" to remain steadfast in its face. At this point,

Hegel employs his most exhilarating eloquence to show the becoming of spirit as the dramatic encounter between life and death. "The life of spirit," he writes, "is not one that shuns death and keeps clear of destruction; rather it endures death and in death maintains its being. In effect, spirit gains its truth only by finding itself in the midst of utter diremption (*Zerrissenheit*)." As he adds, spirit has its power only "by looking the negative in the face and remaining steadfast near it. This steadfastness is the magic power which converts the negative into being."[6]

As previously indicated, the becoming of spirit—as recounted in the *Phenomenology*—is closely intertwined with modernity or the unfolding of modern life. In Hegel's view, the chief characteristic of the modern age is the breakthrough to subjectivity or the rational ego—a breakthrough that coincides with the division between subject and world and the unleashing of the power of negativity. By contrast, ancient and medieval periods—in his assessment—were basically marked by an undifferentiated or "substantive" community spirit in which individual consciousness and freedom were largely submerged. As one should note, however, the distinction between historical ages signaled for him not a simple linear progress, given the enormous struggles triggered by the "power of the negative." Although a firm defender of modernity and its rational acquisitions, Hegel's deepest motivation was to remedy the modern proclivity for atomistic individualism and thus to "sublate" negativity again in a viable modern community (or modern *polis*). In the *Phenomenology*, this point is clearly made in a passage following the comments on death. In ancient life, we read, the preoccupation was predominantly with the cultivation of "natural" or substantive consciousness as the latter is embedded in a given community or generality. In modern times, by contrast, individualism has taken root and staked out its terrain, at least "in an abstract form." The main effort in modernity is concentrated on unfolding the "inner sense" of particular individuality without any process of mediation—a focus whereby concern with the universal is abridged. Hence, Hegel observes, "nowadays the task before us consists not so much in extricating the individual from sensuous immediacy and making him into a 'thinking substance' [*res cogitans*]; rather it consists in the very opposite: by breaking down and sublating limiting concepts to actualize universality and give it spiritual vitality."[7]

Hegel's ambivalent—or better: balanced—assessment of modernity is not confined to the *Phenomenology*, but surfaces as a persistent theme in many of his other writings. Thus, already in texts written before the *Phenomenology*—texts known under the broad label of *Jenaer*

Realphilosophie—Hegel traced the lines of both individual and collective maturation, that is, the story of onto- and phylogenesis. The story begins on the level of immediate sensation where individual consciousness is still fully immersed in the customary fabric of families and clans. In the political arena, customary networks are predominantly held together by patriarchal despots or autocratic monarchies. Only occasionally and under special circumstances is political despotism set aside in favor of a regime of public freedom; the most prominent case was ancient Greece. In the Greek *polis*, Hegel notes, free citizens were able to participate in administering the affairs of the city in such a manner that policies were, at least to some extent, grounded in popular will. Yet, even here, this grounding was at best embryonic and often illusory: public freedom was not yet anchored in, or mediated through, the freedom of individual-particular consciousness. "This," he writes, "is the beautiful happy liberty of the Greeks which has been and is admired so much. The people is dispersed into citizens while at the same time constituting *one* collective individual, the *polis*; the people only interacts with itself [without mediation]: the same will is hence particular and universal." For Hegel, this public *ethos* of the *polis* holds a strong appeal; its beauty resided in "the immediate unity of the universal and the particular," as in a work of art "where no part separates itself from the whole but forms a genial unity." Yet, Greek unity came at a price: "self-consciousness or absolute self-being of the individual was lacking. Like the Spartan state, Plato's *Republic* signals the erasure of self-conscious individuality."[8]

As an antipode to the "beautiful" but confining Greek *ethos*, Hegel portrays modernity as the upsurge of self-conscious individuality and personal freedom. As he notes, by contrast to the narrowly communal spirit of the past, the modern age made room for individual self-consciousness and thereby discovered layers of a "deeper spirit" and a deeper conception of ethical life (*Sittlichkeit*). By gaining some distance from the surrounding world, the individual at this point is able to descend into his or her inwardness, to discover selfhood and autonomous self-will while simultaneously grasping self-conscious subjectivity as the gateway to absolute truth and spirit. To be sure, descent into individual consciousness and self-will also implies a (initial) separation or diremption, a tearing apart of the bond linking individual and the world and individuals among each other. Especially in modern economic life, with its division of labor, self-will is quickly pitted against self-will, leading to a struggle for economic wealth and possessions and ultimately for power. As Hegel comments sharply: Under modern conditions of production, "whole masses of people are abandoned to poverty without remedy. A contrast emerges between vast wealth and vast poverty—a poverty that finds it impossible to make any headway." In this situation, the communal fabric tends to be torn asunder and peaceful social relations tend to give way to class conflict and enmity. "This inequality between wealth and poverty," we read, "this condition of need and necessity turns into the utmost diremption of will, into inner indignation (*Empörung*) and even hatred."[9]

To remedy this inequality and the glaring fissures unleashed by modern life a further step is required: the move to a new *polis* imbued with a higher *ethos* where divergent self-wills are again mediated and reconciled. For Hegel, this move cannot be accomplished contractually or through the simple aggregation of individual self-wills; rather, what is needed is the advance to a new public consciousness where individual wills are sublated (*aufgehoben*) in a more general or universal spirit. On the level of economic relations, the modern *polis* shoulders the task of reducing extreme disparities by curbing excessive profits and securing a minimum standard of living for all. In the words of *Realphilosophie*, modern government "comes onto the scene and must see to it that every sphere [of the *polis*] is preserved." The role of modern government, however, is not limited to mitigating the disparities of status and wealth. For Hegel, public life in the modern *polis* has a higher, ethical goal: the task of mediating particularity and universality, of individual self-will and public spirit. It is on the level of public life that private individuals are rescued from atomistic dispersal, segregation, and alienation—and not through governmental constraint or the intervention of a miraculous force. They are rescued through participation in the workings of the absolute spirit that is essentially their own. According to *Realphilosophie*: "The [modern] state as the rich manifold is the sublation of both particularistic existence and of the pure self-being of the person. Human beings have their genuine being and thinking in [public] law—which is the absolute authority."[10]

As readily can be seen, these comments in Hegel's early texts clearly foreshadowed the much fuller development of similar ideas in his *Philosophy of Right*, a work composed more than a decade after the *Phenomenology*. As is commonly known, the work grew out of a series of lecture courses that Hegel offered first at the University of Heidelberg and later, after 1818, in Berlin. One of the courses in Berlin reflected again on the character of modernity and its difference from antiquity. As a prelude, the course distinguishes philosophy from empirical inquiry, noting that philosophy seeks to penetrate to the inner core of phenomena as revealed in a given context. Seen from this angle, Greek philosophy—and above all Plato—was able to grasp the "inner reality" of the Greek world by formulating "the principle of ethical life (*Sittlichkeit*) in its simple immediacy," thereby disclosing the essence of the "Greek spirit." Yet, as in his earlier texts, Hegel emphasizes the need to transgress the stage of simple immediacy; following its own trajectory, human consciousness grows and matures over time—a development giving rise to multiple tensions: between subject and object, between private inwardness and external reality. This movement reached full fruition in modernity, in the so-called "age of reason." At this point, concentrated inwardness blossomed forth, promoting the growth of individual freedom or autonomy: "When this concentration took the shape of division, when [old-style] public life disintegrated setting individuals free, great enlightened thinkers [like Descartes and Kant] came onto the scene" to capture the development. Again, however, division is not the final stage of consciousness or philosophical reflection. Propelled by the quest for deeper understanding, spirit moves beyond divisions and conflicting particularities, in the direction of reconciliation and the cultivation of a higher mode of public life.[11]

   In the final text of *Philosophy of Right*, ethical life is portrayed as moving through the successive stages of family, civil society, and the state. In Hegel's account, "civil society" (*bürgerliche Gesellschaft*) denotes a "stage of difference" or diremption where the accent is placed on individual particularity and the diversity of human interests. This mode of life was basically unknown to antiquity still wedded to "substantive" communal life. The idea of such life was also unknown to Greek philosophy and hence not thematized in Plato's *Republic*. Although portraying the substance of ethical life "in its ideal beauty and truth," Hegel states, reiterating earlier formulations, Plato's thought could not cope with the emerging diversity except by erecting a substantively unified *polis* that downgraded individuality and private property. The notion of individual autonomy only gained recognition slowly in the post-classical age: it "first dawned in inward form in Christianity and, in external form (linked with abstract universality), in the Roman world." As a distinct mode of ethical life distinguished from family and the state, however, civil society arose only much later: it is "the achievement of the modern world which, for the first time, gives their proper due to all the elements of the idea [of freedom]." At this point in the text, Hegel's ambivalent or balanced attitude toward modernity again comes to the fore. On the one hand, he notes, modern society, by encouraging individual initiative, makes room for the display of individual freedom that is a key ingredient in developed ethical life. On the other hand, emancipation of private freedom also unleashes

a torrent of needs, desires, and preferences—which can be the har-
binger of moral depravity and corruption. Despite the latter danger,
however, there is no shortcut to maturity: "Spirit attains its actuality
only by undergoing division or diremption, by imposing on itself—in
the midst of natural needs and external necessity—this inner limit and
finitude and by proceeding, through the labor of education (*Bildung*),
to overcome this limit and thus obtain objective reality."[12]

Proceeding to the highest level of ethical life, the modern state,
Philosophy of Right correlates (as in earlier texts) the aspects of onto-
genesis and phylogenesis, that is, the growth of individual and public
maturation, placing the accent now squarely on the latter. Again the
Greek *polis* serves as main contrasting foil. In the classical state, and
especially in Plato's *Republic*, individual particularity had not yet
been "released," as individuals had their duties assigned to them
by guardians. The same limitation, even in aggravated form—Hegel
adds—prevailed in Oriental or Asiatic states where functions were
determined by birth and individuals were not granted any "inwardness and personal right." In opposition to this heteronomy or public
tutelage, individuals in modernity demand to be respected in their
"inner life" and to be able to nurture their "own opinions, preferences,
and individual conscience." The nature of the modern state thus has
this distinctive quality that the universal or common good is bound
up with "the complete freedom of particularity and the happiness
of individual members." Accordingly, there is here an interlacing or
reconciliation of perspectives in such a way that public unity is maintained while individuality experiences "full and lively development."
In the words of a well-known and often-cited passage:

> The principle of modern states has this prodigious strength
> and depth of allowing the principle of subjectivity to develop
> to the extreme of personal singularity and independence,
> while at the same time guiding the latter back into substan-
> tive unity, and thus maintaining this unity in and through
> subjectivity itself.[13]

Negation and Negative Dialectics

In his sustained reflections on modern life, Hegel can serve as mentor today by putting us on guard against two main pitfalls: on the
one hand, the lure of an antimodern communalism or fundamentalism disdainful of individual freedom and social differentiation; and

on the other hand, the radical disaggregation of public life in favor
of selfish or particularistic interests—a disaggregation sailing today
under such labels as neo-liberalism and libertarianism. To the extent
that many Western societies today are in the grip of neo-liberal
or *laissez-faire* doctrines, they clearly fall short of Hegel's vision of
modernity—and for this reason alone cannot possibly represent the
culmination of ethical life or the "end of history." However, there
are other reasons calling into doubt such a culmination—reasons
having to do with internal quandaries of Hegel's philosophy. In one
of his many writings on Hegel's work—his text on the meaning of
"negativity" (1938–39)—Martin Heidegger offers a helpful suggestion
on how to read that work (an advice I try to follow here). A genuine
engagement with Hegel, he writes, has to meet "simultaneously these
two demands": on the one side, "to grasp his basic insights in their
intrinsic momentum" (bypassing empty formalism); and on the other
side, "to find a still more originary, and yet not externally imposed
perspective." Pondering the second demand, and especially the possibility of a "critical" reflection, Heidegger raises the question: "What
is the basic premise of Hegel's philosophy whose further analysis
can lead back to a more originary standpoint," while still remaining
somehow faithful to Hegel's agenda? His answer: "We claim that this
basic premise is 'negativity.' "[14]

On the face of it, this claim initially seems farfetched. As shown
previously, Hegel's writings repeatedly make reference to negation or
negativity; this is particularly true of his *Phenomenology of Spirit*. Thus,
in discussing the emerging split in consciousness between subject
and world, the preface attributes this split explicitly to "difference"
(*Unterschied*) and the factor of "negativity." In the same context, Hegel
speaks of "the immense power of the negative" and relates this power
to the encounter between life and death. Spirit, he further adds, has
its intrinsic strength and potency only "by looking the negative in
the face." Passages of this kind could readily be multiplied; yet, it is
necessary to take a closer look at Hegel's statements. What emerges
on inspection is that the "negative" in Hegel's thought is always ancillary to, or in the service of, positive affirmation. Thus, the phrase that
speaks of "the immense power of the negative" immediately adds that
this power is "the energy of [rational] thought, of the pure ego." This
point is underscored when Hegel notes that the power of the negative is "just what we spoke of previously as the subject" or that the
subject is "pure and simple negativity, and on that account a process
of splitting up what is simple and undifferentiated." The correlation
is most clearly expressed, however, in a later passage in the preface

delineating conceptual thought as the *telos* of consciousness: "In the case of conceptual thought, the negative belongs to the content and constitutes, both as its immanent movement and its completed *telos*, the positive [or positive knowledge]."[15]

As one can readily see, in formulations of this kind the role of negation appears muffled or muted. This is precisely Heidegger's complaint when he notes that Hegel's negativity is nothing but "the division (*Unterschied*) happening in consciousness." For Hegel, he adds, negativity is simply "the 'energy' of unconditional thought which, from the beginning, has absorbed everything negative." In a way, negativity from this angle remains something "taken for granted (*fraglos*)": it is "the essence of subjectivity." In an emphatic sense, Hegel's notion of negativity as "negation of negation" is anchored "in the affirmation of absolute self-consciousness."[16] For Heidegger, the ancillary and fugitive character of negativity is closely linked with the fugitive or problematic status of "Being" in Hegel's philosophy. In this respect, his earlier *Being and Time* had already demarcated the parting of ways. In the very first section, dealing with the need to "re-open the question of Being," Heidegger points to Hegel's *Logic* where "Being" is defined as "indeterminate immediacy"—that is, as a pre-reflective empty foil—and where this definition serves as the basis for all further "categorial explications." In the subsequent development of the "becoming" of consciousness, "Being" turns into a synonym for objective beings perceived by subjects, until it finally merges with absolute consciousness or spirit. The problematic status of Hegel's Being is matched by the purely ancillary quality of his notion of negativity—an issue discussed in the concluding sections of *Being and Time*. As Heidegger observes there, negativity for Hegel is initially simply "nothing determinate"—the empty foil of reflection, in order to emerge later as the internal division of consciousness. Hegel, we read, "is able to define the nature of spirit formally and apophanti-cally as the negation of negation. This 'absolute negativity' provides a logically formalized interpretation of Descartes' '*cogito me cogitare rem*,' wherein he sees the essence of *conscientia*." In the end, absolute negativity culminates in absolute spirit, in the "absolute restlessness (*Unruhe*) and self-manifestation of spirit."[17]

As is well known, Heidegger's *Being and Time* presents "Being" neither as an empty immediacy nor as an abstract concept but rather as an urgent "question" prompting the human search for (the meaning of) truth. In a similar manner, negativity or nonbeing is not simply ancillary to the becoming of consciousness; propelled in their quest beyond the realm of things or objects, human beings encounter the original power of "no-thing" or nonbeing (*das Nichts*)—a power eloquently described as a "nihilating" force in Heidegger's lecture "What is Metaphysics?" (presented shortly after *Being and Time*). As we read there: "The nothing is neither an object nor any being at all"; is comes forward "neither for itself nor next to beings [things] to which it would be, as it were, attached." Instead of merely serving as a counter-concept of beings, nothing "originally belongs to their essential unfolding: in the Being of beings the nihilation of nothing occurs."[18] This accent on the independent or nonsubsidiary force of nothing is emphatically reiterated in Heidegger's text on "negativity" cited above. As he observes there: "For the metaphysical thinking [of Hegel], negativity is entirely swallowed up in positivity" and this for the simple reason that Hegel allows autonomy neither to "Being" nor to nothing. Instead, in his dialectical thought, both Being and nothing are initially only a vacuity—the "mere unmediated indeterminacy"—and hence not properly distinguished in their correlation. What needs to happen, by contrast, for Heidegger is the attempt to see "the nothing as the primordial counterforce to Being, and at the same time as its intrinsic nature"—that is, to grasp their differentiated unity. As he adds: Hegel's negativity is muted because it does not take seriously the nihilation operating in nothing. But this nihilation is not just a negative abyss: "The nothing as nihilation is the profound difference from Being while also sharing its nature. The abyss (*Abgrund*) is no-thing-like grounding (*nichthafter Grund*)."[19]

From a very different angle, the muted character of Hegelian negativity has also been pointed out by Theodor Adorno—with a more critical sociopolitical slant. In many ways, Adorno's thinking always revolved around Hegel; but the issue of negativity was most directly addressed in one of his later texts, *Negative Dialectics* (of 1966). Although paying tribute throughout to Hegel's intellectual verve, the text complains about the persistent preponderance of the metaphysics of "subjectivity" and the ultimate "sublation" of negativity—or everything transgressing the rational-conceptual fold—into the positivity of spirit. According to Adorno, the entire course of modern [Western] philosophy revolves around the steady accentuation of consciousness or subjectivity—motivated by the aim "to reduce more and more aspects of [nonsubjective] reality to categories of the thinking subject." In maintaining and even intensifying this trajectory, Hegel's philosophy remained basically heir of Cartesian and Kantian teachings—notwithstanding his strenuous efforts to extricate himself from their rationalism. Being wedded to the paradigm of his predecessors, *Negative Dialectics* states, Hegel's thought did not fully capture the

concrete dynamism he meant to grasp, because his so-called "dialectics"—including the phase of negation—happens within the confines,
and within the internal divisions, of consciousness: The entire fabric
of the dialectical movement "is implicitly pre-thought or conceptu-
ally pre-arranged in every detail," with the result that every concrete
phenomenon appears as "the exemplification of its concept." Adorno
does not hesitate to refer to some sociopolitical dangers inherent in
the philosophy of consciousness or subjectivity. Despite the seeming
innocence of rational reflection, he observes, subjectivity and mastery
or domination have long been reciprocally contaminated: "In its depth,
'spirit' suspects that its stable predominance is not purely spiritual
but has its *ultima ratio* in the physical force at its disposal." Using
even stronger language, he intimates that the primacy of subjectivity,
celebrated in [Western] modernity, "continues in spiritual guise the
Darwinian struggle for survival."[20]

The main shortfall of Hegel's thought, however, resides for
Adorno in its sidelining of negativity as "otherness"—an otherness
exceeding conceptual consciousness and not subsumable under the
rubric of subjectivity or reason's identity with itself. This shortfall was
certainly not what Hegel initially intended. "In his early Introduction
to the *Phenomenology of Spirit*," Adorno writes, "Hegel came close to
the negative character of his dialectical logic." The motto of his *Logic*
to explore every concept so thoroughly until trembles and becomes
"non-identical with itself," clearly showed the strength of his analysis. In this moment of nonidentity, conceptual thought opens itself
to "otherness" (*Anderes*) without absorbing it. Unfortunately, in the
further development of the dialectical system, nonidentity began to
be integrated and ultimately be "sublated" into positive synthesis. In
Adorno's words: Contrary to Hegel, "non-identity cannot be translated
into positivity, not even through the negation of the negation—which,
for Hegel, ends in affirmation." This equation of the negation of negation with positivity is "the quintessential core of identification," which
is the "formal principle" of traditional logic. Against this shortfall
of Hegel's dialectics, Adorno pits the idea of a "negative dialectics"
more attentive to nonconceptual difference. "The endeavor to change
the thrust of conceptualization, turning it toward non-identity," he
writes, "is the emblem of negative dialectics. Insight into the constitutive character of the non-conceptual would terminate the constraint
of identity which conceptual reason otherwise engenders." The aim
of such a different dialectics would be "literally to submerge itself in
heterogeneity, without reducing it to prefabricated categories." There
is a further implication of this kind of dialectics. Seen from this angle,

a concluding section of the text states, Hegel's notion of the so-called "march of the world spirit" derails, rendering illusory the notion of an actual or predictable completion or "end of history."[21]

Toward a Democratic Ethos

With this turn toward a more primordial negativity, subjectivity and conceptual reason are dislodged from their hegemonic or triumphalist position; in the political realm, the same happens to the (monarchical) state construed as the apex of objective spirit. With this change, a chastened and subdued philosophical reflection returns again to the search for, and love of, wisdom—a return that leads it back into the thick fabric of concrete human lives. In this domain, a re-interpreted Hegel can again serve as a present-day mentor. As previously indicated, Merleau-Ponty found inspiration in some of Hegel's works, and especially in his *Phenomenology* where he detected not an abstract system of ideas, but an exploration of "the mind at work" in concrete situations, in "customs, economic structures, and legal institutions." In that early text, he writes, the point of departure was not "a consciousness in full possession of its own clear thoughts" but rather "a life with its own responsibility which tries to understand itself." What proves to be particularly helpful in this context is Hegel's notion of "experience" (*Erfahrung*) seen not as mere sensation nor as a rational construct. Again, Merleau-Ponty eloquently captures its meaning. "Experience," he states, "means here no longer our purely contemplative contact with the sensible world (as it did in Kant)"; rather, "the word reassumes the tragic resonance it has in ordinary language when a man speaks of what he has lived through. It is no longer a laboratory test but rather a trial of life."[22]

As it happens, Hegel's notion of "experience" has also been the target of a lengthy discussion by Heidegger focused on the introduction to the *Phenomenology of Spirit*. As one needs to recall, one of the titles Hegel initially gave to his *Phenomenology* was "Science of the Experience of Consciousness." As Heidegger points out, "experience" here means basically an inner movement or transformation whereby consciousness discovers the true nature of an object of cognition which ultimately turns out to be the truth of consciousness itself. What matters to Heidegger is the transformative movement of experience that, he notes, does not have the character of a mere empirical change but rather involves a breakthrough to a new level or a deeper "*parousia*" of truth. To be sure, viewed as a mere movement within consciousness, Hegelian "experience" remains within the confines of traditional metaphysics, denoting simply the progressive unfolding of "the subjectivity of the absolute subject." However, the term can also be given a more radical (ontological) meaning whereby it designates the transformative "inversion (*Umkehrung*) of consciousness itself," an inversion that does not happen "for consciousness" but points ek-statically beyond—possibly in the direction (not chosen by Hegel) of a new openness to "Being" and nonbeing (or nothingness). The point for Heidegger at this juncture, however, is not the particular construal but rather the idea of "inversion" or radical turning-around itself. Some of the most eloquent and dramatic passages in his exegesis are devoted to this turn-about. The Hegelian movement of spirit, he writes, is "the path of despair on which consciousness loses its not-yet-true character and sacrifices it to the *parousia* of truth." It is a path where consciousness "suffers its own death under the power of the absolute." Toward the end of his *Phenomenology*, Hegel hence calls his work "the golgatha of absolute spirit."[23]

Apart from, and in close connection with, the notion of experience as undergoing or suffering, Hegel's mentoring role is also manifest in his conception of "ethical life" (*Sittlichkeit*). In contrast to widespread misreadings, ethical life for Hegel does not just mean habitual behavior in accordance with factually prevailing customs; nor does it denote a series of abstract norms or principles that—limited to theoretical cognition—fail to animate practical conduct in concretely lived situations. Moreover, living ethically for Hegel is not just a private-individual venture but always occurs in a social and political context. Hence, harking back to Aristotelian teachings, *Sittlichkeit* means the instantiation of ethical aspirations in actual conduct, the cultivation of duty (*Pflicht*) in everyday praxis, and the mediation or reconciliation of "universal" demands with the contingencies of particular life situations. This mediated character was already clearly outlined in one of Hegel's early texts: his *System der Sittlichkeit* (*System of Ethical Life*, 1802–1803). As Hegel emphasized at the time, ethics is not merely a mode of theoretical knowledge, but involves practical engagement on a variety of levels, primarily the levels of family, civil society, and the *polis*. On all these levels, ethical conduct manifests itself in interaction with other human beings, an interaction triggering a complex formative or learning process (*Bildung*). By virtue of this learning process, individual agents are gradually released from the grip of narrow particularity or immediacy in favor of a greater openness toward others; in this manner, the individual becomes in due course "a universality for the other, just as the other is for him."

The highest stage of this mutual engagement or recognition (*Anerken-nung*) is the *polis* where the particular living individual is gradually imbued with the "absolute concept" and hence comes to exist in a universal or "eternal mode."[24]

A much fuller account of ethical life is presented in Hegel's *Philosophy of Right*, particularly in its third part dealing with the different levels of *Sittlichkeit*. The part starts with this lapidary sentence: "Ethical life is the idea of freedom seen as living [or enacted] goodness, a goodness whose knowing will is anchored in self-consciousness and its reality in its enactment, just as the latter finds in the ethical idea its absolute foundation and motivating goal." As can be seen, *Sittlichkeit* for Hegel is the mediation between normative demands and concrete human motivations or aspirations. The tension implicit in this media-tion is explicated clearly in subsequent sections. On the one hand, we read, the ethical idea with its norms and demands has for the human individual the character of an "independent higher reality," the character of "an absolute, and infinitely greater authority and power than the reality of nature." On the other hand, the demands of ethics are for the individual not "something alien" (*ein Fremdes*), but rather testify spiritually to the individual's "own deeper being," to his/her own "feeling of selfhood." Accordingly, ethical demands operate for the individual as "duties (*Pflichten*) binding his/her will"; at the same time, however, the latter function as the gateway to "freedom" liberating the individual both from subservience to natural instincts and from the sense of "oppression" or "depression" (*Gedrücktheit*) felt by individuals in the face of moral imperatives. Hence, in ethically inspired conduct the individual gains "substantial freedom," a freedom consonant with the practice of "virtue" (*Tugend*). To qualify as virtue, however, ethical conduct must be not only sporadic or occasional but—echoes of Aristotle again—the reflection of a continuous disposi-tion reflecting steadiness of character. Once virtue achieves this kind of steadiness, Hegel concludes, *Sittlichkeit* turns into "custom" (*Sitte*), a habitual practice where ethical conduct appears as second nature replacing a "purely natural will."[25]

Properly modified—stripped, above all, of the apotheosis of subjectivity—Hegelian *Sittlickkeit* clearly has relevance today (as an alternative to fashionable moral theories, from utilitarianism and consequentialism to an "oppressive" deontology one-sidedly stressing moral duties). A chastened and quasi-Hegelian mode of ethics, on the level of ordinary life experience, has been formulated by Adorno in his *Minima Moralia*, subtitled *Reflections from Damaged Life*. In his text, Adorno pays explicit tribute to Hegel as the teacher of a method disclosing the mediated character of subjectivity and every isolated phenomenon; at the same time, rebelling against the lure of absolute synthesis, he marshals the power of negativity against this very method, insisting (with and against Hegel) that spirit gains its truth "only in and through absolute diremption," that is, in and through the interplay of concrete particularities.[26] From another perspective and employing a different (ontological) idiom, Heidegger at various points has delineated the contours of an ethics seen as concretely lived "*ethos*," a conduct situated beyond the confines of description and prescription, of sensation and duty (and hence also beyond naturalism and deontology). As he observes in one text (composed roughly at the same time as *Minima Moralia*): "If, in keeping with the basic meaning of '*ethos*,' the term 'ethics' is taken to designate the human situatedness (*Aufenthalt*) in the world, then it follows that a thinking which conceives human life as 'standing-out' into the truth of Being, contains already implicitly an originary ethics." As in the case of Adorno, this originary ethics is nurtured by an emphatic closeness to negation or nothing (*Nichts*). This closeness is revealed in the fact that good and evil—or, in Heidegger's idiom, the "hale" and the "malice of rage"—are not simply subjective human preferences, but are anchored in the power of Being and nonbeing. "Both of these," he writes, "the hale and the rage, can only occur insofar as Being itself is divided or contested (*das Strittige*), concealing the basic upsurge of nihilation. What nihilates, however, illuminates itself as the no-thing-like (*das Nichthafte*)."[27]

Yet, to be viable today, *Sittlichkeit* has to extricate itself not only from the apotheosis of subjectivity but also from the hegemony of the modern "state" seen as apex of objective spirit. At a time when "states" in Western countries are nearly synonymous with military-industrial complexes, there is a strong need to reinvigorate ethics on an everyday, social level. Differently put: in lieu of a state-centered *Sittlichkeit* operating in "top–down" fashion, we need a democratic *ethos* cultivated "from the ground up." Apart perhaps from John Dewey, no one has formulated the gist of such an *ethos* better than Merleau-Ponty. As we read in one of his early writings: "A society is not the temple of value-idols that figure on the front of its monuments or in its constitutional scrolls. . . . To understand and judge a society, one has to penetrate its basic structure to the human bond upon which it is built"—which "undoubtedly depends upon legal relations, but also upon forms of labor, ways of loving, living, and dying."[28] Transgressing the hegemony of the state also means to call into question the totalizing or homogenizing quality of the Hegelian vision. In this respect, the contemporary upsurge of "multiculturalism" demands a greater respect for societal pluralism and diversity than was tolerated by the traditional state. William Connolly has eloquently articulated this demand for a greater acceptance or recognition of diversity under the rubrics of an enlarged ethical "generosity" or an expanded democratic "sensibility" toward others. The "most urgent need today," he writes, is to cultivate "presumptively generous sensibilities" and to open them up to the prevailing variety of "theistic and nontheistic creeds" and cultural aspirations. As he adds—embracing the register of *Sittlicheit*—such cultivation in turn presupposes the nurturing of concrete practical virtues: "The public *ethos* of pluralism . . . solicits the active cultivation of pluralist values by each faith [or tradition] and the negotiation of a positive *ethos* of engagement between them."[29]

Connolly's text also intimates another transgression of the state, a transgression pointing in a different direction: that of a global pluralism or a pluralist cosmopolitanism. Without simply bypassing state structures or treating them as obsolete, he observes, "what is needed are creative modes of intervention . . . in the service of reducing economic inequality, fostering intra- and inter-state pluralism, and promoting ecological sanity"—thus laying the groundwork for a global democratic *ethos*.[30] It is at this point that we seem to reach the outer limit or most important shortfall of Hegel's philosophy: its deeply engrained Eurocentrism or Western-centrism. In all of his writings, including the *Phenomenology* and *Philosophy of Right*, Hegel treats non-Western societies or modes of life as basically backward, underdeveloped, and in need of "catching up" with Western modernity. The assumption underlying this treatment seems to be that people living in the modern West have reached the highest stage of rational maturity and hence are masters and no longer pupils.

As opposed to this premise, the contemporary age of globalization discloses vast new arenas of further learning experiences—experiences held in store precisely for those whose "school days" are claimed to be over. In an essay titled "Hegel's Philosophy and Its Aftereffects until Today," Heidegger's student, Hans-Georg Gadamer, stressed the need for such new learning experiences. In light of Hegel's historical teleology, Gadamer writes, has the "end of history" really arrived? With his announcement of the "principle of freedom" has the need for learning stopped? Or is it not rather the case that we are now faced with the issue of translation and implementation—an issue that "points to the unending march of world history into the openness of its future tasks and gives no becalming assurance that everything is already in order"?[31] To be sure—and as Gadamer would agree—implementation does not just involve the application of a fixed doctrine to particular cases; rather, the learning works both ways. To grasp the complexity of this process, it is good to return to Merleau-Ponty who has admirably pinpointed the issue. "Civilizations lacking our philosophical or economic equipment," he writes at one point, "take on an instructive value." In particular, "the Orient's 'childishness' has something to teach us, if it were nothing more than the narrowness of our adult ideas." The relationship between Orient and Occident, he adds (in a passage summing up a genuine post-Hegelian *ethos*),

> like that between child and adult, is not that of ignorance to knowledge or non-philosophy to philosophy. . . . Simply rallying and subordinating "non-philosophy" to true philosophy will not create the unity of the human spirit. It already exists in each culture's lateral relationships to the others, in the echoes one awakes in the other.[32]

3

Democratic Action and Experience

Dewey's "Holistic" Pragmatism

The pragmatic legacy will only be recovered and revitalized when we try to do for our time what Dewey did in his historical context—to articulate, texture, and justify a vision of a pragmatically viable ideal of communal democracy.

—Richard Bernstein

Hegel's philosophical system did not persist long beyond his lifetime. As Karl Marx noted on his arrival in Berlin (in 1836), the system was in a state of complete disintegration.[1] This does not mean that fragments of the Hegelian corpus were not invoked and used for diverse partisan purposes. Thus, Left or "Young" Hegelians (so-called) appropriated Hegel's emphasis on social reform to overturn elitist legacies—but usually without concern for *Sittlichkeit* or public *ethos*. On the other hand, Right Hegelians were intent on bolstering the modern state bureaucracy—but without attention to individual freedom in civil society. Hence, what atrophied was not so much the "*disjecta membra*" (disjointed pieces) but the synthesis and "holistic" integrity of Hegel's philosophical vision. Academic philosophy, in any case, proceeded on its own, thoroughly non-Hegelian paths. From the vantage of "objective spirit," these paths led into either "upward" or "downward" directions. Thus, through a variety of restorative movements (from neo-Thomism to neo-Kantianism), some philosophers aimed to retrieve "perennial" truths located beyond time and space; countering this speculative ascent, other philosophers curtailed their reflective ambitions so as to become "handmaidens" of modern science or scientific positivism. Curiously, by the end of the nineteenth century, Hegel's holistic vision found resonance and at least a partial revival in an unexpected setting far from its native habitat: democracy in the New World as envisaged by American pragmatist thinkers.

Among leading American philosophers of that period, John Dewey was most strongly influenced by Hegel and exhibited the strongest affinity for the integral quality of his German precursor. This does not mean, of course, that Dewey was in any way an orthodox disciple or intent on recapitulating German idealist teachings. As is well known, after an initial period of infatuation, Dewey broke with the idealist model, in an effort to replace it with a more concrete, down-to-earth perspective. Yet, innovation did not entirely erase some continuity. Basically, what the change amounted to was an attempt to replace Hegel's spiritual holism with a more organic or "naturalistic" holism—something he (misleadingly) labeled "instrumentalism" or instrumental pragmatism. The continuing influence of Hegel, however, remained evident in a number of key terms or categories structuring the pragmatist's work—most importantly the category of "experience." Some of his most important texts employ the term in their titles: *Experience and Nature*, *Art as Experience*, and *Experience and Education*. As in the case of his German precursor, "experience" for Dewey did not just mean a sensory impact but rather a complex learning process whereby human beings expose themselves to the lessons of the world while simultaneously integrating these lessons in evolving interpretive frameworks.

This interactive process, in turn, remained faithful to Hegel's deepest aims: the aim of healing the modern divisions or diremptions between subject and object, knowledge and *praxis*, agency and social institutions. In the present context, I can only lift up some aspects of Dewey's sprawling work. While in a first step, I examine his notion of "philosophizing" as a mode of learning experience or ongoing inquiry, I turn in a second step to his prominent role as a pedagogue or philosopher of democratic education. In two concluding sections, I assess Dewey's contribution to democratic agency, while also reviewing some recent attempts to move beyond his kind of pragmatism.

Philosophy as Inquiry

During the early period of his life, when Hegel's influence was still pronounced, Dewey wrote a book on philosophical thinking that laid out the basic contours of his pragmatic approach. Titled *How We Think* (and first published in 1909), the text ranged over a broad array of relevant issues and problem areas (only some of which can be highlighted here). Differentiating the term from more superficial conceptions, the text made it clear that, for Dewey, the main concern was with "reflective thinking" seen as a kind of sustained inquiry relying on available evidence in the face of possible objections. In his words, thinking as inquiry involves "active, persistent, and careful consideration of any belief or supposed form of knowledge in the light of the grounds that support it, and the further conclusions to which it tends." Thinking of this kind is not entirely spontaneous or self-generated. In a quasi-Platonic or Socratic vein, Dewey stipulates that reflective thought always proceeds from a puzzle or quandary that triggers wondering and a desire to search for clarification or better understanding. "The origin of thinking," we read, "is some perplexity, confusion, or doubt. Thinking is not a case of spontaneous combustion; it does not occur just on 'general principles.' " Because it is not generated by abstract principles, inquiry itself does not amount to a purely logical or cerebral exercise. Properly conducted, reflective thinking involves the human being as a whole and often entails agony or a kind of existential transformation. To cite Dewey again: "Reflective thinking is always more or less troublesome because it involves overcoming the inertia that inclines one to accept suggestions at their face value; it involves a willingness to endure a condition of mental unrest and disturbance."[2]

Being triggered by quandaries and resulting in possible transformative change, reflective thinking in Dewey's account exhibits a certain worldly "concreteness" reminiscent of Hegel's work (especially the latter's *Phenomenology of the Spirit*). At the same time, not being confined to cerebral manipulations, Deweyan reflection maintains the correlation—although not identity—of theory and *praxis* familiar from Aristotle's "practical" philosophy (and also from Hegel's *Philosophy of Right*). Throughout his text, Dewey takes a critical stance toward two prominent (mis)conceptions of philosophy: on the one hand, an abstract idealism or else "intellectualism" confining thought to an internal process in the mind; and on the other hand, a shallow empiricism or positivism that reduces thinking to the passive reception of sense data. Adopting a superior and decontextualized outlook, intellectualism prides itself in being purely "theoretical" and not being "associated with practical concerns." What remains when these concerns are bracketed? "Evidently only what has to do with knowing considered as an end in itself." For a "theorist" of this kind, thought is adequate and self-contained "just because it engages and rewards thought" while being severed from any "end or good beyond itself." On the other hand, empiricism is content to gather sense impressions randomly without any concern for their broader meaning or implications for lived *praxis*. What happens in both of these approaches is that reflective thinking comes to a stand still, being stalled either in the abstractions of mind or in the randomness of sense data. Turning sharply against devotees of a thoughtless "empirical method," Dewey states that "mental inertia, laziness, unjustifiable conservatism, are its probable accompaniments." But the same inertia can also result from an abstract perennialism: "Certain men or classes of men come to be accepted as guardians and transmitter of established doctrines. To question the beliefs is to question their authority. . . . Passivity, docility, acquiescence come to be primal intellectual virtues."[3]

Against the sketched derailments of philosophy Dewey pits the notion of "experience" in its rich concreteness. As used by him in the text, the term denotes a sustained attentiveness to the diverse phenomena of the world coupled with an alert curiosity and eagerness to derive some integral sense or meaning from them. "Experience," we read, "is not a rigid and closed thing; it is vital, and hence growing." When dominated by the past, by custom and routine, "it is often opposed to the reasonable, the thoughtful. But experience also includes the reflection that sets us free from the limiting influence of sense, appetite, and tradition." Although open or receptive to sensory phenomena, reflective thought intervenes creatively to distill meanings or coherent frameworks—and does so mainly with the help of language and symbol systems: "Learning in the proper sense is not learning 'things,' but the *meaning* of things, and this process involves the use of signs or language in its generic sense." The bestowal of meaning is not mechanical or detached but rather is guided by a concrete concern or what Dewey calls a "sympathetic interest," which provides "the medium for carrying and binding together what would otherwise be a multitude of items, diverse, disconnected, and of no intellectual use." It is at this point that something like an "active intellect" is operative in transforming passive observation into an "*active* process." For, properly construed, Dewey notes, "observation is exploration, inquiry for the sake of discovering something previously hidden and unknown." Without being arbitrary or whimsical, reflective thought always displays a "phase of originality," where the latter means "personal interest in the question, personal initiative in turning over the suggestions furnished by others, and sincerity in following them out to a tested conclusion." By working over dispersed, fragmentary materials, Dewey concludes (in Hegelian fashion), thought "unites what was isolated and therefore puzzling, and thus generalizes."[4]

In analyzing the notion of reflective thinking, commentators often have emphasized the close connection between Deweyan "inquiry" and the methods of modern natural science—and not entirely spuriously. There can be no doubt that, especially during his middle years, Dewey was strongly impressed by the progress of modern science, and especially by the new vistas opened by Darwinian evolutionism. Given that (apart from "pure" knowledge) modern science typically is in the service of ulterior ends—such as the furthering of "man's estate" (in Bacon's phrase)—Deweyan pragmatism has often been narrowly identified with "instrumentalism" (a phrase he not always disdained) or a coldly calculating utilitarianism. Despite certain overtones or affinities, however, great care must be taken (I believe) not to forget Dewey's holistic or integral leanings—leanings that persisted even in his more naturalistic or "scientistic" phase. Hence, notwithstanding his appreciation of modern innovations, scientific method should be considered only as one type or example of reflective inquiry; moreover, the very meaning of "science" and "scientific method" requires renewed scrutiny.[5] The unorthodox character of Dewey's notion of "science"—a notion closer to the German "*Wissenschaft*" as employed in Hegel's "Science of Experience" (*Wissenschaft der Erfahrung*)—is evident in an essay composed toward the end of World War I, in 1917, entitled "The Need for a Recovery of Philosophy." The essay takes aim again at the twin antipodes of pragmatism seen as a concretely practical philosophy. The first antipode is now termed abstract "rationalism," a perspective anchored in a radical dualism. Modern rationalism, Dewey notes, "accepted the account of experience given by traditional empiricism and introduced reason as extra-empirical." What remained mysterious, however, was "how a reason extraneous to experience could enter into a helpful relation with concrete experiences." For, by definition, "reason and experience were antithetical," so that the concern of reason was not the guidance of experience "but a realm of considerations too sublime to touch, or be touched, by experience."[6]

Even more strongly rebuked is the other antipode of pragmatic thought: empiricism or fact-gathering positivism. Like rationalism, the empiricist paradigm also rested on a dualism, but shifted the accent to the factual side. In Dewey's words: "One of the curiosities of orthodox empiricism is that its outstanding speculative problem is the existence of an 'external world' " (outside of mind). Not surprisingly, this accent gives rise to the quandary how this external world can at all be known, that is, to the dominant "problem of knowledge as conceived in the industry of epistemology." Typically, empiricist epistemology predicates the possibility of knowledge on the "correspondence" between statements or mental states and external phenomena—but without being able to show how the notion of correspondence is itself factually grounded (or "corresponds" itself to external facts). Seen in this way, empiricist epistemology remains suspended in midair. It is against the implicit dogmatism of this paradigm that Dewey marshals the powerful legacy of Hegelian holism with its bent toward relieving the diremptions between subject and object, mind and matter, "knower" and the "known." Taking a stand against the so-called "spectator theory of knowledge," Dewey challenges the presupposed subject–object gulf whereby "knowing is a viewing from outside." But, he continues,

> if it be true that the self or subject of experience is part and parcel of the course of events, it follows that the self *becomes* a knower. It *becomes* a mind in virtue of a distinctive way of partaking in the course of events. The significant distinction is no longer between the knower *and* the world; it is between different ways of being in and of the movement of things.

Viewed in this light, pragmatism takes indeed its stand with "science"—but a science that is sufficiently open and nonepistemological to resonate generously with "daily life" and the unfolding "texture of events."[7]

With this accent on the "becoming" or maturation of knowledge, philosophical inquiry emerges as an ongoing learning process in which both the target of inquiry and the inquirer undergo a formative, and possibly transformative, experience. Differently put: reflective thought is not a mechanical operation whereby a fixed "knower" pursues and reaches a pre-established goal or target; rather, what happens—in near-Hegelian fashion—is that the inquiring mind (or consciousness) is itself challenged and reversed, leading to a seasoning of reflective intelligence. It is this seasoning of intelligence that, in Dewey's account, captures the deepest "need for a recovery of philosophy." What pragmatism aims at, he insists, is not some external utility or usefulness; rather, its deeper concern is with the quickening of intelligence so as to free it from stale dogmas, mindless customs, and base inclinations. In his words: "The pragmatic theory of intelligence means that the function of mind is to project new and more complex ends—to free experience from routine and caprice." The endeavor to attain pregiven or fixed goals may display great technical efficiency; but the envisaging of new possibilities or potentialities is the very "opposite of a doctrine of mechanical efficiency." For Dewey as a pragmatist, thought or intelligence is "inherently forward-looking" beyond the scope of the status quo; attaching oneself to possibilities not previously staked out is the emblem of "a quickened and enlarged spirit." Continuing this train of thought, the essay concludes with a captivating expression of faith or hope (far removed from a timid instrumentalism): "Faith in the power of intelligence to imagine a future which is the projection of the desirable in the present . . . is our salvation. And it is a faith which must be nurtured and made articulate: surely a sufficiently large task for our philosophy."[8]

The forward-looking character of Deweyan philosophizing or reflective thinking was steadily intensified during the later period of his life. The dreadful experiences with fascism and the persistence of totalizing ideologies in the post-war world persuaded him that, now more than ever, the urgent task ahead was a "recovery of philosophy," the latter term taken not as an abstract, perennial pastime but as a practical and ethical engagement with the pressing crises of the time. In an essay composed in 1949 and titled "Has Philosophy a Future?," Dewey placed his pragmatic approach in opposition to this outlook, focused on timeless issues in abstraction from human concerns. To a large extent, he noted, traditional philosophy has been preoccupied with "all-embracing" themes such as "Being, Reality, the Universe, Nature at large," themes that were implicitly marked off from everything that is partial and merely human. In opposition to this outlook, Dewey recommended to approach philosophy "the other way around and about," that is, a way that would not abscond beyond time and place, but concentrate on "what is most comprehensive *within* human affairs and occupations." Such preoccupation, he added, was particularly crucial in the present context that is marked by a "crisis of human affairs," a crisis attested to by its "literally worldwide occurrence": "The expression 'One World' has to do with a world which is *one* only in the sense that it is unsettled and disturbed throughout all its parts and in the relation of these parts to one another. Moreover, the crisis is as intensive as it is extensive."[9]

The essay of 1949 is important both for clearly differentiating pragmatism from a narrowly partisan activism and for clarifying the role of "science" in relation to the future of philosophy. Dewey minces no words in castigating intellectual perspectives that, although dressed in philosophical garb, place themselves entirely in the service of unreflective ideologies. As he notes, there are some "aggressive" intellectual movements that claim to be relevant today but in fact are entirely subservient to a particular institution or authority. Two varieties are prominent: one on the extreme Left, the other (of older vintage) on the extreme Right. The older variety appeals to historical tradition and to some spiritual authority upholding that tradition. In its aggressive form, the authority invoked is claimed to be "final and absolute"; some advocates of this variety authoritatively demand a return to premodern times and a rejection of modernity with its emphasis on science and reason. In this rejection of modernity, political traditionalism stands worlds apart from the devotees of the "extreme Left" movement; for the claim or dogma of that movement is precisely that it is "the very climax and completion of all that is genuinely modern and scientific." For Dewey, this claim is lopsided if not entirely spurious. For one thing, the "science" invoked by the movement is itself old-fashioned and "now scientifically outgrown"; the modernist aura is derived from Newtonian physics, whereas newer developments—like relativity and quantum theories—are neglected. The dogmatic character of the movement is also shown in the treatment of history where the entire course of historical change is penned within "fixed limits"—on the assumption "that history has revealed its complete meaning and taught its final human lesson in the middle of the twentieth century." As Dewey sharply retorts: "The denial of the occurrence of the novel, the unforeseen, the unexpected in history, would be comic were it not tragic in its consequences. . . . The whole scheme is monolithic. It holds that unity, whole-ness, is necessarily structural and static."[10]

These comments throw further light on Dewey's broad-minded and flexible conception of science—in contrast to the narrow "scientism" with which he has often been charged. Important additional contours of this conception emerge in the concluding part of the 1949 essay. Basically, Dewey at this point distinguishes between an early phase of modern science focused on physics and the development of socially beneficial techniques; and a later phase when the benefits of that science have become ambivalent. "The incoming of science," he observes, "was hailed as the initial stage of an era of rational illumination; its conclusions were welcomed as ushering in an age of prosperity and mutual understanding." Of late, however, this positive estimate has given way to a mood of "equally indiscriminate pessimism and condemnation." For Dewey, the point is not to choose for or against science, for or against the Enlightenment. Rather, the task is to recapture the initial inspiration that guided science as a mode of inquiry, as the medium of a general learning process. As indicated before, his intent is to reorient philosophy, to guide it "the other way around and about." In large measure, this "turn-*about*" (*Kehre?*) involves a "*re*-turn" to the view of philosophy "put forward of old by Socrates," to the view of philosophy as "a *moral* undertaking in the sense in which the moral and the deeply and widely human are identical." What is involved in this turn is not a rejection of science as such, but a turning-way from older physicalist models that by now have become stale and doctrinaire. Although glorified by progressivists, Dewey comments, "our science is technical rather than widely and deeply human"; it would be a "measure of sanity and sober wisdom" to cultivate a broader inquiry suitable for present-day needs. Allowing Galileo and his successors directly to address contemporary philosophers, the essay concludes with a passage far removed from a shallow instrumentalism:

> It is for you to do for the very life of man what we did for the physical and physiological conditions of that life. . . . It is for you to use [the results of our search] to carry forward the establishing of a more human order of freedom, equity, and nobility. We accomplished the simpler and more technical part of the work. It is for you, possessors of a torch lit by our toil and sacrifice, to undertake, with patient and courageous intelligence, a work which will hand on to *your* successors a torch that will illuminate a truly human world.[11]

Philosopher of Education

From his emphasis on reflective thought as inquiry—an inquiry continuously to be cultivated—the pedagogical thrust of Dewey's work can immediately be gleaned. It seems fair to say that, among late modern philosophers, no one in fact has paid more attention than Dewey to education and its role in social and political life. Like his concern with inquiry, this preoccupation persisted throughout the different stages of his career. An early expression of this commitment was penned in 1897, while he was teaching at the University of Chicago, and is titled "My Pedagogic Creed." In this creed, every child is perceived as the heir or heiress of the accumulated treasures of human civilization: "I believe that all education proceeds by participation of the individual in the social consciousness" of the species.

The process begins unconsciously at birth; but gradually the child comes to share consciously "in the intellectual and moral resources which humanity has succeeded in getting together." What needs to be noted here is the participatory aspect of education. Dewey's pedagogical outlook is sometimes charged with favoring a one-sided, child-oriented approach stressing the child's "natural" abilities. But this misconstrues the point. Dewey does indeed want the child to participate experientially (and creatively) in the learning process—not to dominate it unilaterally. What Dewey wants to guard against is both the glorification of the *"bon sauvage"*—exempt from the need for education—and the lure of social conformism fostered by a detached formalism, that is, the stress on rote learning and memorization characteristic of much traditional schooling.[12]

At the time the "Creed" was composed, modern psychology was just emerging as a professional discipline, supplementing the somewhat older sociological profession. Some of the terms used in Dewey's text reflect these developments (and should probably be taken with a grain of salt): "I believe that this educational process has two sides—one psychological and one sociological; and that neither can be subordinated to the other or neglected without ill results." On the psychological side, the child's own inclinations and talents furnish "the material and the starting point for all education." However, "knowledge of social conditions, of the present state of civilization," is for Dewey equally necessary in order properly to channel the child's abilities. For, although the child has his or her tendencies, we do not know what they mean "until we translate them into their social equivalents." As Dewey emphasizes, the two aspects should not be construed as two separate dimensions or as replicas of the Cartesian mind–matter or inner–outer bifurcation—a construal that would entirely vitiate Dewey's holistic pragmatism. The two "sides," the psychological and social, are rather mutually implicated and contaminated—or, as he says, they are "organically related" leaving no room for mere compromise or super-imposition. In a pithy formulation that eloquently captures his pedagogical outlook, Dewey states: "I believe that the individual who is to be educated is a social individual and that society is an organic union of individuals. If we eliminate the social factor from the child we are left only with an abstraction; if we eliminate the individual factor from society, we are left only with an inert and lifeless mass." In more overtly political terms, the outlook makes room for both "individualistic and socialistic ideals," thus endorsing something like a social liberalism or a liberal socialism.[13]

To be sure, the latter terms needs to be used cautiously, given Dewey's strong aversion to fixed systems or totalizing ideologies. Thus, the term *socialism* needs to be cleansed of an oppressive collectivism incompatible with his attachment to human freedom. In turn, the meaning of *liberalism* needs to be rethought, precisely with regard to its implications for education. For Dewey, one of the unacceptable (and even unintelligible) axioms of early liberalism was the assumption of a "foundational" *a priorism*: the idea that human beings "by nature" (or by "nature's God") are endowed with certain fixed traits or qualities, completely apart from cultivation or education. In line with certain late-modern innovations, Dewey preferred to consider human beings as bundles of possibilities or potentialities, bundles whose maturation depends on appropriate social contexts and educational guidance. This view is articulated with particular cogency in one of his most prominent texts on education: his *Democracy and Education* of 1916. As he points out there, early modern philosophy was basically a reaction or rebellion against past constraints. In opposition to perceived forms of authoritarianism, early modern thinkers took refuge in such conceptions as "mind-free-from-world" or "individual-free-from-society." "The reaction against authority in all spheres of life," we read, "and the intensity of the struggle, against great odds, for freedom of action and inquiry, led to such an emphasis upon personal observations and ideas as in effect to isolate mind and set it apart from the world to be known." Despite the undeniable advancement of science and enlightenment, early liberalism—in Dewey's account—ignored a premise needed for the success of its own enterprise: the sociality of knowledge: "As a matter of fact, every individual has grown up, and always must grow up, in a social medium. His/her responses grow intelligent, or gain meaning, simply because he/she lives and acts in a medium of accepted meanings and values."[14]

With these comments, Dewey takes a stand—once again—against the Cartesian *cogito* and a "spectatorial" view of knowledge, showing them to be at odds with education. Underscoring his pragmatic (or *praxis*-oriented) outlook, he insists that it is "through social intercourse, through sharing in the activities embodying beliefs" that the individual "gradually acquires a mind of his/her own." Hence, contrary to the claims of *a priorism*, "the self *achieves* mind in the degree in which knowledge of things is incarnate in the life about him." To avoid misunderstanding, the emphasis on interactive nurturing—in Dewey's case—does not amount to an endorsement of social or contextual determinism destructive of individual freedom. As with regard to "mind," individual freedom is also presented as a shared achievement, as the corollary of a long historical learning process—not as an instantaneous, unilateral initiative. Perhaps remembering Hegelian teachings, *Democracy and Education* sketches the historical development of individual freedom from antiquity to the present, always with concrete attention to social context. As in the case of Hegel's work, the Greek *polis* is presented as a society not entirely devoid of individual freedom, but where freedom is limited to a few and even then sharply subordinated to communal needs. In contrast to this tradition, modern Western Enlightenment celebrated a strictly "individualistic ideal" and a human freedom seen as "nonsocial or even antisocial." Although helpful as a weapon to combat inveterate customs and abuses, the ideal was ultimately unable to account both for individual freedom and social institutions: "Merely to leave everything to 'nature' was, after all, but to negate the very idea of education; it was to trust to the accidents of circumstance." Going beyond the Hegelian narrative, Dewey finds many nineteenth-century intellectuals intent on overcoming the social void, but filling it (inadequately) with the conception of a unified nationhood. Only an open-ended democratic society, he concludes, can provide the proper educational context for human freedom.[15]

In this and subsequent writings on the topic, education has the quality of a broadly formative process akin to *Bildung*—though minus the elitist features sometimes attached to that notion. Moreover, education in its proper sense extends beyond narrowly instrumental career training—without dismissing such training on some levels and for some purposes. The need to balance the different dimensions of education, but with an eye toward fostering noninstrumental concerns, is clearly stated in an essay of the same period titled "American Education and Culture." The essay calls attention to the concrete historical situation of America: the situation of an expanding industrial society in a country whose land has barely been tamed and settled. Under prevailing conditions, attention to utilitarian and narrowly practical pursuits could not be readily dismissed. However, as a forward-looking pragmatist, Dewey was intent on supplementing awareness of existing reality with an appreciation of future possibilities. Like "mind" or human "freedom," culture—especially refined or noninstrumental culture—was not an *a priori* possession but a task to be achieved. As Dewey noted candidly: "Stripped of egoistic illusions" the fact is "that we have as yet not culture: that our culture is something to achieve, to create." Achievement of this kind requires more than a merely marginal or sporadic effort: "The enterprise is of heroic dimensions." Putting himself entirely in the service of this effort, Dewey's essay articulated a breathtaking pedagogic vision: "To transmute a society built on industry which is not yet humanized into a society which wields its knowledge and its industrial power in behalf of a democratic culture requires the courage of an inspired imagination." Given the immensity of the undertaking, the effort may fail. Some well-intentioned people may resign prematurely and surrender themselves to "the meshes of a mechanical industrialism." But others may persist trying to "subdue the industrial machinery to human ends until the nation is endowed with soul."[16]

Dewey's refusal to identify education with narrowly instrumental training is evident from the important role he assigned throughout his life to art and artistic expression. His *Democracy and Education* contains an important chapter on "educational values" that makes broad room for art, including the "fine arts." "Literature and the fine arts," he observes there, "are of peculiar value because they represent appreciation at its best—a heightened realization of meaning through selection and concentration." Yet, for the pragmatist, the fine arts should not be separated too neatly from other art forms and ordinary activities—because such a segregation would rob the latter of their own humanistic (and noninstrumental) integrity: "Every subject at some phase of its development should possess, what is for the individual concerned with it, an aesthetic quality." *Democracy and Education* also devotes a chapter to the significance of "play" and playfulness in the curriculum—perhaps in memory of the famous "play drive" (*Spieltrieb*) formulated by Friedrich Schiller.[17] During the later years of his life, Dewey composed a lengthy study which still ranks as a major landmark of twentieth-century aesthetic theory: his *Art as Experience* (1934). As one should note right away, aesthetics here does not mean a recondite, specialized discipline removed from other domains of thought. Given the pervasive role of "experience" in all of Dewey's philosophy, it is clear that art is not "absolute" in the sense of being "absolved" from ordinary experience and reflective thought in general. As he states in the opening chapter of his treatise: "The odd notion that an artist does not think and a scientific inquirer does nothing else [but think] is the result of converting a difference of tempo and emphasis into a difference in kind. The thinker has his esthetic moment," while "the artist has his problems and thinks as he works" (although his thought is "more immediately embodied in the object").[18]

More than any of his other writings, *Art as Experience* displays the holistic or "relational" character of Dewey's outlook. Without neglecting differences of focus and accent, his treatise refuses to divorce the artist rigidly from other human beings as well as the artwork from the artist. In the words of Abraham Kaplan who introduces the study: "In the perspective of cultural dualism, art is counterposed to science [or inquiry] as subjective rather than objective, private rather than public, concrete rather than abstract, particular rather than general, sensory rather than intellectual." But the distinctions are far from solid; for, we speak of "understanding art," even such nonrepresentational art as music and poetry, and the term *intellectual* simply names the fact "that the experience has meaning." In contrast to certain theories concentrating on "taste," the experience of art for Dewey does not coincide with private enjoyment or passive consumption; nor does it derive from a unilateral transfer of "inside" emotions to external expressions in a display of "genius." Rather, art resides in the consummation of active–passive human experience, in the disclosure of a world through the artwork itself. The integral quality of artistic disclosure has a transformative and deeply educational significance—but precisely when the artwork is not instrumentalized for ideological purposes. It is the inner freedom of the artwork from internal or external compulsions that liberates and brings into view new possibilities of life. In Dewey's words: "Literature conveys the meaning of the past that is significant in present experience and is prophetic of the larger movement of the future. Only imaginative vision elicits the possibilities that are interwoven within the texture of the actual." The treatise concludes with these lines: "Art is a mode of prediction not found in charts and statistics, and it insinuates possibilities of human relations not to be found in rule and precept, admonition and administration."[19]

Mentor of Democracy

During his lifetime, Dewey shared the limelight with several prominent philosophers; but he managed to stand out in an important respect. In the words of Raymond Boisvert: "Dewey distinguishes himself at a stroke from his younger contemporaries, Martin-Heidegger, Ludwig Wittgenstein, and Alfred North Whitehead. Each of these thinkers held strong beliefs and cared deeply about social goods; none of them, however, articulated a detailed sociopolitical philosophy consistent with their overall outlook."[20] Although surrounded by a host of ancillary features, the centerpiece of Dewey's "sociopolitical" philosophy is the rethinking and attempted revitalization of democracy as a political regime. In this respect, his contribution has often been sidelined or else thoroughly misunderstood. In popular parlance, democracy is often closely linked with liberalism and even identified with the latter.

This linkage, however, misses the character of democracy as a form of government, specifically of self-government. As widely construed, liberalism basically means a policy seeking to promote individual freedom from societal and governmental constraints (what Isaiah Berlin called "negative liberty"). Under the aegis of globalization, neo-liberalism has emerged as a dominant global ideology—with odd results for democracy. For if people want to be freed or liberated from self-government, then democracy vanishes. Moreover, someone will quickly step in to fill the gap—but not on democratic terms.[21]

As previously indicated, human freedom for Dewey is not an *a priori* possession but an ongoing achievement requiring cultivation and struggle. The same holds true, and even more emphatically, for democracy. In some of his writings, Dewey reflects explicitly on the character of democracy as a potentiality—in broad accord with the pragmatic view of philosophy as an "inquiry." As we read in "Philosophy and Democracy" (1919), the pragmatic outlook is linked with a conception of the world in which "there is real uncertainty and contingency," a world that "in some respects is incomplete and always in the making." This outlook stands in necessary opposition to a mode of philosophizing claiming to yield absolute or transtemporal truth, a truth often buttressing a rigid rank order of people and things. As Dewey writes sharply, much of traditional philosophy was committed to a "metaphysics of feudalism," that is, a foundational doctrine assigning to people and things fixed grades of value and significance. Wittingly or unwittingly, such a philosophy always tended to work "on behalf of a regime of authority," for it was held to be right and morally correct that "the superior should lord it over the inferior." Without necessarily rejecting all forms of rank, a pragmatic mode of reflective thought has no truck with this foundational conception. To a philosophizing seen as ongoing inquiry, "any notion of a perfect or complete reality, finished, existing always without regard for the vicissitudes of time, will be abhorrent." Such a philosophy will think of time not as just a repetitive series of moments but as "a genuine field of novelty, of real and unpredictable increments of existence, a field for experimentation and invention." Translated into political terms, such a field is modern democracy.[22]

Viewed from this angle, the relation between philosophy and democracy is not just fortuitous or the effect of a personal idiosyncrasy. Rather, the two are linked by a deeper affinity—as demanded by a "holistic" perspective that correlates mind and matter, thinking and doing. To illustrate this affinity further, the essay draws attention to the founding triad of modern democracy: liberty, equality, and fraternity. What is indicated by this triad is not a set of immobile ideas but rather an actively motivating hope or aspiration—such that democracy "means" the hope or love for liberty, equality, and fraternity. Regarding liberty, Dewey distinguishes democratic freedom again from the older "liberal" conception whereby liberty is an *a priori* endowment imprinted on human rationality or rational insight into first principles. In Dewey's account, this is not the kind of freedom inspiring a society that "has set its heart on democracy." Similarly, with regard to equality, democracy is not concerned with fixed equations measured in quantitative or mathematical terms. While erecting a barrier against traditional rank orders, democratic equality is an ethical motivation respecting distinct individuality (although not abstract individualism). In Dewey's words, it means that "every existence deserving the name of existence has something unique and irreplaceable about it," that "it does not exist to illustrate a principle, to realize a universal or to embody a kind of class." Put differently, it means that "no matter how great the quantitative differences of ability, strength, position, wealth, such differences are negligible in comparison with something else—the fact of individuality, the manifestation of something irreplaceable." Once liberty and equality are construed in this manner, the essay concludes "there is nothing forced in understanding fraternity as continuity, that is to say, as association and interaction without limit."[23]

With this interpretation of the democratic triad, Dewey clearly followed Montesquieu's lead in assigning to democracy a distinct ethical quality or aspiration. Emphasis on this ethical quality—not necessarily in opposition to, but always as a premise of governmental arrangements—was in fact a hallmark of Dewey's approach throughout his life. One of his earliest and most widely cited essays, titled "The Ethics of Democracy" (first published in 1888), clearly sets forth his approach. Basically, the essay takes aim at two highly influential conception of politics: first, the modern "social contract" formula whereby government is nothing but an artifact created by individual wills; and second, as a counterpoint, the tempting lure of an aristocratic order of public life. In polemical fashion, both conceptions had been put forth by Sir Henry Maine in his *Popular Government* (1886). For Maine, democracy was basically "a form of government" and nothing else, a form regulating in a certain way the (Hobbesian) relation between the ruler and the ruled, the sovereign and the subjects. More importantly, the basis of this government was purely quantitative or numerical, in that it established "the rule of the many, of the mass." Being simply a numerical aggregate, the popular multitude was unable to exercise actual power and hence had to delegate it to a minority: democratic government thus is "an external power formed by a process of delegation." The way that democracy or democratic government, according to Maine, comes into being is through the formulation of a "social contract"—a process that relies on the idea that "by nature" human beings are "mere individuals without any social relations *until* they form a contract." Being the result of fragmented initiatives, the contract itself brings into being nothing more than a haphazard regime, with "sovereignty" (so-called) coinciding with arbitrary whim on the part of rulers or multitude. In Dewey's words: "To define democracy simply as the rule of the many, as sovereignty chopped up into minced meat, is to define it as abrogation of society, as society dissolved, annihilated."[24]

From Dewey's (still strongly Hegelian) perspective, the conception of democracy—or any political regime—as a mere artifact or machine was unacceptable because it violates the qualitative or ethical dimension of social life. In his words: "The student of society [one might add: the student of politics] has constantly to be on his guard against the abstract and purely mechanical notions introduced from the physical sciences." If alerted to the danger of such abstractions, the student will remember that "men cannot be reduced for political purposes" to mere numbers, whether in the voting booth or in opinion surveys. To the mechanical construal of public life Dewey opposes an "organic" or quasi-organic conception—although he is careful to differentiate it from a purely physical or physiological type. In the animal body, he writes, "the organic relation is incomplete" whereas in human society the relation is transformed and completed. In society, "the whole lives truly in every member, and there is no longer the appearance of [mere] physical aggregation. The organism manifests itself as what it truly is, an ideal or spiritual life, a unity of will." In this respect, democracy approaches most nearly the "ideal" of social organization: one in which "the individual and society are organic to each other" or organically related to each other. Although, like in any form of government, democracy also exhibits a distinction between rulers and ruled, the distinction is merely temporary and ultimately submerged in "relationism" and even coincidence. Herein resides ultimately the difference between democracy and the aristocratic idea because, in the latter, human relationship is limited and truncated in favor of subordination. Dewey at this point invokes the testimony of a fellow intellectual who, in referring to democracy, stated that he was "speaking of a sentiment, a spirit, and not a [mere] form of government." Endorsing this approach, his essay insists on the ethical fiber or *Sittlichkeit* of democratic politics. In opposition to

Maine's mechanical formula, he writes, democracy

> has been finely termed the memory of an historic past, the
> consciousness of a living present, the ideal of the coming
> future. Democracy, in a word, is a social, that is to say, an
> ethical conception, and upon its ethical significance is based
> its significance as governmental. Democracy is a form of
> government only because it is a form of moral and spiritual
> association.[25]

Subsequent traumatic events—the experiences of war and the
rise of totalitarianism—did not basically change Dewey's confidence
in democracy. His *Democracy and Education,* penned during the World
War I, did not waver in this commitment. A democratic society, we
read there, "repudiates the principle of external authority" and hence,
only can rely on "voluntary disposition" and ultimately on education.
But, Dewey adds, "there is a deeper explanation" for this feature: "A
democracy is more than a form of government; it is primarily a mode
of associated living, of conjoint communicated experience."[26] It was,
however, the later spreading of totalitarianism that elicited Dewey's
most eloquent defense of democracy seen as an open-ended and nonrepressive political regime. A 1937 essay, titled "Democracy is Radical," denounced allegedly "left-leaning" regimes or movements that
did not disdain to use oppressive and violent methods to accomplish
their goals. This derailment betrayed a complete misunderstanding of
democracy and its inherent radicalism—which is a radicalism of both
means and ends. As Dewey acknowledged, the end of democracy is
indeed "a radical end" for it is an end "that has not been adequately
realized in any country at any time" and requires profound changes
in social and economic arrangements. But it was equally imperative
for democrats to insist on "democratic methods" for effecting change:
methods relying on "voluntary activities of individuals in opposition to
coercion"; on "assent and consent in opposition to violence"; on "the
force of intelligent organization versus that of organization imposed
from outside or above." For Dewey, a "revival of democratic faith" as
an antidote to totalitarianism was something to be "devoutly wished
for." But the hope was bound to be dashed unless it was nurtured
by trust "in our common human nature" and the power of voluntary
action based on "public collective intelligence."[27]

Two years later, at the onset of the next big war, Dewey switched
from the critique of derailments to a renewed expression of hope.
Titled "Creative Democracy—The Task Before Us," the new text

portrayed genuine democracy as a creative challenge—in fact, as the emblem of the highest human creativity. As he pointed out, the origin of liberal democracy a century and a half ago was largely the result of a "fortunate combination of men and circumstances"; however, the reservoir of these happy circumstances was by now largely exhausted. Confronted with unprecedented political and technological challenges, the renewal of democracy today requires a large dose of "inventive effort and creative activity." The old assumption that the founders of liberal democracy had succeeded in "setting up a machine that solved the problem of perpetual motion in politics" has turned out an illusion. In opposition to this mechanical conception, it has become clear that democracy is a continuous human endeavor, in fact, "a *personal* way of individual life" involving "the possession and continual use of certain attitudes." One of the attitudinal premises is the assumption of open-ended potentialities or "possibilities" of human beings instead of the stipulation of fixed traits or qualities. Among these potentialities in need of cultivation, for Dewey, is the capacity of human beings for "intelligent judgment and action if proper conditions are furnished." Another crucial potentiality is mutual generosity and tolerance—because intolerance and abuse based on "differences of opinion about religion or politics or business, as well as because of differences of race, color, wealth or degree of culture, are treason to the democratic way of life." To cultivate these potentialities means to unleash creative human imagination—for, Dewey concludes, the task of democracy is forever that of "the creation of a freer and more humane experience in which all share and to which all contribute."[28]

Beyond Pragmatism?

Democracy as an ethical community? We have certainly moved a long distance from this view both in actual practice and intellectual commitment. In lieu of Dewey's democratic *ethos*, we have reinstated the doctrine of rugged individualism, the cult of the isolated "self-made" ego—a cult often associated with unilateral aggressiveness. This return of the Social Darwinist creed is not of very recent origin, but can be traced back to the onset of the Cold War (when two monolithic ideologies, individualism and collectivism, came to confront each other). Students coming to New York after the war to visit Dewey must have found the intellectual atmosphere not very congenial to his ideas. To this extent, Dewey's fate resembled that of Hegel at the time of the July Revolution. Like Hegel's comprehensive system, Dewey's holistic vision by the time of his death had disintegrated into the dispersed fragments, the *disjecta membra* of his reflective thought. Thus, the diremptions that both Hegel and Dewey had sought to remedy—the divisions between mind and matter, subject and object, theory and *praxis*, norm and fact—reemerged again with full force. Dismissing the pragmatic search for unity, logic and epistemology became the dominant branches of official (analytical) philosophy. In terms of political thought, devotees tended to devote all their energies to the study of past texts (thus converting, in Dewey's words, philosophy into history). In lieu of learning from experience broadly conceived, empiricists confined themselves to positivist fact-gathering without deeper inquiry. Shunning educational guidance, ethics and practical life turned into a matter of private preference and idiosyncrasy.[29]

During the later part of the last century, anti-holistic tendencies were reinforced by an intellectual orientation originating mainly on the European continent: the trend often labeled "postmodernism." Although initially highly diversified—with some versions challenging "modernist" diremptions—the arrival of the trend in America had a curious (although perhaps not entirely unexpected) result: the quick absorption of European ideas into the maelstrom of American individualism, libertarianism, and solitary ego-centrism. What was baffling about the transformation was the initial use of dramatic formulas—like the "end of man" or the "end of the subject"—formulas which, at least in some instances, quickly gave way to stunning celebrations of the absolute uniqueness, "otherness," and incommensurability of individuals (beyond any social relationism). In this respect, although perhaps overstating his case, Charles Taylor was surely on solid ground when, in 1991, he remonstrated against (what he called) the ongoing "slide into subjectivism" and the tendency to replace authentic "individuality" (in Dewey's sense) with something closer to narcissism—a tendency encouraged by some postmodern rhetoric. As he wrote: By "deconstructing" or exorcising modern subjectivity yet welcoming it through the back door, such rhetoric leaves social agents—despite all the doubts about selfhood and agency—with "a sense of untrammeled power and freedom before a world that imposes no standards," ready "to enjoy 'free play,' or to indulge in an aesthetics of the self." As an antidote to the galloping "fragmentation" of social life and the steady "weakening of the bonds of sympathy," Taylor recommended a revitalization of "democratic will-formation," arguing that "a serious attempt to engage in the cultural struggle of our time requires the promotion of a politics of democratic empowerment."[30]

The sketched developments had a curious effect also on pragmatism. Although frequently hailed as the most significant and "genuinely American" philosophy, pragmatism was either exiled from America or else transformed so as to reflect the dominant fashions of libertarianism, solitary individualism, and (versions of) postmodernism. What goes under the label of "neo-pragmatism" in large measure follows the second option. While emphasizing the merits of liberalism and the expansion of individual rights, comparatively little attention is given by neo-pragmatists to the economic and communal downside of neo-liberal markets. While celebrating (in postmodern fashion) the diversity of private-individual lifestyles, little more than lip service is given to the Deweyan stress on "radical" or "creative" forms of democracy. With some grains of salt, these comments also apply to perhaps the leading neo-pragmatist of recent times: Richard Rorty. Despite his unquestionable accomplishments, one notices with chagrin in his work the resurgence of a number of dichotomies or diremptions that Dewey had spent his lifetime to overcome: the bifurcations between private "irony" and public involvement; between individual ethical relativism and social conformism; between scientific "epistemology" (traditionally committed to empirical truth) and the broad arena of "edification" (apparently only governed by private taste). In this and other respects, one must agree with Larry Hickman, the renowned Dewey expert, when he writes that Rorty at one point "claimed Dewey's authority in advancing the view that there is no real distinction between the sciences and the arts since both are just types of literature. [Yet] Dewey regarded both of these views—scientific realism and extreme relativism—as flawed and he vigorously opposed them."[31]

Critiquing some shortfalls of neo-pragmatism, of course, does not mean to plead for pragmatist orthodoxy. Just as in the case of Hegel, faithfulness to Dewey requires an effort to recapture the inner spirit motivating his work—or to "rethink the unthought" of his writings. Here several issues demand attention: one is precisely the issue of holism. Again as in Hegel's case, Dewey's quest for holistic unity sometimes was perhaps premature and not sufficiently flexible to accommodate emerging forms of complexity and differentiation. The attempt to translate Hegel's objective spirit into a mode of "organic naturalism"—although in keeping with the scientific temper of his time—was bound to conjure up apprehensions or misunderstandings, especially the misprision of a "totalizing" system averse to deeper (Kierkegaardian or Nietzschean) aspirations. Closely connected with this issue is the status of "pragmatism" itself—a term whose meaning remains vague and confused due to Dewey's own ambivalent usage (wavering between pragmatism, instrumentalism, and experimentalism). Probably the most central unresolved problem, however, is the meaning of action or *praxis*—crucial terms in any "pragmatic" theory. Here, one would have wished for Dewey to differentiate more clearly between "action" as doing, instrumental "making," and artistic "creation" or creativity. In many of his writings, Dewey presents action (alias making or creating) simply as the intentional pursuit of a goal by a pregiven individual or collective agent. Thus, his *Liberalism and Social Action* (1935) portrays action simply as a process that "effects actual change in institutions" and also "the needed change in patterns of mind and character"—a formulation that seems predicated on a Cartesian self. However, at other points, speaking of the "unity of the act," Dewey suggests that agent and the goal of action are actually "constituted at one and the some time." Moreover, seen as interaction, action involves not only doing but also "undergoing" or "suffering"—hence an "intensely receptive activity." Sometimes termed "speaking in the middle voice," this kind of action/passion would surely deserve to be spelled out more fully by contemporary Deweyans.[32]

In other respects, however, Dewey's thought seems to be far ahead of his time—projecting itself into our age of globalization and global terror wars. An important, and not always sufficiently noted, feature is Dewey's own incipient cosmopolitanism—manifest especially in his interest in Asian culture and philosophy. As is well known, after World War I Dewey lectured extensively in China and in 1920 received an honorary degree from the Chinese National University (with a citation calling him the "second Confucius"). During the same years, he also lectured at the Imperial University of Tokyo and at universities in Turkey (where he prepared a report on the Turkish educational system). Contemporary students of "comparative philosophy" with good reason celebrate Dewey as a pioneer and mentor of their own endeavors. Thus, Roger Ames and David Hall in several of their writings, but especially in *Thinking Through Confucius*, have emphasized the role of Dewey, and American pragmatism in general, as a gateway facilitating access to Chinese classical thought in our time.[33] On a more general level, Dewey's thought has lessons for our globalizing age—a time overshadowed by "clashes of civilizations" and seemingly unending terror wars. In a stunning manner, his essay on "creative democracy" links the latter not with conquest but the pursuit of peace fostered by "the habit of amicable cooperation." "To take as far as possible," he writes, "every conflict which arises—and they are bound to arise—out of the atmosphere and medium of force, of violence as a means of settlement into that of discussion and of intelligence is to treat those who disagree—even profoundly—with us as those from whom we may learn, and insofar, as friends." Dewey concludes with a passage that might have been penned by Mahatma Gandhi or Martin Luther King, Jr.:

> A genuinely democratic faith in peace is faith in the possibility of conducting disputes, controversies and conflicts as cooperative undertakings in which both parties learn by giving the other a chance to express itself, instead of having one party conquer by forceful suppression of the other—a suppression which is none the less one of violence when it takes place by psychological means of ridicule, abuse, and intimidation instead of by overt imprisonment or in concentration camps.[34]

4

Agency and Letting-Be

Heidegger on Primordial Praxis

Martin Heidegger opens his famous *Letter on Humanism* with these words: "We are still far from pondering the nature of action decisively enough." These words are baffling and provocative—especially in our present (so-called) "post-metaphysical" age when all the emphasis is placed on action, doing, and busy work. Intellectually, there is no shortage of theories trying to ponder and explain the nature of action. Typically, such theories place the agent in the "driver's seat," by depicting action as the intentional pursuit of a goal or effect by an individual or collective "subject." Most prominent among these theories today is the "rational choice" model that portrays as most rational an action that accomplishes its goal most efficiently, that is, with the greatest benefit (or utility) for the agent at the smallest cost. Seen against this background, Heidegger's opening line is startling and untimely. Its baffling character is deepened or exacerbated when Heidegger continues: "We know action only as something causing an effect, with the actuality of the effect being valued according to its utility. But the [real] nature of action is fulfillment (*Vollbringen*)." Here the reader suddenly finds himself on the open seas, with no banisters or handy utility maxims to cling to. The hope of finding such banisters vanishes entirely in the following lines: "To accomplish or fulfill means: to unfold something into the fullness of its being, to lead it forth (*producere*) into this fullness. Capable of being accomplished in this sense is really only what already is. But what 'is' above all is Being."[1]

In opening his *Letter on Humanism* with these lines, is Heidegger abandoning concern with action or agency, preferring to find a refuge in aloof contemplation or quietism? Although often interpreted precisely in this way, perhaps—instead of abandoning it—the lines invite or lure us into a deeper reflection on agency, into a domain transgressing or transcending self-seeking pursuits and "rational choice." Perhaps, instead of absconding into a "metaphysical" retreat, Heidegger wishes to draw our attention to a mode of action that is more genuinely human and even constitutive of our humanity. This, in any event, is the intuition or assumption guiding the following pages. As it happens, dimensions of Heidegger's work are sometimes compared with American-style pragmatism or pragmatic philosophy. Thus, in discussing the pathways of "modernity," Jürgen Habermas detects some pragmatist affinities in *Being and Time*, especially in the emphasis on instrumental conduct (*Zuhandenheit*). From a very different angle, Charles Taylor finds even stronger parallels in Heidegger's "holistic" approach, his insertion of meanings and actions into the contextual framework of "being-in-the-world."[2]

Without contesting or strongly disagreeing with such readings, I enter a certain caveat. As it seems to me, Heidegger's *pragmatism*—if this is the term one wishes to use—is clearly far removed from popular or run-of-the-mill versions of this perspective (especially versions claiming that "truth is what works"). In the following, I start out by delineating affinities with a certain (mainly Deweyan) conception of pragmatism, by focusing on Heidegger's approach to philosophy and philosophical education. Next, I turn to Heidegger's notion of action or agency, in an attempt to flesh out what might be meant by "accomplishment" and by unfolding something into "the fullness of its being." I conclude by pondering the implications of Heideggerian agency for contemporary ethical and political life.

Heidegger as a Pragmatist

Approached straightforwardly and without great definitional scruples, Heidegger's work has a loosely pragmatist cast—where "pragmatism" stands for a concern with action, doing, or some form of practical engagement. As is well known, his *Being and Time* presents human beings not as "rational animals"—with an accent on abstract, epistemic reason—but as "beings-in-the-world," that is, as creatures dealing with the rich fabric of the world and first of all with those features that appear "handy" or ready for use (*zuhanden*). This dealing is guided by a mode of "caring" (*Besorgen*) or carefulness (*Sorge*) that undergirds human involvement in the world generally. In Heidegger's words: human involvement in, or dealing (*Umgang*) with, the world "is dispersed into manifold ways of caring. The kind of dealing closest to us . . . is not bare perceptual cognition but rather a caring or concern which 'handles' things and puts them to use." Next to or in conjunction with the dimension of "handiness," *Being and Time* delineates other forms of involvement in the world: among them, the perceptual knowledge of natural things or objects (*vorhanden*)—which requires a distinct kind of attentiveness and discovery (*Entdeckung*)—and the engagement with fellow human beings (*Mitsein*) guided by modes of interhuman care or solicitude (*Fürsorge*). All these types of dealings or engagement are not isolated or parceled out into separate rubrics, but are held together by a holistic context in which the significance of the diverse aspects (*Bewandtnis*) and hence the comprehensive "worldliness" of the world is disclosed: "The significance thus disclosed is the existential structure of *Dasein* [human being], of its being-in-the-world, and as such the . . . condition of the possibility of discovering the wholeness of its involvements."[3]

Apart from these broadly pragmatist features, another—clearly central—aspect of *Being and Time* needs to be taken into account: its preeminent focus on the "question of Being" (*Seinsfrage*). In adopting this focus, one should note, Heidegger does not propose to offer a conceptual analysis of "Being" nor to establish a fixed (perhaps perennial) doctrine about "Being," a doctrine that could be memorized and rehearsed. In contrast to such a conceptualism or intellectualism, the book places the entire emphasis on the "*question* of Being" or on Being as a question. Hence, the central issues pervading and agitating the entire study are these: What does it mean for us to be? What is the point of our being? What is the sense of the world and other beings in the world? And ultimately: What are the meaning and the "truth" of Being as such? These issues cannot be settled (or rather evaded) by arbitrary decision or a retreat into subjective preferences. For Heidegger, human beings in their "existence" are "ek-static" creatures—that is, beings "standing out" or catapulted into the open arena of the meaning and truth of Being (which foils all pat answers). At this point, the unusual or uncanny character of Heidegger's "pragmatism" comes to the fore. Although accepting that human beings, as beings-in-the-world, have an initial preunderstanding of, and hence familiarity (*Vertrautheit*) with their world, this familiarity is contested and criss-crossed by a dimension of the "question of Being" that exceeds familiarity and cannot be domesticated. As the opening pages of *Being and Time* state: "Being is *transcendence* as such. . . . Hence, every disclosure of Being as transcendence is *transcendental* knowledge."[4] With these lines, every cozy form of pragmatism, every comfortable kind of human familiarity is blown out of the water. Seen in this light, pursuit of the "question of Being" cannot be stabilized in a system, but requires continued existential engagement. It requires a willingness to be underway, to venture onto open seas where Being and nothing (*Nichts*) are entwined and where the latter is perhaps the only gateway to meaning.

The peculiarity of Heideggerian pragmatism is not confined to *Being and Time*; it emerges even more clearly in a lecture course presented shortly afterward (in 1928/1929) under the title "Introduction to Philosophy" (*Einleitung in die Philosophie*). As Heidegger emphasizes at the very beginning of his lectures, such an introduction cannot just mean the gathering or piling up of information *about* philosophy: about the historical sequence of "systems" and philosophical doctrines and the differences among these doctrines. Nor can introduction mean a guided tour among the so-called branches of philosophy, like logic, ethics, and aesthetics, and their historical development. What such a piling up of information accomplishes is an expansion of knowledge without any engagement. In Heidegger's words: if, at the end of the semester, students have completed such an "historical and systematic overview," they are the "proud owners of sundry modes of knowledge" about the subject matter; but they have learned nothing about philosophy as "philosophizing," as a *praxis* or practical engagement. The entire notion of an "introduction" is misguided—he adds—if it implies a movement from a place outside or exterior to philosophy to an insider's perspective. The assumption is misguided because philosophy does not mean an idle rummaging in ideas but has an existential, perhaps an existential-pragmatic status. In the poignant words of the lecture course: "Even if we do not explicitly know anything about philosophy, we are already inside philosophy, because philosophy is something that belongs to us in the sense that we are always already philosophizing." This passage is followed by the still more lapidary formulation: "To be human (*Menschsein*) means to philosophize. Human *Dasein* as such—in its very nature and not occasionally or accidentally—is anchored in philosophy."[5]

To be sure, in most human beings, philosophy exists initially as a latent potential or in a dormant state requiring awakening; to this extent, "introduction" means an attempt to actualize a dormant possibility. In Heidegger's words: "Introducing now means to mobilize (*in Gang bringen*) philosophizing, to allow philosophy to become in us an actual happening (*Geschehen*)." In the language of *Being and Time*, to mobilize philosophy or put it to work means to awaken and activate the "inner-most" possibility of human beings: namely, to ponder and care for the "question of Being." To arouse or awaken this central possibility, in turn, can be construed as a mode of emancipation or liberation: liberation *from* extraneous preoccupations and liberation *of* the deepest human potential and task, that of the "humaneness" (*Menschsein*) of human beings. In the words of the lecture course: "Philosophy must become free [or unfold freely] in us. . . . But what thus is freed or set free, we in turn most sustain in our freedom: we must freely awaken and entertain the task of philosophizing." As Heidegger makes it abundantly clear, mobilizing the freedom to philosophize does not all mean to indulge in private-subjective opinions or to jettison the historical legacy of philosophizing: "It would be a rash mistake to assume that we can cultivate philosophy by totally rejecting historical traditions." Even less does the freedom implicit in philosophizing sanction a retreat into self-centered subjectivism or solipsism. "The liberation of philosophy in human *Dasein*," the lecture course insists, "has nothing whatever in common with a psychological or egotistical narcissism (*Selbstbegaffung*)." At this point, the unusual or uncanny side of Heidegger's "pragmatism" comes again to the fore: the emphasis on the "eccentricity" of human *Dasein*. Contrary to the popular view of human centeredness or "self-familiarity," he states, human *Dasein* "is in its core ek-centric, which means that by its very nature it can never occupy the center of beings." If this is so, however, then it is precisely the task of philosophizing to show "that *Dasein* is catapulted out of and beyond itself and can never possess itself."[6]

As can readily be seen, philosophizing as a form of liberating and awakening has inevitably a transformative and, in a sense, pedagogical quality. Heidegger's lecture course draws the attention of readers and students explicitly to the connection between philosophizing and the Greek notion of "*paideia*" meaning educational guidance, formation or "*Bildung*." If, he states, human *Dasein* is animated by the "question of Being" and oriented toward the "understanding of Being" (*Seinsverständnis*), then philosophizing inevitably has the character of "*paideia*": "It is for this reason that, in antiquity, philosophy was for a long time equated with '*paideia koinōs*,' which we can translate approximately as '*Bildung*.' " Understanding of Being, he adds, is not instantaneous but requires sustained labor, a labor that, in turn, has to be propelled by an existential desire or inclination, in Greek "*philein*"—which discloses the inner connection between "*paideia*" and the original Greek meaning of "*philo-sophia*." In the words of the lecture course: "Understanding requires a sustained effort which, from the outset, has to be nurtured by an original inclination or sympathy (*Neigung*) toward things. This sympathy, this inner friendship with beings is what is meant by the Greek '*philia*'—a friendship which, like every genuine liking, has to struggle with and for the target of its love." With this accent on loving and struggling, the notion of philosophizing is clearly far removed from detached observation or mere conceptual analysis and inserted again into a mode of *praxis* or existential-ekstatic pragmatism: "Understanding is not something that can happen without engagement (*Zutun*); rather, it needs to be lifted up into the freedom of human existence in order to be actualized."[7]

In this context, it seems appropriate to draw attention to Heidegger's comments on educational formation or "*Bildung*" in another context: his essay on "Plato's Theory of Truth" (1930–1931; subsequently developed into a longer lecture course). In his essay, Heidegger interprets Plato's "parable of the cave" in the sense of a learning experience whereby human beings are freed from dark compulsions in favor of a deeper understanding of truth. This learning experience does not involve the mere accumulation of cognitive information but rather a thoroughgoing transformation or "turning-about' (*Umwendung*) of the whole human being. For Plato, he notes, educational formation does not consist in expansion of knowledge such that "bits of new information are poured into an empty container"; rather, genuine formation "grips and transforms the soul itself and as a whole, namely, by placing human beings into their proper abode and habituating them in that abode." The movement from the cave to the light beyond the cave is thus not just a spatial or geographical excursion, but rather a "periagogé" or *Umwendung* (perhaps *Kehre*?). Moreover, the movement does not involve an exit from ordinary humanity to a trans- or extra-human condition; instead, it liberates or awakens a latent human potentiality that has not been actualized. In Heidegger's words: "The exemplary disposition resulting from the transformation has to be unfolded or cultivated out of a potential condition into a stable conduct. This transformative habituation of human beings into the respective domain is the core of what Plato calls *paideia*."[8]

Elaborating further on educational formation, the essay on Plato emphasizes that *paideia* is not a static possession or privilege but an ongoing process of learning: a process leading from ignorance to growing insight. *Paideia*, Heidegger observes, "is basically a transition (*Übergang*), namely, from un-learning or non-learning (*apaideusía*) to learning (*paideia*). In line with this transitional character, *paideia* always refers back to *apaideusia*." Trying to find an equivalent for the Greek term, Heidegger adds that "the German word *Bildung*" perhaps "comes closest"—provided some precautious are taken. What is important here is to return to *Bildung* its original semantic power and to release it from the grip of later (bourgeois?) misconstruals. The important point for Heidegger is that *Bildung* is not just a unilateral, intentional project anchored in the modern subject or individual (which would reduce *Umwendung* to the work of the "self-made man"). Rather, a broader, holistic reciprocity has to be taken into account. Deriving from *"bilden"* (to form), *Bildung* in one sense means an act of formation. However, in the Platonic sense (which Heidegger here endorses), active "forming" takes place in anticipation of a guiding "form," measure, or "image" (*Bild*) that solicits the forming act. Given its formative or guiding role, this image can also be called "exemplary image" (*Vor-bild*). Hence, *Bildung* means "simultaneously active forming and guidance by a *Bild*." In Heideggerian language, exiting from the "cave" means emerging from the grip of "beings" into a growing understanding of "Being"—which is not merely a cognitive principle but a life-sustaining, exemplary guidepost.[9]

Letting-Be as Primordial Praxis

As can be recalled from *Being and Time*, understanding (of Being) is one of the primary modalities of human existence, joined by such other modalities as mood (*Befindlichkeit*) and speech. What unites and holds together these "existential" attributes is the undergirding quality of "care," which again can assume different shapes or connotations. A point often debated in the literature concerns the character of care: whether it should be seen as a personal predilection or else as a response to something demanding attention. One way to clarify this issue is by resorting to the notion of "letting-be" (*Seinlassen*) seen as a correlate of care. The lecture course "Introduction to Philosophy" elaborates in great detail on this notion. As Heidegger observes there: in all our dealings with the world—whether we deal with "handy" or not-handy things and even in aesthetic appreciation—we participate in the world and its beings in a special way: the mode of "letting-be." In this mode, we are not foisting our desires or predilections on beings and we certainly do not try to maximize our own benefits; at the same time, we are not in a state of utter noninvolvement. "This letting-be of things," we read, "occurs in a broad sense prior to any special interestedness or disinterest. Basically, in thus letting-be, we allow beings or things to be themselves," while adopting on our part a stance of (existential-metaphysical) "equanimity" (*Gleichgültigkeit*) which is not indifference. As Heidegger adds, linking this point with the discussion in *Being and Time*: "Such equanimity is possible only in the modality of care (*Sorge*). The letting involved in this allowing, however, is not a bare omission (*Unterlassen*)." Above all, letting-be is not simply a nullity—although we certainly cannot (and do not wish to) add or superimpose anything on the being of nature. Without any imposition or manipulation, "letting-be is a *praxis* (*Tun*) of the highest and most primordial sort and possible only on the basis of the inner core of our existence: its freedom."[10]

In linking letting-be with *praxis* or doing, Heidegger is keenly aware of the danger of misunderstanding. In trying to ward off possible miscontruals, he insists on the need to differentiate "*praxis*" from sheer activism and from forms of instrumental action (*poiesis*) seeking to produce a specific outcome or effect. The distinction is difficult today, he observes, given the prevalent opinion "that 'action' and 'doing' occur only where life is hectic, where business booms, and power or mastery holds sway." Invoking classical Greek teachings at this point, the lecture course takes a stand far removed from everyday busy-ness. Referring specifically to Aristotle's *Politics* and *Nicomachean Ethics*, Heidegger emphasizes that *praxis* in the Greek sense does not at all denote the production of ulterior effects; instead, such action carries its goal and accomplishment within itself—with the result that it can be termed autonomous and self-fulfilling (*autarkes* and *autoteles*). As Aristotle has continuously stressed, *praxis* is "a doing which reaches its end or fulfillment in itself" and in this manner also completes or "fulfills the agent" or actor. Seen in this light, *praxis* clearly happens before the traditional distinction between "theoretical" and "practical" orientations. Properly construed—or construed in the classical sense—"*theoria*" is itself an eminent and even preeminent form of *praxis* because it is oriented to the understanding and disclosure of the "manifestness" (*Offenbarkeit*) of beings in their truth. Such understanding and disclosure, however—Heidegger adds—is precisely the basic concern of human *Dasein* in its care for "Being." Hence, understanding of Being is a *theoria* (in the Greek sense) that is also *praxis*—and in fact, the most "primordial *praxis*" (*Urhandlung*): Letting-be means "to allow beings to become manifest (in their truth). This is the primordial *praxis*."[11]

Carrying its accomplishment or fulfillment within itself, *praxis* in Heidegger's (and Aristotle's) sense is not a linear goal-directed pursuit with the actor firmly in the driver's seat. In a sense, one may say that *praxis* occurs in "middle voice," a voice combining action and passivity, doing and experiencing or undergoing. In Heidegger's words, *praxis* seems to proceed from "a spontaneity located entirely in ourselves"; however, by encountering and letting things and beings "be," it displays "a peculiar passivity or receptivity." This receptivity implies openness and a kind of "self-surrender (*Sichfreigeben*) in favor of beings so that they can show themselves how they are" (or in their truth). This self-surrender or self-giving is the very opposite of a self-enclosed or self-possessed subjectivism or individualism—an enclosure that has been the emblem and the shortfall of modern Western philosophy at least since Descartes. The construal of human existence as an "ego" or, more generally, as a "subject"—the lecture course states—has been a philosophical derailment, because it has stripped human beings of their worldliness and of their embroilment with "Being" (in all its forms). Stressing the basic openness (*Erschlossenheit*) of human *Dasein*, Heidegger elaborates again on the transgressive or self-transcending quality of human understanding of, and care for, Being: its orientation toward the disclosure of (the meaning of) truth. As Heidegger observes: Human *Dasein* is that kind of being that is "constitutively engaged" with the meaning of Being and its truth. For this to be possible, however, truth cannot simply be an external state of affairs, or a statement corresponding to such a state; rather, it has to be anchored in the very depth of human existence. Differently phrased: disclosure of truth has to belong to the "accomplishment or fulfillment" of *Dasein* itself. For this to be possible, however, a transgressive or transformative movement has to happen, opening the path to disclosure: Insofar as "understanding of Being" belongs to *Dasein*—we read—there must be a "transgression" (*Überstieg*) of the initial opacity of beings. This means "*Dasein* is as such transcending.... With this transcending move, *Dasein* attests to its own special ascent or elevation (*Erhöhung*)."[12]

Self-transcending, for Heidegger, is by no means easy or ready-made; this is so because every height implies a depth, every ascending the possibility of a descent. This brings to the fore a feature central to Heidegger's thought: the interlacing of revealment and concealment, of being and nonbeing. Although oriented toward the understanding of Being, the finitude of human *Dasein* foils or derails a complete grasp or comprehension. Moreover, every openness toward Being includes a possible self-enclosure, every move toward understanding the possibility of a slippage into busyness, absent-mindedness or oblivion (what he elsewhere calls "*Verfallen*" or "fallenness"). Hence, care for Being implies a difficult venture; in the language of Plato's *Phaidros*, it involves "labor and struggle" (*ponos te kai agon*) of the soul. Yet again, this venture or struggle is not simply a willful initiative, an activity reflecting the spontaneity of an ego. As suggested before, activity and struggle occur here also in the middle voice. Differently phrased, the search for understanding of Being (and its truth) is not a unilateral project but is also a response: a response to the call or solicitation of

Being. This solicitation, in turn, is not the dictate of an exterior force or power seeking to level *Dasein* into blind submission; rather, it is a call resonating with the innermost design of *Dasein*: its openness and its freedom to be. In Heidegger's words: "Since transcending is a constitutive feature of *Dasein* as such, it follows that in the explicit letting-be of transcendence the basic [ek-static] character of *Dasein* is made manifest." This letting-be, however, was previously pinpointed as the "primordial *praxis*" (*Urhandlung*) of *Dasein*. Thus, one can now say that the *praxis* of letting-be discloses the "free being" (*Freisein*) of *Dasein*. Differently put: "The explicit act of transcending is a primary *praxis* of *Dasein's* freedom."[13]

To repeat and underscore a previous point: freedom is not the property of an ego, nor is the act of transcending an isolated private venture. Here one has to be on guard against one of the most popular misconstruals of Heidegger's work: the equation of *Dasein*, especially "authentic" *Dasein*, with a solitary existence. The misreading is baffling given the entire thrust of this work: the emphasis on "being-in-the world" which always and necessarily includes a "being-with" (*Mitsein*) or "being-with-others" (*Miteinandersein*). Whatever doubt may have been left by *Being and Time* is entirely removed by the "Introduction to Philosophy." In fact, "being-with" and "being-with-others" (or "being-with-one-another") is a central theme of the course. Given the recurrent emphasis on action and "primordial *praxis*," it should come as no surprise that "being-with," for Heidegger, does not primarily involve mutual cognition or awareness but rather shared action or participation (*Teilnahme, Teilhaberschaft*) in a shared *praxis*. As the course repeatedly emphasizes, being-with does not involve a juxtaposition of egos or a mutual cognitive grasp (*Erfassen*); nor does it imply a mutual introspection or psychic analysis. On the contrary, mutual awareness is always predicated on, or anchored in, a prior "being-with-one-another"—which, in turn, is made possible by the openness of *Dasein* to all forms of Being (including that of fellow beings). Thus, in being with others, *Dasein* is engaged not primarily in a process of knowing, not even of mutual "recognition," but rather in a shared orientation toward the disclosure of the truth of Being. This sharing, Heidegger stresses, provides a common ground (*ein Gemeinsames*) that is not instrumentally fabricated or engineered but is a corollary of the "*Urhandlung*" of letting-be: "The 'with' in being-with-others discloses a commonality that derives from the fact that self and others are equally projected or catapulted [toward truth]."[14]

As can readily be seen, commonality for Heidegger is not the out-growth of arbitrary choice nor of contractual agreement or negotiation.

More importantly still, in its "ek-static" orientation, commonality must not be confused with an empirical communalism or "communitarianism" (based on national, ethnic, or religious bonds), a communalism neglectful of *Dasein's* transcending freedom. In the words of the lecture course: "*Dasein* has to be free in its own being if it is to be supported or guided by others, if it is to open itself genuinely for co-being or commit itself to others." What is shared between fellow human beings is the care for and openness toward Being; however, given human finitude and diversity, the latter does not mean the same thing for everyone, nor is it approached in the same way. The meaning could only be the same for all if Being were a finished doctrine, an abstract concept, or an external "thing-in-itself"—options that were clearly ruled out in *Being and Time*. Hence, for Heidegger, commonality or participation in a shared *praxis* is compatible with "difference" (*Unterschied*) and a strong form of pluralism (which does not coincide with relativism). As he states, human beings are oriented toward something shared "in common" (*ein Gemeinsames, ein Selbiges*) that does not at all coincide with "sameness" or identity; thus, it is possible and even assumed that "several people relate in quite different ways to commonality." In the lecture course, this thought is also expressed in the statement that human orientation toward Being is neither identical nor purely relativistic but "relational." Given that care for Being is also defined as "primordial *praxis*," commonality can be described as diversified participation in the disclosure (or letting-be) of truth. What needs to be noted above all is that, contrary to a certain kind of pragmatism, truth is not simply something useful but a standard of *praxis*: "Being together with others means a participation in truth."[15]

Agency in Ethics and Politics

Heidegger's "Introduction to Philosophy" throws into relief several aspects of his thought that are not always fully appreciated. A prominent aspect is the emphasis on human freedom seen as a corollary of *Dasein's* "ek-static" openness to Being. Among students of Heidegger, the centrality of this aspect has been recognized above all by Günter Figal who states that Heidegger's thought was marked from the outset by "concern with freedom" and that his entire philosophy should in effect "be read as a philosophy of freedom."[16] This conception, as can readily be seen, collides head on with widespread associations of Heidegger's thought with oppressive forms of totalitarianism or collectivism (and this despite Heidegger's own notorious political meanderings). To be sure, accepting the centrality of the notion, the meaning of "freedom" has to be clarified and sorted out; above all, its "ontological" status (for Heidegger) has to be carefully differentiated from such popular ideological doctrines as libertarianism, *laissez-faire* liberalism, and possessive (or self-possessed) individualism. This sorting out is facilitated by another prominent theme in the "Introduction to Philosophy": the importance of "being-with" or "being-with-others." As indicated before, "being-with" or co-being for Heidegger does not mean a random togetherness nor a mutual cognitive exploration; above all, it does not denote a merger or fusion of egos that would rob *Dasein* of its own freedom or its being free for others. What seems to be required for Heidegger—at least at this point in his intellectual journey—is a careful balancing of self-being and being with and for others, a balancing accomplished in the context of a shared participation (*Teilnahme*) in the quest for meaning and truth.

Another important feature underscored (although certainly not initiated) in the lecture course is the affinity of Heidegger's thought with a certain kind of pragmatism. This affinity is illustrated by his equation of philosophy with practical "philosophizing" as opposed to the detached cognition of philosophical doctrines or systems (as well as a rummaging in popular opinions). The same proximity—at least to Deweyan pragmatism—is reflected in the emphasis on philosophical education or *paideia*, the latter being sharply distinguished from indoctrination. Undergirding and amplifying these affinities is the perhaps most crucial aspect of Heidegger's thought (at this stage of his life): the concern with *praxis* or agency (*Handlung*). As has been shown, this concern is mediated significantly through classical Greek philosophy, especially the teachings of Aristotle and Plato. The closeness or indebtedness of the early Heidegger to Aristotle has been recognized for some time; his focus on the "question of Being" has generally been construed as a renewal of Aristotelian impulses. With the publication of additional Heideggerian writings during recent years, this Aristotelian connection has been further documented and corroborated. Fastening attention on this connection, scholars have pointed to the "movement" character of Aristotelian "being" (*kinesis*), the "two-folded" character of his metaphysics (anticipating Heidegger's "ontological difference"), and the inherent power or force pervading "being" (*dynamis, entelechy*).[17] To be sure, Aristotle's legacy is significantly modified and redirected in Heidegger's thought—as is evident in his rejection of "substance" metaphysics and the notion of a "causality" in Being. Also, as the "Introduction" makes clear, Aristotelian "ontology" is always coupled with a Platonic (or Neoplatonic) emphasis on ascent, elevation, and transcendence. Moreover (and perhaps most importantly), Heidegger's turn to finitude and temporality injects into Greek thought an element of biblical (particularly Protestant) eschatology alien to the classical sources.[18]

Instead of delving further into the recesses of metaphysics and theology, I return attention here to the issue of *praxis* and agency. As it happens, one of the most hotly debated topics in contemporary social and political thought is precisely the status and meaning of action; for good or ill, Heidegger's work is often drawn into this controversy. According to some observers, Heidegger's preoccupation with the "question of Being" erected a gulf between theory and *praxis*, between thinking and the concerns of practical life, thereby rendering his work ethically and politically irrelevant (despite some egregious derailments). In opposition to this view, other readers have charged him with a hyperactive bent, specifically with a blind "decisionism" or the espousal of arbitrary individual or collective "projects."[19] As the preceding discussion should have made clear, both readings are far off the mark. As "Introduction to Philosophy" as well as later writings demonstrate, Heidegger was by no means willing to abandon or jettison action in favor of a mystical "quietism"—or else a postmodern "end of man" or "end of the subject." His intense engagement with Aristotle's legacy was precisely designed to rescue for our time a viable notion of human *praxis*—a notion not tarnished by modern (Cartesian, neo-Kantian, or positivist) dilemmas. A constitutive feature of these dilemmas was their implicit egocentrism or anthropocentrism, that is, their insistence on placing the human actor in the driver's seat, thereby reducing the goal of action to the achievement of instrumentally chosen ends. With the help of Aristotelian—and (in part) Platonic—teachings, Heidegger was able to debunk this kind of instrumentalism and self-centered decisionism, and to re-enlist human *praxis* as a pathway in the search for meaning and truth.

In the classical tradition, searching for truth was always closely linked with the quest for goodness or "the good" (*to agathon*)—a linkage that renders Heidegger's Aristotelian connection relevant also for contemporary ethics. Although often sidelined or else polemically dismissed, this relevance has of late been recognized a least by some scholars. Thus, in his study on *Ethics and Finitude*, Lawrence Hatab translates Heidegger's "being-in-the-world" somewhat boldly or pointedly as "being-ethical-in-the-world." The justification for this translation, in his view, resides in the fact that *Dasein* means an engaged "being-with" the world and fellow human beings—an engagement marked by care or solicitude and not reducible to aloof or detached spectatorship. For

Hatab, contemporary moral thought is characterized by a plethora of theorizing and a shortfall of engaged practice or attentiveness to the "holistic" quality of human life. Contemporary moral discussion, he notes, is dominated by such theories as "emotivism" (focusing on desire or feeling), utilitarianism or "consequentialism" (focusing on desired effects), and "deontology" (privileging standards of duty). What these theories have in common is a "splitting" operation, the tendency to separate the desiring "subject" from social outcomes or "objective" standards. Here a Heideggerian approach, channeled through Aristotelian ethics, can provide a remedy by pointing to the contextual-holistic quality of human conduct. As Hatab observes, conduct for Heidegger is never a purely solitary venture, but always a response to the "beckoning" of the world and of Being. This responsiveness in a way replicates the Aristotelian linkage between desire (*oreksis*) and virtue (*arête*) as a shared mode of ethical life. Seen against this background and following this example, "Heidegger associates desire (*oreksis*) with a double movement that suggests the kind of 'middle voice' between subjectivity and objectivity, activity and passivity, that has always marked his reflections on Being."[20]

The implications of the discussed writings for contemporary politics also deserve to be explored. No claim is made here that Heidegger was at any point a supporter or great friend of democracy, especially in its presently prevailing forms. Yet, it is possible to imagine other forms that might perhaps have found his approval. Combined with the pervasive emphasis on care, the centrality assigned to human freedom suggests at least the possibility to vindicate, on Heideggerian grounds, a socially responsible and pluralistic regime of democratic freedom—far removed from dominant forms of *laissez-faire* liberalism and any kind of monolithic collectivism.[21] This possibility is predicated on what I consider to be the most significant legacy of Heidegger's work for political thought: his reformulation of action or *praxis* in terms of letting-be, and especially his refusal to equate action with the production of outcomes or effects.

According to the opening lines of his *Letter on Humanism* (cited above), the nature of action does not reside in this kind of production but rather in accomplishment or fulfillment whereby something is unfolded into "the fullness of its being." Read in conjunction with "Introduction to Philosophy," the meaning of these opening lines now becomes clear. For Heidegger—borrowing a leaf from Aristotle—action in the genuine sense is self-revealing and self-fulfilling (*autoteles*). What such action reveals above all, or unfolds into fullness, is the nature of the human agent—an agent who, as "being-in-the-world," is involved in the "primordial *praxis*" of letting the truth of Being manifest itself. In disclosing *Dasein's* freedom as self-transcendence toward truth, *praxis* thus basically humanizes or fulfills the intrinsic humanity of agency. To the extent that democracy is based on popular action, these reflections bring into view the prospect of an "other" democracy—perhaps a "democracy to come"—which friends of democratic regimes might fruitfully wish to ponder.[22]

5

Action in the Public Realm

Arendt Between Past and Future

Remembering Hannah Arendt today, more than three decades after her death, is urgent and rewarding, but also difficult; it is the latter because of our inability to "place" her, to fit her into usual labels. When seen from the angle of customary labels, Arendt inevitably appears as a kind of "misfit"—certainly as a "displaced" person or what she herself (in a remarkable self-description) called a "conscious pariah." Born in Old Europe at the end of the "Belle Epoque," she experienced the shattering and collapse of old European traditions in two World Wars and the Holocaust. These experiences expelled or displaced her to the New World, to America where she achieved a degree of fame—but without ever fully renouncing her status as an immigrant or refugee. Although trained or educated by two of the most distinguished European philosophers—Martin Heidegger and Karl Jaspers—she never considered herself properly speaking a "philosopher," and certainly not a metaphysician, preferring instead the more modest title of "thinker" or "political thinker"—which does not simplify matters. In comparison with most of her colleagues in political theory, Arendt did not concentrate her energies on recapitulating the "canonical" teachings of the past but preferred to focus her attention (pragmatically) on what was "underfoot," that is, on the civilizational watershed that she perceived was happening during her lifetime.[1]

To be sure, dislocation cannot mean here a placement completely "outside" of time and space—which would equal a retreat into a timeless no-man's land. Following the teachings of both Heidegger and Jaspers, Arendt always considered herself a "worldly" thinker, a being-in-the-world marked by a distinct temporality bounded by birth and death. In remembering her now, we are inevitably constrained to "place" her somehow into her period, her own space–time coordinates that are no longer quite our own. Although fully respecting and seeking to retrieve her situatedness, we cannot pretend to be able to melt completely into her thought, into her understanding of herself and her world. Having died in 1975, Arendt was not a witness to some of the more dramatic developments shaping our lives: the collapse of the Soviet Union; the rapid advances of globalization; September 11; and (on an intellectual plane) the advent of so-called "postmodernism" and the return of religion to political prominence. Without being anachronistic, we cannot help wondering how Arendt might have responded to some of these recent developments. This, in any event, is the angle adopted in the following pages. While honoring the integrity of her thought, a main endeavor will be to derive lessons from her reflections for today's predicaments and our own "crises of the republic."[2]

Needing to be brief and selective, my accent is chiefly on three questions. First, what, in Arendt's view, is the nature of political theorizing in contradistinction from "pure" theoretical philosophy and traditional metaphysics? In this respect, I highlight affinities of her thought with pragmatist (especially Deweyan) and existentialist perspectives. Next, what (for Arendt again) is the nature of politics and the "public sphere" in opposition to the modern penchant for social engineering and totalizing ideologies? And the final question is: What is the status of her thought in light of recent phenomena like multiculturalism, postmodernism, and globalization? What light do these phenomena shed on her conceptions of public "action," of the plurality of agents in the public realm, and of the purpose of political agency—where individual "immortality" seems to blot out concern for the good life?

Thinking What We Are Doing

As practiced today in most Western societies, political theory—like philosophy—is a "professional" discipline, more specifically a subdiscipline within a larger profession called "political science." To the extent that it is fully integrated in the latter profession, political theory necessarily adopts the stance of neutrally disengaged analysis characteristic of the natural—and all "positive"—sciences. Under such labels as "formal" and "empirical" theory, some analysts in fact aim to distill invariant "laws" of political behavior—while remaining completely removed from the lived concerns of their contemporaries. In a different guise, professionalism also prevails among theorists strongly opposed to "positivist" models and dedicated rather to the rehearsal of the great "tradition": that is, the major "canonical" texts of traditional political thought (hence the label "traditionalist" sometimes attached to this group). What—despite surface skirmishes—links canonical theorists with the positivists is their shared spectatorial stance, or what has been called their "view from nowhere": what in one case are called invariant natural "laws" of behavior are restyled in the other case as invariant "essences" or perennial ideas. Curiously, spectatorship is also shared by some anti-essentialist theorists willing to descend into the thick of history: by limiting their focus to past periods, "historicists" again tend to shun involvement with what is "underfoot," with the predicaments of their own time.[3] Generally speaking, what is discouraged on all sides is practical involvement or engagement—something that, although perhaps of private interest, lies strictly beyond "professional" conduct.

To the extent that the preceding picture is correct (or even only partially correct), it clearly reveals Arendt's displacement in the ranks of her colleagues, her inability to "fit" into prevailing formulas. Arendt herself was keenly aware of her distinctive and "un-fitting" status; she articulated the difference on several occasions, most prominently in the preface to her book *Between Past and Future*, subtitled *Six Exercises in Political Thought*. By calling the chapters in her book "exercises," she clearly wanted to highlight this difference: the fact that they conveyed not some invariant laws or essences but rather attempted to come to terms with what was "underfoot," more specifically to "work through" the situation "between past and present." To quote from her preface: the essays in her book are "exercises," and their only aim is "to gain experience in *how* to think; they do not contain prescriptions on what to think or which truths to hold." In adopting this stance, Arendt's outlook clearly resembles Dewey's stress on experimentalism and "inquiry" guided by experience. As one should note as well, the essays in her book are reflective endeavors; they do not offer appeals for blind activism nor ideological blueprints—although they do involve practical engagement. To continue with her preface: What is offered in her book is "an experience in thinking," and that experience can be won "like all experience [only] in doing something, through practice, through exercises." And here is a passage (with clear Deweyan resonances) that admirably summarizes Arendt's approach to political theorizing: "These are exercises in political thought as it arises out of the actuality of political incidents, . . . and my assumption is that thought itself arises out of incidents of living experience and must remain bound to them as the only guideposts by which to take its bearings."[4]

What this passage reveals is Arendt's closeness not only to pragmatism but also to Continental philosophy, and especially to existential phenomenology with its commitment to the reflective scrutiny of experienced phenomena. Similar passages—although without the explicit reference to political incidents—can be found in the writings of her European mentors. As Jaspers wrote in one of his texts: "Instead of having some total overview of our condition, we philosophize in awareness of a situation that, time and again, leads us to the final limits and bases of human reality." And Heidegger likewise is famous for stressing the linkage of thinking with lived human experience.[5] To be sure, neither of her mentors—although being anti-metaphysical (in a sense)—ceased to be philosophers on that account. In her preface, Arendt guards herself against confusion with a certain kind of existentialism that she identifies with mindless activism. Without mentioning names, she writes that some existentialist thinkers of the twentieth century "turned to politics for the solution of philosophical perplexities" and "tried to escape from thought into action." In the case of these thinkers, existentialism signaled primarily "an escape from the perplexities of modern philosophy into the unquestioning commitment to action." The very opposite position was adopted (she notes) by some philosophers of the same period who, disenchanted with the failures of politics, turned from action "back into thought," into the empyrean of ideas. Disillusioned with concrete experiences, such philosophers came to maintain either that ideas had "become altogether meaningless" or that it was necessary to retrieve "old verities" even if they have "lost all concrete relevance."[6]

In order to remain attentive to the "actuality" of concrete incidents, political thought cannot escape nostalgically into the past nor project itself into a utopian future, but has to take its stand in the present—a present not conceived, however, as a point in a linear sequence, but rather as a lived moment lodged in the interstices of competing temporalities. With this emphasis on lived time—as opposed to clock time or linear chronology—Arendt's text again reveals the influence of her European mentors, particularly of Heidegger's insistence on the nonlinear temporality of human existence or being-in-the-world.[7] Her preface to *Between Past and Future* describes the present as a "gap" or "interval" seen not as an empty abyss but as a collision or "thought-event" in which both past and future struggle for significance and meaning. Arendt, in this context, refers to a story penned by Franz Kafka where the latter depicted the human condition as a battle between past and future, with the former "pressing from behind" and the second seeking to "block the road ahead." This story, she notes, admirably captures the gist of a "thought-event": "The scene is a battleground on which the forces of the past and the future clash with each other; between them we find the man whom Kafka calls 'he,' who, if he wants to stand his ground at all, must give battle to both." Despite her fondness for the great storyteller, Arendt is not entirely uncritical of certain accents in his parable. Notwithstanding flashes of insight, she writes, Kafka did not manage to break out of the "traditional image" according to which we think of time "as moving in a straight line" or as reducible to a "unidirectional flow" of moments. The only antidote to this rectilinear movement for Kafka resided in an exit from time or temporality as such—an exit that landed him (Arendt remonstrates) in "the dream of a region over and above the fighting line," which is nothing but "the old dream which Western metaphysics has dreamed from Parmenides to Hegel." What is missing in the opposition between linear time and perennial timelessness is a third possibility: namely, a dimension "where thinking could exert itself without being forced to jump out of human time altogether."[8]

The dimension opened up by Arendt's notion of a "thought-event" is a force field of interlocking temporalities—a field not far removed from the tensions implicit in the "hermeneutical circle." Taking her bearings from William Faulkner's adage that "the past is never dead, it is not even past," Arendt offers a striking formulation of the complexities of this circle, saying:

> This past, moreover, reaching all the way back into the origin, does not pull back but presses forward, and it is, contrary to what one would expect, the future which drives us back into the past. Seen from the viewpoint of man, who always lives in the interval between past and future, time is not a continuum, a flow of uninterrupted succession; it is broken in the middle, at the point where "he" stands; and "his" standpoint is not the present as we usually understand it but rather a gap in time which "his" constant fighting, "his" making a stand against past and future, keeps in existence.

For Arendt, thought and particularly political thought is inevitably lodged in this antagonism or this "force field" of competing temporalities; only here can it gain traction and disclose its significance. In her words: this force field "whose origin is known, whose direction is determined by past and future, but whose eventual end lies in infinity, is the perfect metaphor for the activity of thought." As one should note again, Arendt here does not speak of sheer activism but of the "activity of thought"—which means a reflective engagement with what is "underfoot." Such engagement does not produce panaceas or ideological blueprints; but it seasons and "humanizes" both human existence and politics. "Only insofar as he thinks," she adds, "does man in the full activity of his concrete being live in this gap between past and future."[9]

Similar reflections on political thought can also be found in Arendt's most well-known text, *The Human Condition* (dating from roughly the same period). In this case, the title reflects the influence of European existential philosophy (where the phrase "human condition" had largely come to replace the older concept of "human nature"). Above and beyond terminology, however, there are deeper resonances or affinities having to do with perceived dangers threatening human existence—above all dangers resulting from the modern infatuation with science, technology, and instrumentalism. In language harking back to the great founder of European phenomenology, Edmund Husserl, the "Prologue" to *The Human Condition* speaks of a "crisis" of modern life arising from "within the natural sciences" and "the modern scientific worldview" as such—a crisis deriving from the growing gulf between scientific analysis and technological construction, on the one hand, and practical human experience or engagement, on the other. In Arendt's presentation, the modern infatuation has triggered a veritable "rebellion" against the human condition and the human life-world—that is, against humanity's "being-in-the-world"—and a relentless attempt to replace this condition with neutral observation and/or technical fabrication. The prologue in this context points to a pervasive process of "world alienation" or flight from worldliness—a flight involving a twofold exodus "from the earth into the universe" (abstractly construed) and "from the world into the self" or the recesses of private inwardness. What is sacrificed in this double exodus is the realm of shared human experience and *praxis*—a realm that, in the view of Aristotle, Dewey, and Arendt's European mentors, is also a domain constituted by ordinary language, speech, and communicative understanding. Quite irrespective of science's "great triumphs," she writes, the chief trouble with scientific and mathematical formulas is that "they will no longer lend themselves to normal expression in speech and thought."[10]

For Arendt, the sidelining of ordinary speech has existential and (most importantly) political consequences. In her words: "The situation created by the sciences is of great political significance," because politics is necessarily a realm of shared speech and action. "Wherever the relevance of speech is at stake," she adds, "matters become political by definition, for speech is what makes man a political being" (a formulation clearly replicating the Aristotelian linkage of *"zoon politikon"* and *"zoon logon echon"*). The point here is not that positive sciences are entirely devoid of language, but rather that their language consists of mathematical symbols far removed from and no longer readily translatable into ordinary speech. This distance also affects the relation between scientific experts and political *praxis*, accentuating the difference between expertise and political judgment. "The reason why it may be wise to distrust the political judgment of scientists *qua* scientists," the prologue states, "is not primarily their lack of 'character' . . . or their 'naïveté' . . . but precisely the fact that they move in a world where speech has lost its power. And whatever men do or know or experience can make sense only to the extent that it can be spoken about." What these lines gesture toward or anticipate is a theme that is central to the later argument of *The Human Condition*: namely, the role of "action" in the "public realm" (a theme I turn to shortly). Replicating insights garnered again from both Aristotle and her European mentors, Arendt's prologue contains a statement that might serve as motto of her entire study: "Men in the plural, that is, men insofar as they live and move and act in this world, can experience meaningfulness only because they can talk with and make sense to each other and to themselves."[11]

Before entering into the dense web of ideas assembled in *The Human Condition*, Arendt reflects once again briefly on the character of her enterprise, that is, on the status of political thought or theorizing. As before, the accent is again on "working through," on carefully assessing what is "underfoot" in our present age. In her words: "What I propose in the following is a reconsideration of the human condition from the vantage point of our newest experiences and our most recent fears." Such an assessment, she adds, is a reflective exercise, an exercise that constitutes a needed antidote to the "thoughtlessness," the "heedless recklessness," the "hopeless confusion," and the "complacent repetition of 'truths' which have become trivial and empty" that are among "the outstanding characteristics of our time." Instead of seeking refuge in reckless activism, absentmindedness, or else abstract perennialism, *The Human Condition* seeks to mend the gulf between thinking and doing, between philosophy and *praxis*: "What I propose, therefore, is very simple: it is nothing more than to think what we are doing."[12]

Vita Activa and the Public Realm

Among Arendt's most important and seminal contributions is her emphasis on engaged action and interaction in political life, on what she calls "action" in a shared "public realm." In the literature devoted to her work, these features tend to be stressed or highlighted—and quite properly so.[13] With this emphasis, Arendt placed herself at odds with powerful tendencies in Western modern life, tendencies bent on sidelining political *praxis* in favor of either social engineering (based on presumed scientific knowledge) or else of private consumerism and self-gratification. Behind these tendencies looms a dominant paradigm of modernity inherited from Galileo and Descartes: a paradigm that splits the world into inside and outside, *cogito* and "extended matter," willing or wanting and knowing—divisions leaving little or no room for political *praxis* in a shared space. In the subtitle to *The Human Condition*, Arendt describes these divisions or splits as "the central dilemmas facing modern man," dilemmas that she discusses more fully in the historical chapter of her book dealing with the rise of the "modern age." There she depicts the basic modern predicament as a dual withdrawal or "alienation" from the world (and the earth): namely, first, a withdrawal into solitary individual inwardness, and second, a withdrawal into an external-scientific spectatorship buttressed by an "Archimedean point" (or a view from nowhere). Both moves are intimately linked. Coupled with the inward move has been an extra-terrestrial flight with the help of Galileo's invention of the telescope—an exodus permitting historians to speak of "a '*véritable retour à Archimède*' that has been effective since the Renaissance."[14]

In *The Human Condition*, the historical narrative concerning the rise of modernity is preceded by the formulation of a theoretical structure delineating modes of human conduct, a structure that is both innovative and stunning (and perhaps disorienting) in its neat compartmentalization. As is well known, Arendt distinguishes between three principal modes of human conduct, held together by the summary label *vita activa*: namely, labor, work, and action (the latter meaning basically political action or *praxis*). As she writes in the opening chapter of her book, each of the three types of conduct "corresponds to one of the basic conditions under which life on earth has been given to man." Among the three, labor is most primitive and entirely prepolitical: it corresponds to "the biological process of the human body whose spontaneous growth, metabolism, and eventual decay are bound to the vital necessities produced and fed into the life process of labor." Whereas labor testifies to our inherence in nature, work by contrast corresponds to "the un-naturalness of human existence" and involves the "artificial" construction or instrumental fabrication of a durable world of objects (hence, it manifests a certain, artificial kind of "worldliness"). Finally and most importantly, action or *praxis* is the emblem of a properly human world of meanings and aspirations: it "goes on directly between men without the intermediary of things or matter" and "corresponds to the human condition of plurality, to the fact than men, not Man, live on the earth and inhabit the world." In addition to being the most distinctively human type of conduct, action for Arendt has the further merit of promising freedom and creative innovation through its linkage with (what she calls) "natality," the new beginning signaled by birth: "Since action is the political activity par excellence, natality, and not mortality, may be the central category of political, as distinguished from metaphysical thought."[15]

The tripartition of modes of conduct stipulated in the text has distant origins in classical antiquity (especially the Aristotelian distinction between *oikos* and *polis*)—although the respective accents are greatly modified. The most innovative contribution, in Arendt's own view, is not the distinction between labor and action, but rather that between labor and work—terms that, in the history of Western thought, have tended to be mingled or confused. "The distinction between labor and work which I propose," she writes, "is unusual"; apart from a few scattered remarks by some authors, "there is hardly anything in either the premodern condition of political thought or in the large body of modern 'labor' theories to support it." For Arendt, the rise of modern science and technology coupled with industrialization renders plausible and even urgent the differentiation between sheer biological life and a realm of civil artifacts (or between what Hobbes called "natural bodies' and "artificial bodies"). In terms of *The Human Condition*, labor signifies human behavior fully immersed in the ever-recurring life cycle and hence governed by physical necessity. The situation changes dramatically once the focus is shifted from *animal laborans* to *homo faber* or "man the tool maker"; at this point, a durable world of instruments and use objects emerges, which ensures a certain reliability of survival. From the angle of life chances, the products of work (and not the products of labor) "guarantee the permanence and durability without which a world would not be possible at all. It is within this world of durable things that we find the consumer goods through which life assures the means of its own survival."[16]

Although providing for the durability of life, the world of instruments and use objects is not yet properly a "human" world, that is, a world constituted essentially by human speech and action.

Distinguished from both the goods of labor and the objects of work, Arendt writes, "there are finally the 'products' of action and speech, which together constitute the fabric of human relationships and affairs." As compared with the durability of artifacts, the latter products are peculiarly vulnerable, fragile, and elusive. Left to them, we read, the products of speech and action "lack not only the tangibility of things, but are even less durable and more futile than what we produce for consumption." In Arendt's presentation, speech and action have a pre-eminently human, existential, and even transnatural quality. Viewed in the context of modes of conduct, action and speech (she claims) "have much more in common than any of them has with work and labor." The only thing that action shares with labor is a certain evanescence or instability. In order to become concretely tangible or manifest, she insists, action and speech must "first be seen, heard, and remembered and then be transformed, reified as it were, into things." In fact, the whole world of politics or human affairs depends for its "reality" and continued existence on this twofold process: "the presence of others who have seen and heard and will remember" and then "the transformation of the intangible into the tangibility of things" in the form of records, stories, documents, or monuments.[17]

For Arendt, speech and action do not really exist unless or until they are openly heard and witnessed—and this can happen only in a shared open space that she calls the "public realm" (a variation on what John Dewey called "the public"). Basically, *The Human Condition* pinpoints two interrelated dimensions of "publicity" or the "public realm." First of all, the term denotes that "everything that appears in public can be seen and heard by everybody and has the widest possible publicity." To this extent, manifest "appearance"—that something is openly seen and heard—"constitutes reality" (at least the reality of a publicly shared human life). By contrast, inner feelings and aspirations, and even the experience of "great bodily pain," are purely "private" because they cannot be publicly communicated or shared. The second aspect highlighted in the text is the "worldliness" of public life, the fact that it is inserted into a shared space or realm as distinguished from "our privately owned place in it." Worldliness here does not refer to a merely natural habitat or to the space of organic life. Rather, the world-character of the public realm is sustained by the artifacts created by work that provide the durable context for speech and action. Thus, the public realm involves both the "fabrication of human hands" and the "affairs that go on among those who inhabit the man-made world together." This linkage of action with the artifacts of work is one of the factors insuring a certain durability of public life over time; the other factor is remembrance, which grants to past political actions or deeds a lasting and (in a sense) "immortal" significance.[18]

As one should note, the shared or "common" quality of public life does not stand in contradiction to the "human condition of plurality" stressed as a corollary of action. As Arendt emphatically asserts, the commonality of public life is predicated neither on a sameness of individual interests, nor on a fixed "common nature" identical among all participants, but only on a range of shared or communicable concerns and purposes. In her words: The "reality" of the public realm relies "on the simultaneous presence of innumerable perspectives and aspects in which the common world presents itself and for which no common measurement or denominator can ever be devised." Although the "common world" is indeed a shared meeting ground for all, "those who are present have different locations in it, and the location of one can no more coincide with the location of another than the location of two objects." For Arendt, public commonality is pluralist in character and must not be confused with any kind of conformism or collectivism, or with a pliant "communitarianism." Drawing some inspiration from both Machiavelli and Nietzsche, she accepts the role of "agonal" contest in public life—although not a contest destructive of publicity. This is precisely the "meaning" of public life, she affirms, that speech and action "derive their significance from the fact that everybody sees and hears from a different position." While shying away from anarchism (and also from a "friend–enemy" conception of politics), The Human Condition construes public life ultimately as a balance of unity and diversity: "Only where things can be seen by many in a variety of aspects without changing their identity, so that those gathered around them know they see sameness in utter diversity, can worldly reality truly and reliably appear."[19]

Arendt Between Past and Future

Many things have happened since Arendt's time. For latecomers studying her work, it is fitting both to look back and to look ahead, and thus to place Arendt herself "between past and future." In order to pay properly tribute to her, latecomers need to practice "memory work" by recalling her seminal teachings—although without "canonizing" them or erecting them into invariant doctrines. As it seems to me, pondering her work from the agonies of our own time, some of her insights have undiminished significance, whereas others need to be rethought or reformulated—precisely in order to keep her spirit alive.

Among her insights that have retained—and even gained added—significance I would count her comments on evil and the "banality of evil"—comments that, although fully acknowledging the reality of evil, can serve as an antidote to political Manichaeism, especially the fashionable rhetoric about an "axis of evil." Of equally undiminished significance are her comments on "lying in politics" and on the importance of maintaining a measure of factual "truth" in public life. Probably at no point in recent history has the importance of such veracity been more clearly evident than in our contemporary political context, a situation marked by widespread media manipulation, "double-speak," and massive efforts of dis-information. Arendt's reflections on the "Pentagon Papers" resonate uncannily with recent political developments, especially her observation (referring to the Vietnam War) that "the divergence between facts—established by the intelligence services, sometimes by the decision-makers themselves . . . and the premises, theories, and hypotheses according to which decisions were made, is total."[20]

The most crucial and seminal contribution of her work is undoubtedly her discussion of action and the public domain. The relevance of these topics is arguably even more acute today than it was at the time of her writing, given the global ascendancy of a "neo-liberal" economic ideology entirely dismissive of public life or else bent on reducing politics to an instrument of economic interests. The ascendancy of the neo-liberal ideology also shows the continued relevance, under completely changed circumstances, of Arendt's penetrating analysis of the nature of "totalitarianism." Although tailored to the historical examples of European fascism and Soviet communism, aspects of her analysis uncannily survive the collapse of these historical regimes. By "totalitarianism" Arendt basically meant a political system that, by abolishing every remnant of shared public life, erects a monolithic structure of domination by means of social engineering aided and abetted by ideological brainwashing and dis-information. Transgressing traditional forms of despotism or tyranny, totalitarian systems in her view are sustained by a pervasive conformism penetrating all layers of society, a conformism generating (she writes) "the fiction of a normal world along with a consciousness of being different from and more radical from it."[21] Once these features are taken into account, even liberal and neo-liberal systems—although posturing as the very antithesis of totalitarianism—can be seen to exhibit totalizing tendencies replicating or at least approximating the Arendtian model.[22]

An intrinsic corollary of the focus on public life and the critique of totalitarianism is Arendt's distinction between public "power" and "violence," between shared republican "empowerment" and violently coercive force. In our time of radically unleashed violence—of globalized and seemingly interminable "terror wars"—this distinction is crucially pertinent. At the present juncture of time, it appears more urgent than ever to recall Arendt's statement that "power and violence are opposites; where the one rules absolutely, the other is absent." In our contemporary period, massive violence is perpetrated by state actors as well as non-state actors, both relying for their purposes on unilateral, radically unaccountable willpower—a strategy deriving ultimately from the modern concept of absolute state "sovereignty." Among twentieth-century political thinkers, Arendt is virtually alone in denouncing this legacy of sovereignty, together with the associated notion of unilateral free will. As we read in *The Human Condition*, "sovereignty is possible only in imagination, paid for by the price of reality," and the same holds true of unilateral freedom and willpower. "If it were true that sovereignty and freedom are the same," Arendt adds, "then indeed no man could be free, because sovereignty, the ideal of uncompromising self-sufficiency and mastery, is contradictory to the very condition of plurality. No man can be sovereign because not one man, but men, inhabit the earth." To these statements one needs to add the strong indictment formulated in *Between Past and Future*:

> Politically, this identification of freedom with sovereignty is perhaps the most pernicious and dangerous consequence of the philosophical equation of freedom and free will. For it leads either to a denial of human freedom—namely, if it is realized that whatever men may be, they are never sovereign—or to the insight that the freedom of one man, or a body politic, can be purchased only at the price of the freedom, i.e., the sovereignty, of all others. . . . If men wish to be free, it is precisely sovereignty they must renounce.[23]

With this condemnation of sovereignty—which is basically a condemnation of the modern Westphalian system—the possibility of a different future comes into view, a post-Westphalian future predicated no longer on unilateralism but on global interdependence, on a global community of peoples. Unfortunately, at this juncture, Arendt only offers us vague hunches or glimpses. To be sure, lodged in the interstices of past and future, Arendt could not have ventured rashly into future scenarios without undermining the internal coherence of her thought. Still, viewed from the perspective of latecomers (and certainly from my perspective), her work sometimes reveals a certain "pastness":

above all, a distinct indebtedness to the very "central dilemmas" of the modern age against which Dewey and Heidegger had struggled and from which she tried so valiantly to extricate herself in other respects. A case in point is the somewhat rigid bifurcation between labor and action, biological processes and public endeavors—a distinction that revives (in modified form) the Cartesian division between mind and body, humanity and external nature.

A corollary of this bifurcation is the sidelining of the "social domain" in favor of the public sphere—a sidelining that undercuts the importance of "civil society" for democracy, especially in our multicultural and globalizing age. An additionally confusing or disorienting factor in this context is the stress placed on birth or "natality" as the gateway to innovative human freedom—a stress sidelining the possibly transformative role of mortality (or human "being-toward-death"). Clearly, birth as such is part of the ordinary biological life process and thus not directly or intelligibly connected with public action. This seems to be acknowledged, at least in part, by Arendt when she observes at another point that the household domain is the "realm of birth and death which must be hidden from the public realm because it harbors the things hidden from human eyes and impenetrable to human knowledge."[24]

In a still more pronounced form, indebtedness to Cartesian dilemmas—or else to a subjectivist type of existentialism—surfaces in the discussion of "action" itself. Although placed in the context of a public domain, action for Arendt involves a form of individual self-display or self-revealment, a disclosure of "who" the actor existentially is. As she writes: "In acting and speaking, men show who they are, reveal actively their unique personal identities and thus make their appearance in the human world." In Arendt's account, this self-disclosure of agents (or acting "subjects") is silhouetted against the "objective" backdrop of the "world of things"—a backdrop also described as an "objective intercourse" or a "physical, worldly in-between" as distinguished from the more intangible realm of words and deeds constituting a "second, subjective in-between." No great acumen is needed to perceive in these formulations remnants of modernist (Cartesian) metaphysics—something she herself recognizes by stating that the chosen concept of action is "highly individualistic, as we would say today." Whatever the values of this individualism may be, it clearly falls short of the insight reached in Dewey's conception of the "unity of action" (the co-constitution of doer and deed) and also of Heidegger's notion of action as "fulfillment" (in the middle voice). The accent on subjective individuality reaches its culmination when the goal of action is portrayed as memorialized personal "immortality," and the standard for judging action as the performance of "great" deeds or the display of public "greatness." As *The Human Condition* states: "Action can be judged only by the criterion of greatness because it is in its nature to break through the commonly accepted and reach into the extraordinary. . . . The art of politics teaches men how to bring forth what is great and radiant."[25]

The modernist slant of these passages fits ill with contemporary ("postmodern") sensibilities. As it seems to me, the accent on personal immortality and great performances exhibits a theatrical cast no longer in tune with a time marked by terror wars, genocides, and ethnic cleansings—all executed on a grand scale. In this situation, one cannot help but regret a certain obtuseness in Arendt's writings having to do with philosophical, ethical, and also religious concerns. It may have been quite proper on her part to demarcate political action against an abstract, otherworldly metaphysics or a spectatorial "view from nowhere." But clearly, not all philosophizing is of this kind. Some philosophical endeavors, both in the past and in the present, have a distinctly practical or *praxis*-oriented bent—Aristotelian philosophy and Deweyan pragmatism being prominent cases in point. Although referring to Aristotle's legacy on numerous occasions—for example, by invoking his notion of "*bios politikos*" involving action and speech "out of which rises the realm of human affairs"—the legacy is ultimately sidelined because of an alleged overemphasis on contemplation (which is surely debatable).

Viewed against the backdrop of practical philosophy—from Aristotle to Dewey and beyond—the deficit of Arendt's work becomes patently obvious, especially in her dismissal of ethical considerations and her sharp refusal to consider democracy an "ethical community" (in Dewey's sense). As it seems to me, one of the most dubious passages in *The Human Condition* is the assertion that "goodness, as a consistent way of life, is not only impossible within the confines of the public realm, it is even destructive of it."[26] As a remedy for this deficit, it is imperative, in my view, to affirm a very different position: namely, that the purpose of political action is to enhance not personal immortality but the "good life" of all participants, and that the standard for judging such action is not greatness but rather justice and equity.

6

Postmodernism and Radical Democracy

*Laclau and Mouffe
on "Hegemony"*

Postmodernism and post-structuralism frequently are seen as mere academic trends, soon to be replaced or outdated by newer fashions. This view is reinforced by their prominent role in literary criticism and aesthetics—fields notoriously prone to quick fluctuations of taste. In application to politics and political theory, postmodernism often appears as little more than a mode of escapism, a display of verbal artistry oblivious of concrete social contexts and power constellations. Against this background, the work of Ernesto Laclau and Chantal Mouffe offers an invigorating breath of fresh air: brushing aside academic cobwebs, their writings relentlessly and almost passionately probe the implications of post-structuralism for political life. Unpretentiously stated (and thus shunning easy notoriety), their arguments touch at the core of contemporary political and philosophical concerns. Countering any association with escapism or a simple-minded anarchism, their work demonstrates the relevance of post-structural themes for the theoretical grasp of liberalism and socialism, and particularly for the future of democratic politics.

From the vantage of Laclau and Mouffe, this relevance manifests itself prominently or with special virulence in the context of traditional socialist thought (as part and parcel of the so-called "crisis" of Marxism). As they observe in their introduction to *Hegemony and Socialist Strategy* (1985): "Left-wing thought today stands at a crossroads. The 'evident truths' of the past . . . have been seriously challenged by an avalanche of historical mutations which have riven the ground on which those truths were constituted." Apart from a host of social and political changes, the authors appeal to more subtle intellectual dislocations, especially the effects of post-metaphysics with its attack on stable foundations: "What is now in crisis is a whole conception of socialism which rests upon the ontological centrality of the working class, upon the role of the Revolution (with a capital 'r'), as the founding moment in the transition from one type of society to another, and upon the illusory prospect of a perfectly unitary and homogeneous collective will that will render pointless the moment of politics." In turning to the concept of "hegemony," the study seeks to do more than add a further refinement or complementary twist to traditional essentialism: instead, the aim is to initiate a paradigmatic shift reverberating through the entire set of categories and providing a new "anchorage" from which contemporary social struggles are "*thinkable* in their specificity."[1] In the following I first recapitulate briefly some of the main themes presented in *Hegemony and Socialist Strategy*. Subsequently, I lift up for closer scrutiny several of the chief theoretical innovations of the study in order to conclude finally with some critical observations or afterthoughts.

Traditional Marxism Contested

Congruent with its paradigmatic ambition, *Hegemony and Socialist Strategy* opens with a backward glance at the history of Marxist or socialist discourse and, more specifically, with a detailed genealogy of the concept of hegemony. As the authors emphasize, the concept entered Marxist discourse initially as a stopgap measure or as a mere supplement designed to patch up evolutionary anomalies. To illustrate the context of the concept's emergence, the opening chapter points to the dilemmas of Rosa Luxemburg as they are revealed in her book on the mass strike.[2] In that work, Luxemburg recognized the fragmentation of the working class as a necessary structural effect of advancing capitalism; at the same time, however, the prospect of revolutionary struggle was ascribed not to the operation of economic laws but to the spontaneous constitution of class unity through the medium of symbolic action. It was the fissure implicit in this argument that called and made room for a supplementary category curbing the reign of economic necessity.

Initially, to be sure, this opening collided head-on with the dominant Marxist model of the time, a framework spelled out and summarized in Karl Kautsky's commentary on the Erfurt Program

(1892). According to the Kautskian text, Marxism was an essentialist doctrine predicated on the indissoluble "unity of theory, history and strategy." The latter unity or totality, in turn, was based on a number of related features or assumptions—among them, that the structure of industrial society was increasingly simplified in the direction of class conflict; that the two chief classes were differentiated in their essence or by nature because of their diverse status in the mode of production; and that the denouement of class struggle was intelligible as resolution of prior contradictions. It was only at the end of the Bismarck era, with the rise of organized capitalism, that the flaws of the essentialist model began to surface. What made itself felt at this point, we read, was a "new awareness of the opacity of the social, of the complexities and resistances of an increasingly organized capitalism; and the fragmentation of the different positions of social agents which, according to the classical paradigm, should have been united."[3]

Reactions to these changes were halting and only slowly affected the structure of traditional premises. Laclau and Mouffe discuss three immediate responses to the perceived crisis of Marxism: the establishment of "Marxist orthodoxy," the formulation of a "revisionist" approach by Eduard Bernstein, and Georges Sorel's "revolutionary syndicalism." Marxist orthodoxy, in their presentation, involved the ascendancy or privileging of abstract theory over concrete social struggles and also over the political practice of social democratic parties. Divergences from theoretical postulates were treated either as deceptive appearances or surface phenomena or else as marginal contingencies unable to alter the predicted course of events: namely, the ascendancy of a unified proletariat under the leadership of the workers' party. Only occasionally—especially in the cases of Antonio Labriola and Austro-Marxism—did orthodoxy grant some space to autonomous political initiative but without proceeding to integrate such initiative within the overall theoretical framework. The issue of the relation of politics and economics, or of superstructure and base, was the central motif underlying Bernstein's revisionist approach—a position that insisted that the fragmentation or division of the working class in advanced capitalism could be remedied only through concrete political intervention. While introducing a breach between politics and economics, however, revisionism never questioned the class-based character of political action or of the workers' party; moreover, Bernstein's Kantian leanings fostered a dualism between the realm of freedom (anchored in the autonomy of ethical subjects) and the determinism of economic laws—a gulf only precariously bridged by the notion of social "evolution" (*Entwicklung*). Moving beyond a simple juxtaposition of domains, revolutionary syndicalism as advocated by Sorel attempted for the first time to conceptualize social autonomy, that is, to "think the specificity of that 'logic of contingency' " on which "a field of totalizing effects is reconstituted." Pursuing this path, Sorel was led to replace economic class unity with more amorphous social "blocs" held together by ideological devices.[4]

A corollary of these reactions to social fragmentation was the emergence of the concept of "hegemony" as the site of a new or ascending political logic. In orthodox discourse the concept occupied only a marginal place, as a marker for theoretically undigested events. In the writings of Georgii Plekhanov and Pavel Axelrod, for example, hegemony designated the multiple (economic and political) tasks imposed on the Russian proletariat as a result of economic backwardness. According to Laclau and Mouffe, hegemonic relations at this point merely "*supplement* class relations. Using a distinction of Saussure's, we could say that hegemonic relations are always facts of *parole*, while class relations are facts of *langue*." The reduction to supplementary status was still operative in Leninism, and especially in the Leninist formula of a "class alliance" cemented under the leadership of a proletarian "vanguard" party. Because of the "ontological centrality" assigned to the proletariat, class alliance in this case did not modify essential class identities in the direction of fusing them with the democratic demands implicit in hegemonic practices. The same centrality was reinforced in the immediate aftermath of the Russian revolution—as is evident in Zinoviev's slogan of the "bolshevization" of communist parties, where "bolshevization" means "a firm will to struggle for the hegemony of the proletariat."[5]

In terms of the study, the crucial break with Marxist essentialism was initiated by Antonio Gramsci whose work is portrayed as the decisive "watershed" offering a formulation of the hegemonic link "which clearly went beyond the Leninist category of 'class alliance.' " Extricating himself from the legacy of fixed class identities, Gramsci focused on broader social groupings called "historical blocs" whose unity of purpose or "collective will" was fostered by intellectual and moral leadership in a context of cultural and political hegemony. As a corollary, moving beyond simple base-superstructure formulas, his approach perceived ideology not as an abstract system of ideas but as an organic ensemble of beliefs and concrete practices partially embodied in institutions and social structures. Yet, despite these important theoretical advances, Laclau and Mouffe note a persistent ambivalence in Gramsci's work curtailing his pioneering role: namely, a tendency to return to an "ontological" or essentialist conception of class identity and to ascribe the ultimately unifying power in hegemonic formations to an economically defined class. To the extent that the Gramscian "war of position" still paid tribute to a zero-sum construal of class struggle—they write—it revealed an "inner essentialist core" in his thought "setting a limit to the deconstructive logic of hegemony." The same ambivalence, in their view, was reflected in social-democratic policies of the period, especially in the "planism" of the post-Depression era and also in later technocratic models of state intervention.[6]

Against the backdrop of this historical scenario, the study embarks on its central and most ambitious task: the theoretical elaboration of a nonessentialist concept of hegemony as cornerstone of a "radically democratic" political theory. On nonfoundational premises, hegemony has the character of a creative "articulation," that is, of the "political construction" of a social formation out of dissimilar elements. Such a creative articulation is radically at odds with a closed "totality" or a view of society as a completely intelligible and homogeneous structure—a view partially operative in Hegelian philosophy and in versions of Marxism. To clarify their conception of hegemony, Laclau and Mouffe proceed through a detour: a confrontation with Louis Althusser's structuralist theory and its aftermath. The most promising feature of Althusser's approach, they note, was the principle of "overdetermination"—the thesis that social formations or phenomena are not causally fixed but the result of a symbolic fusion of plural elements. As it happened, however, overdetermination remained vague in Althusser's work and was progressively overshadowed by other structuralist ingredients, especially the claim of determination by the economy "in the last instance"; as a result of this claim, symbolic construction functioned merely as a contingent margin of causal necessity.

The theoretical critique of Althusser's model—as inaugurated by Etienne Balibar and continued by spokesmen of British Marxism (like Barry Hindess and Paul Hirst)—focused on the logical connections among ingredients of the model and ultimately on the role and status of "structural causality." Although promising in many respects, this critique, according to the authors, so far has resulted only in logical disaggregation and not in a radical reformulation of basic categories. Moving in the latter direction, the study advances these definitional propositions: "We will call *articulation* any practice establishing a relation among elements such that their identity is modified as a result of the articulatory practice. The structured totality resulting from the articulatory practice, we will call *discourse*." Whereas differential positions articulated within a discourse are termed *moments*, the label *elements* is reserved for differences not discursively structured. Discursive formations are said to be unified neither logically nor empirically nor transcendentally but only through an ambivalent symbolic coherence (akin to Michel Foucault's "regularity in dispersion"). Most importantly, as articulatory enterprises discourses only selectively structure the social domain without reaching definitive closure; due to their inherent finitude and multivocity, they never exhaust the broader "field of discursivity" with its available surplus of meaning. Hegemony here denotes the selective structuring of the social field around distinct "nodal points" seen as privileged discursive accents.[7]

Fleshing out the notion of discursive practices, Laclau and Mouffe comment in some detail on the role of the subject (or subjectivity) in such practices; on the contest or antagonism prevailing between discursive formations; and on the relation between hegemony and democracy. In line with the unfixity of social identities, subjects in their view cannot function as the constitutive origin of social formations—which does not entail the elimination of human agents but rather their construal as "subject positions" within a discursive structure (possibly as nodal points in such a structure). On the level of Marxist analysis, economic classes likewise are only articulated ingredients (possibly nodal ingredients) within a selectively structured social field. Because of their finite and selective character, discursive formations inevitably are in tension with alternative possibilities. In a critical review of Marxist literature, the study sharply demarcates antagonism from such notions as "logical contradiction" and "real opposition" (*Realrepugnanz*): whereas the latter are objectively given relations, the former derives precisely from ambiguity and the contestation of givenness.

Seen as the limit of social formations, antagonism results not merely from the confrontation between different empirical structures, but rather operates as an intrinsic negative potency in every formation challenging its presumed positivity or its objective givenness. According to the authors, this negative potency manifests itself chiefly through a system of equivalence that subverts all positive differences, reducing them to an underlying sameness. "The *ultimate* character of this unfixity (of the social)," they write, "the *ultimate* precariousness of all difference, will show itself in a relation of total equivalence, where the differential positivity of all its terms is dissolved. This is precisely the formula of antagonism, which thus establishes itself as the limit of the social." Yet, just as social positivity can never fully be stabilized, negativity or negative equivalence cannot become a total or all-embracing enterprise (without canceling the very possibility of social articulation). Instead, social formations are predicated on a precarious blend of the "opposed logics of equivalence and difference"—with full integration and total rupture only signaling the extreme ends of a spectrum.[8]

This aspect brings into view the relation between hegemony and democracy. Viewed as a social formation, democracy cannot be reduced to total equivalence or a bipolar conflict between self-enclosed camps—despite the possible presence of deep fissures. Differentiating between "popular struggles" (in a Jacobin sense) and "democratic struggles," the study presents the former only as extreme variants within the broader framework of hegemonic democratic relations: "The existence of two camps may in some cases be an *effect* of the hegemonic articulation but not its *a priori* condition. . . . We will therefore speak of *democratic* struggles where these imply a plurality of political spaces, and of *popular* struggles where certain discourses *tendentially* construct the division of a single political space in two opposed fields. But it is clear that the fundamental concept is that of 'democratic struggle.' "[9]

The theme of hegemony and democracy is further explored in the concluding chapter of the study. In the authors' view, the relation between socialism and democratic politics has involved a difficult process of adjustment: namely, the move from an essentialist doctrine—treating the bipolar division of society as *"an original and immutable datum*, prior to all hegemonic construction"—toward a more diversified democratic conception acknowledging the basic "instability of political spaces" and the fact that "the very identity of the forces in struggle is submitted to constant shifts." The last approximation of a factual bipolarity occurred during the French Revolution, with the pervasive opposition between "people" and *"ancien régime."* Since that time, however, the dividing line between social antagonisms has become increasingly "fragile and ambiguous" and its formulation has emerged as the "crucial problem of politics." As discussed in previous chapters, Marxism sought to reconstitute an essential polarity on economic grounds—but without succeeding in translating the distinction of classes into an automatic sociopolitical conflict.

According to Laclau and Mouffe, the development of radical democracy has put in question the "continuity between the Jacobin and the Marxist political imaginary," and more generally the assumption of a privileged point of rupture and the "confluence of struggles into a unified political space." Returning to the period of the French Revolution, the study portrays the insurgent "logic of equivalence" as the basic instrument of social change and as the beginning of a long-term "democratic revolution." This process of democratization has gained added momentum in recent decades, due to antagonisms triggered by the so-called new social movements. The targets of insurgency in this case are chiefly the bureaucratization, commodification, and growing homogenization of life in advanced industrial societies. In theoretical terms, what these movements bring into view is the specificity of contemporary struggles constituted on the basis of "different subject positions" (in lieu of a fixed or foundational polarity); more generally, they highlight the emergence of a "radical and plural democracy" with a close intermeshing of radicalism and pluralism.[10] As the authors recognize, the shift from essentialism to plural struggles does not by itself guarantee a progressive democratic outcome. Pointing to the rise of the "new Right" and of neo-conservatism in Western countries, the study detects in our time a new valorization of positive social differences and also of individual autonomy seen as a counterpoint to mass democracy. What this counter-insurgency accentuates—Laclau and Mouffe argue—is the importance of political hegemony and the need to intensify broad-based political struggles in line with the modern process of democratization.

Such struggles, they write, should locate themselves fully "in the field of the democratic revolution" and its expanding chains of equivalence; their task, in any case, "cannot be to renounce liberal-democratic ideology, but on the contrary, to deepen and expand it in the direction of a radical and plural democracy." Socialist strategy in the past was ill equipped to shoulder this task, mainly because of its hankering for an "essentialist *a priorism*"—a hankering manifest in its reliance on privileged subjects ("classism"), on a privileged social basis ("economism"), and on a privileged policy instrument ("statism"). Once *a priorism* is abandoned, socialist or social-democratic strategy has to insert itself into the precarious web of hegemonic democratic relations, particularly into the interplay of positivity and negativity or of the logic of difference and the logic of equivalence—an interplay that also may be phrased as the tension between equality and liberty or autonomy. As the authors conclude: "Between the logic of complete identity and that of pure difference, the experience of democracy should consist of the recognition of the multiplicity of social logics along with the necessity of their (hegemonic) articulation"—an articulation that needs to be "constantly re-created and renegotiated."[11]

Radical Democracy and Hegemony

As should be clear from the preceding synopsis, *Hegemony and Socialist Strategy* is a richly textured and often provocative work; it is also

tightly argued and intellectually uncompromising—in a manner barring easy access. In terms of contemporary labels, the study inserts
itself in the broad movement of post-structuralism and postmodernism—but without facile trendiness (and without entirely abandoning
structuralist themes, from Ferdinand de Saussure to Althusser).[12]
Contrary to aestheticizing tendencies or construals, the work clearly
demonstrates the relevance of post-essentialism or "deconstruction" for
political theory; in fact, *Hegemony and Socialist Strategy* can and should
be viewed as a major contribution to a present-day understanding of
democracy. Most importantly, the study counteracts the widespread
association of deconstruction with anarchism or with complete social
and political randomness. Although devoid of essentialist moorings or
ontological fixity, post-structuralist politics—as presented by Laclau and
Mouffe—operates in a complex relational web endowed with distinct
parameters or constraints, parameters shielding radical democracy from
the perils of despotism, totalitarianism, and unmitigated violence.

   Although amenable to diverse interpretations, the study (in my
view) is basically a political text, an example of innovative political
theorizing. Apart from its historical resonances, the accent on hegemony involves centrally a revalorization of politics against all forms
of reductionism (which would subordinate politics to other domains).
A crucial assault launched in the study is directed at sociologism as
well as economism. In a bold formulation—challenging prominent
portrayals of sociology as "master social science"—Laclau and Mouffe
speak of the "impossibility of society," that is, the inability of the social
domain to provide a firm grounding of analysis.[13] What society needs
in order to gain contours is some kind of political articulation, that is,
the formulation and establishment of hegemonic political relationships.
Reminiscent vaguely of Arendtian arguments, the study defines politics
as "a practice of creation, reproduction and transformation of social
relations," a practice that cannot be located at a "determinate level
of the social" because the problem of the political is "the problem of
the *institution* of the social, that is, of the definition and articulation
of social relations in a field criss-crossed with antagonisms." Moving
beyond Arendt, however, the authors do not accord to politics a stable
space or a completely autonomous sphere. In effect, radical democracy
in their text is presented as a form of politics that is founded "not
upon dogmatic postulation of any 'essence of the social,' but, on the
contrary, on affirmation of the contingency and ambiguity of every
'essence,' and on the constitutive character of social division and
antagonism. Affirmation of a 'ground' which lives only by negating
its fundamental character; of an 'order' which exists only as a partial
limiting of 'disorder.' "[14]

The attack on the constitutive character of society applies with particular force to economism as it has operated in traditional Marxism. Challenging the presumed determination of the labor process and of class struggle by an abstract "logic of capital," Laclau and Mouffe assert the dependence of the latter on antagonisms linked with a pervasive "politics of production." A number of recent studies, they write, "have analyzed the evolution of the labor process from the point of view of the relation of forces between workers and capitalists, and of the workers' resistance." They reveal the presence of a "politics of production" at odds with the notion that capitalist development is the effect "solely of the laws of competition and the exigencies of accumulation." To be sure, attacking economism is not the same as postulating a rigid separation between economics and politics or ascribing a foundational status to the latter. According to the authors, such a view could only be maintained "if political practice was a perfectly delimited field whose frontiers with the economy could be drawn *more geometrico*—that is, if we excluded as a matter of principle any overdetermination of the political by the economic or vice versa." Given that politics is a matter of hegemonic articulation, the relationship between politics and economics cannot be permanently fixed or stabilized and depends on circumstances and prevailing articulatory practices.[15]

The dismantling of univocal fixity and the accent on complex relationships lends to the study a quasi-Hegelian or (more properly) post-Hegelian flavor—a circumstance readily acknowledged by the authors. In terms of *Hegemony and Socialist Strategy*, Hegel's philosophy is precariously and ambiguously lodged at the intersection between metaphysics and post-metaphysics—more specifically between a theory of totality and a theory of hegemony. In the authors' words, Hegel's work is at once the "highest moment" of German rationalism and idealism and simultaneously "the first modern—that is to say, post-Enlightenment—reflection on society." The ambiguity has to do chiefly with the ability of reason to grasp reality as a whole; differently phrased: with the respective weights assigned to absolute logic and a more opaque and contingent "cunning of reason." Occupying a watershed between two epochs, Hegel is said to represent on the one hand the culmination of rationalism: namely, "the moment when it attempts to embrace within the field of reason, without dualisms, the totality of the universe of differences." On the other hand, however, Hegel's totality or synthesis contains "all the seeds of its dissolution," as the rationality of history can be affirmed "only at the price of introducing contradiction into the field of reason itself." The continued significance of Hegel's thought resides basically in the second dimension: namely, in its midwifing role for a theory of hegemony, opening reflection up to the flux of contingent and not purely logical (or essential) relationships.[16]

The post-Hegelian quality of the study—or its Hegelianism with a deconstructive twist—surfaces at numerous points and most prominently in the discussion of hegemony and its relation to "antagonism." As previously indicated, antagonism denotes not simply a juxtaposition of objective entities (either on a logical or a factual level), but rather involves a process of mutual contestation and struggle. In general philosophical terms, antagonism arises from hegemony's inability to effect social and political closure—that is, from the polysemy and "surplus of meaning" constantly overreaching and destabilizing discursive practices. In language reminiscent of Hegel, the study situates social formations at the crossroads of positivity and negativity, where negativity designates not simply a lack but a "nihilating" potency. The tensional relation between presence and absence resurfaces or is rearticulated as the interplay of two social logics, namely, the logics of equivalence and difference. Here again it is important to notice that, although pointing in opposite directions, neither logic is able to achieve foundational status or complete self-enclosure. In the authors' words: if negativity and positivity exist only "through their reciprocal subversion," this means that "neither the conditions of total equivalence nor those of total differential objectivity are every fully achieved." Translating the interplay of logics into the more traditional correlation of liberty and equality, another passage asserts: "The precariousness of every equivalence demands that it be complemented/limited by the logic of autonomy. It is for this reason that the demand for *equality* is not sufficient, but needs to be balanced by the demand for *liberty*, which leads us to speak of a radical and *plural* democracy."[17]

The notion of the correlation and interpenetration of social logics presents politics—particularly democratic politics—as an arena of contestation and interrogation, but not as a field of total domination or else mutual destruction. The accent on the relational character of antagonism injects into politics a moral or qualitative dimension, an aspect hostile to the reduction of politics to a simple organism (or mechanism) or else to a naturalistic state of war. If social identities are acquired only through agonal interaction, then it is impossible or illicit either to impose stable identity through a model of integral totality or to foreclose interaction through a system of radical equivalence. Integral closure—the lure of complete social positivity—is chiefly the temptation of the logic of difference. As the authors point out, however, because of its negative potency, antagonism signifies the "limit" of any given social order "and not the moment of a broader totality in relation to which the two poles of the antagonism would constitute differential, i.e., objective-partial instances." The opposite temptation arises from the logic of equivalence: radically pursued, equivalence either totally negates discursive formations and social identities or else polarizes society into two hostile forces of which each operates as the negation of the other. An example of the latter alternative—Laclau and Mouffe observe—can be found in millenarian movements where "the world divides, through a system of paratactical equivalences, into two camps" related only in the mode of negative reversal. More recent instances are terrorism, the notion of an "axis of evil," or totalitarian absolutism.[18]

The implications of this relational conception are multiple and significant: only a few can be highlighted here. Although the study's post-Hegelian thrust is directed against all forms of integral closure or "sutured" totality, the proposed remedy or antidote is not random fragmentation. While critical of the pretense of universal principles or discourses, the authors do not simply opt for particularism—that would only entail a new kind of self-enclosure or a "monadic" essentialism. As they indicate, a mere dismantling of totality readily conjures up the peril of "a new form of fixity," namely, on the level of "decentered subject positions." For this reason, a "logic of detotalization" cannot simply affirm "the *separation* of different struggles and demands," just as "articulation" cannot purely be conceived as "the linkage of dissimilar and fully constituted elements." Through a strategy of disaggregation we are in danger of moving "from an essentialism of the totality to an essentialism of the elements." The means for overcoming this danger is provided by the logic of "overdetermination." For, we read, if the sense of every identity is overdetermined, then "far from there being an essentialist *totalization*, or a no less essentialist *separation* among objects, the presence of some objects in the others prevents any of their identities from being fixed. Objects appear articulated not like pieces in a clockwork mechanism, because the presence of some in the others hinders the suturing of the identity of any of them."[19]

Similar considerations apply to the issue of pluralism. Although endorsing a "radical and plural democracy," the study holds no brief for group egotism. In the authors' words, both an absolute pluralism and a "total diffusion of power within the social" would blind us to the operation of overdetermination and to the presence of "nodal points" in every social formation. With slight modifications, relationism or the interpenetration of identities also affects the status of individual autonomy or liberty. Segregated from equality or equivalence, such autonomy only fosters new modes of totalization—which points up the need to reformulate "bourgeois individualism": "What is involved is the production of *another* individual, an individual who is no longer constructed out of the matrix of possessive individualism. . . . It is never possible for individual rights to be defined in isolation, but only in the context of social relations which define determinate subject positions."[20] Among the most significant contributions of the study are its caveats against total antagonism or against the polarization and militarization of politics. In our violence-prone age when many flirt with theories of radical discord—as an antidote to co-optation—*Hegemony and Socialist Strategy* offers a welcome corrective.

Polar vocabulary was still present—although ambiguously—in the Gramscian notion of "war of position." For Gramsci, war of position involved the progressive disaggregation of a social formation and the construction of a new hegemony of forces—but along a path that left the identity of the opponents malleable and subject to a continuous process of transformation. Thus, the military imagery was in this case "metaphorized" in a direction colliding with its literal sense: "If in Leninism there was a militarization of politics, in Gramsci there is a demilitarization of war"—although the reformulation reached its limit in the assumption of an ultimate class core of every hegemony. Once the latter assumption is dropped, Gramsci's notion can be metaphorized further in a manner compatible with radical democracy. At this point, the distinction between popular struggles and democratic struggles becomes relevant. Whereas Gramsci still presupposed the division of political space along the lines of popular identities (although granting their constructed character), relinquishing this premise opens the way to a fluid and nondichotomous concept of hegemony: "We will thus retain from the Gramscian view the logic of articulation and the political centrality of the frontier effects, but we will eliminate the assumption of a single political space as the necessary framework for those phenomena to arise." Democratic struggles are precisely those that involve a plurality of political spaces.[21]

Some Post-Hegelian and Deweyan Caveats

Despite the impressive depth and rigor of the reviewed work, there is room for critical comments or afterthoughts. Basically, these comments are not meant to deprecate the cogency and overall thrust of its arguments, but rather to amplify and strengthen them in the

direction of a viable post-Hegelian democratic theory. Precisely from
the latter perspective, some of the accents of the study appear to
me lopsided or skewed. In tracing the genealogy of hegemony, the
opening chapter places a heavy—and probably excessive—emphasis
on autonomous action and initiative. Thus, in the discussion of Luxemburg, the "logic of spontaneism" is singled out as an important
counterpoint to class-based essentialism and the literal fixation of
social meanings. Similarly, Sorel's myth of the great strike is held up
for its focus on "contingency" and "freedom," in contradistinction to
the chain of social and economic necessity. Influenced by Nietzsche
and Henri Bergson, Sorel's philosophy is said to be "one of action
and will, in which the future is unforeseeable, and hinges on will."
Formulations of this kind are liable to inject into the study a flavor of
voluntarism not entirely congruent with the authors' broader outlook.
The impression is reinforced in the central portion of the study, namely,
in the equation of hegemony with articulation and of the latter with
a mode of "political construction from dissimilar elements." The term
construction seems to place hegemony in the rubric of a "purposive"
and voluntaristic action (in the Weberian sense)—thus obfuscating
the distinction between *praxis* (or practical conduct) and technical-
instrumental behavior.[22]

Once voluntarism is eschewed, the study embarks on hazardous
terrain. In fact, its theory of hegemony is lodged at one of the most
difficult junctures of Hegelian thought (and of traditional metaphysics in general): the juncture marked by the categories of "freedom"
and "necessity," or "determinism" and "contingency." Occasionally,
hegemony is portrayed almost as an exit route from necessity and
all modes of social determinism. Thus, whereas Marxist essentialism
is said to have banished contingency to the margins of necessity, the
relationship is claimed to be reversed in hegemonic articulation—in
the sense that necessity now "only exists as a partial limitation of
the field of contingency." As the authors somewhat exuberantly add:
"If we accept that a discursive totality never exists in the form of a
simply *given and delimited* positivity, the relational logic will be incomplete and pierced by contingency. . . . A no-man's-land thus emerges
making the articulatory practice possible."[23] Elsewhere, however, this
reversal is called into question—which opens the road to a complex
conceptualization of hegemony in terms of an intertwining and mutual
subversion of necessity and contingency. Once the goal of final fixation
recedes, Laclau and Mouffe observe, a profound ambivalence emerges:
at this point "not only does the very category of necessity fall, but it
is no longer possible to account for the hegemonic relation in terms

of pure contingency, as the space which made intelligible the necessary/contingent opposition has dissolved." What emerges at this point is no longer a simple external delimitation of two contiguous fields, but rather a relationship of mutual interpenetration and contestation. As they write, the relations between necessity and contingency cannot be conceived as "relations between two areas that are delimited and external to each other . . . because the contingent only exists within the necessary. This presence of the contingent in the necessary is what we earlier called *subversion*"—and what, in effect, must be called reciprocal subversion.[24]

What the preceding comments adumbrate is a theoretical relationship that is recalcitrant both to dualism and to monism (in their traditional metaphysical sense). The opposition to dualism is a recurrent theme of the study. Thus, Bernstein's revisionism is chided for embracing a "Kantian dualism" pitting autonomous ethical subjects against economic determinism. Similarly, Marxist orthodoxy is taken to task for harboring a "permanent" and "irreducible" dualism between the logic of necessity and the logic of contingency, with each side being merely the "negative reverse" of the other. Such dualism, the authors note, establishes merely a "relation of frontiers," that is, an external limitation of domains devoid of reciprocal effects. The distinction between "elements" and "moments" in articulatory practices is, in fact, predicated on the persistence of a nondualistic mode of nonidentity. If articulation is a practice, we read, "it must imply some form of separate presence of the elements which that practice articulates or recomposes"; it must also exclude the complete transformation of elements into integral moments or components. What comes into view here is a term placed midway between identity and total nonidentity, a term that some post-structuralist thinkers have thematized under such labels as *intertwining* or *duality*; Heidegger's "*Zwiefalt*" (twofoldedness) and the Derridean notion of "*différance*" point in the same direction.[25]

In a prominent manner, the notion of intertwining or duality would seem to be applicable to the relation between positivity and negativity or between the logics of difference and equivalence (as these terms are used in the study). As the authors repeatedly affirm, negativity is not simply a void or a logical negation but a nihilating ferment exerting real effects: "The presence of the Other is not a logical impossibility; it exists—so it is not a contradiction." The same thought is expressed in the argument that negativity and positivity exist only "through their reciprocal subversion," and also in the view that antagonism as the negation of a given order operates as the intrinsic limit of that order—and not as an alien force imposing external constraints. Unfortunately, passages of this kind collide with occasional formulations that approximate the interplay to a Sartrean kind of antithesis (of being and nothingness). Small wonder that on such premises antagonism begins to shade over into total conflict—as happens in a passage that finds the "formula of antagonism" in a "relation of total equivalence where the differential positivity of all . . . terms is dissolved."[26] Flirtation with nothingness is also evident in the statement that experience of negativity is "not an access to a diverse ontological order, to a something beyond differences, simply because . . . there is no beyond." Yet, the fact that negativity is not another objective (or positive) order does not mean that what lies "beyond differences" is simply a vacuous nothingness. In fact, if differences were related strictly by nothing, the result would be total segregation or equivalence—and by no means the complex web of relationships thematized under the label of *hegemony*. In Heidegger's vocabulary (which, to be sure, has to be employed cautiously), different elements in order to enjoy a relationship are linked on the level of "being"—a term denoting a nonobjective type of matrix in which positivity and negativity, ground and abyss (*Abgrund*) are peculiarly intertwined.[27]

The quandary of positivity and negativity carries over into the conception of democracy—surely a centerpiece of *Hegemony and Socialist Strategy*. In this context, the quandary surfaces as the opposition between democracy construed as a system of radical equivalence and democracy as a social formation intrinsically marked by the tension between equivalence and difference. The first alternative is stressed in the historical narrative tracing the emergence and spreading of "democratic revolution." Referring to the beginning of this process, the study detects a "decisive mutation in the political imaginary of Western societies" at the time of the French Revolution, a mutation that is defined in these terms: "the logic of equivalence was transformed into the fundamental instrument of the production of the social." The same kind of principle is said to govern the subsequent process of democratization: "The logic of democracy is simply the equivalential displacement of the egalitarian imaginary to ever more extensive social relations, and, as such, it is only a logic of the elimination of relations of subordination and of inequalities" and "not a logic of the positivity of the social."[28] Not surprisingly, in order to constitute a viable social order, democracy defined in this manner—as a pure "strategy of opposition"—needs to be supplemented with a "strategy of construction of a new order" bringing into play the "element of social positivity." Actually, however, the construal of democracy as radical equivalence or as expression of a purely "subversive logic" stands in conflict with the conception of "plural democracy" emphasized in the study—a conception in which equivalence and difference, equality and liberty (or autonomy) are inextricably linked. Against the background of this tensional experience, the pursuit of pure equivalence emerges in fact as a sign of political deformation—provoking the specter of despotism and totalitarianism.[29]

This leads me to a final comment. If democracy involves a complex relationship of forces and groupings (recalcitrant to total opposition or essentialist fixation), then antagonism does not necessarily have to have a hostile and mutually coercive character. If hegemony denotes a nonexclusive articulation—fostering an intertwining of exteriority and interiority—then room seems to be made for a more friendly or sympathetic mode of interaction (which, to be sure, cannot entirely cancel negativity and thus an element of equivalence and power). Above all, radical democracy must valorize a distinct political agency, an agency located beyond subjugation or control and pliant passivity, that is, an agency in the "middle voice." Against this background it may be possible to reinvigorate the Deweyan notion of democracy as an ethical community—although a community composed of multiple, more limited communities standing in open (and sometimes agonistic) interaction.[30] Extending the study's post-Hegelian leanings, it seems likewise feasible and legitimate to view democratic politics as permeated by ethical concerns or by the Hegelian category of *Sittlichkeit*, now operating on the grassroots level. Along the same lines, there may be an opportunity today to rethink the Hegelian state—in such a manner that "state" no longer signifies a positive structure or totality, and certainly not simply an instrument of coercion, but rather the fragile (perhaps hegemonic) link holding social interactions in check or in balance. Democracy under these auspices is still an arena of struggle—but a struggle not simply for self-centered advantage or domination but for an equitable relation between liberty and equality: that is, a struggle for justice and mutual recognition of differences.

7

Jacques Derrida's Legacy

Democracy to Come

Martin Heidegger writes somewhere that "higher than actuality is possibility." With this statement, the philosopher lifts the weight of prevailing conditions and makes room for untapped future scenarios—not in the sense of utopian blueprints but of open horizons and uncharted transformations. To be sure, preoccupied with the linkage of "being and time," Heidegger always remained aware of the interlacing of temporalities—of the future direction of the past as well as the past sedimentations in the future—and hence of the correlation of actuality and possibility. Yet, even in his case, the burden of an oppressive present tilted the balance sometimes in the direction of radical transgression—as is evident in his writings on Nietzsche and some other texts penned during the 1930s.[1] Suffering under the same oppressive weight, some of his later students or followers shifted the accent steadily toward transgression of, or noncompliance with, actuality; easily the most resolute thinker in this respect is Jacques Derrida. Influenced by both Nietzsche and Heidegger (and some French Nietzschean thinkers), Derrida placed his focus entirely on "overcoming" of the past—something he called "deconstruction" and which involved the dismantling of the metaphysical-ontological premises or underpinnings of inherited frameworks and traditions of thought. Proceeding in this manner, Derrida's life work amounted to a restless journey or peregrination, a relentless exodus from all forms of positivism, conformism, and habitual practices—including the prevailing practices of democracy.

In large measure, the fascination exerted by Derrida is rooted precisely in this transgressive spirit, this radically deconstructive élan. To be sure, over the decades, this élan was manifest in different guises and varying contexts. During his early years, a central preoccupation of his work was with language, grammar, and linguistic signification; a main effort at this point was to disrupt traditional humanistic conceptions of meaning and understanding, conceptions construing language as a pliant vehicle for the expression of human thought. During subsequent decades, attention began to shift toward broader philosophical and political topics, including the themes of friendship, Marxism, and Eurocentrism; again, the chief endeavor was to challenge or unsettle traditional premises undergirding these themes. It was during this phase of deconstruction that the notion of a "democracy to come" first surfaced in his writings. During ensuing years, Derrida's outlook came increasingly under the influence of Emmanuel Levinas, especially the latter's opposition between "totality and infinity"—a bifurcation pitting an immanent actuality against a radically "transcendent" possibility (or what Derrida came to call an "impossible possibility"). A major manifestation of this later shift was the concern with questions of religion and with a resolutely trans-national cosmopolitanism.

For purposes of illustration, I select the following three texts corresponding to the mentioned phases. From among the writings of the early phase, I select Derrida's critique of humanism, published under the title "The Ends of Man." Regarding the middle period, I turn to his attack on Eurocentrism launched in *The Other Heading: Reflections on Today's Europe*. Concerning the final period, I discuss his book *Rogues: Two Essays on Reason*, which contains his most extended reflections on trans-national (or post-sovereign) politics and the (im)possibility of a "democracy to come." I conclude with brief comments on the (im)possibility of democratic *praxis*.

The Ends of Man

In the context of French (and more broadly European) intellectual life, the year 1968 constituted a kind of watershed: namely, a turning away from a certain subject-centered phenomenology and existentialism in the direction of a radical decentering or dispersal of the "subject." In many ways, this change was intimately linked with the status of "humanism" in Western thought. Derrida's essay "The Ends of Man" was first presented in fall 1968 as a lecture at a colloquium dealing with "Philosophy and Anthropology" (the latter term being largely a stand-in for humanism). The lecture refers explicitly to the turbulent events of that year: the opening of the Vietnam peace talks, the assassination of Martin Luther King Jr., and (later that year) the French student rebellion and the invasion of the universities by "the forces of order." For Derrida, these events carried both a political and a philosophical significance because of their impact on cherished French (and European) thought patterns of the past.

After World War II, he notes, "under the name of Christian or atheist existentialism, and in conjunction with a fundamentally Christian personalism, the thought that dominated France presented itself essentially as humanist." The focus of existentialist and personalist thought was on "human reality," which was a translation of Heidegger's *Dasein* but actually closer to the traditional concept of "human nature." Among authors exemplifying the outlook, Derrida mentions such idealists as Brunschwicg and (more importantly) the leading existentialist Jean-Paul Sartre. In the writings of these authors, he maintains, the meaning and "unity of man" was never really examined but simply presupposed. To this extent, "not only is existentialism a humanism [as Sartre had insisted], but the ground and horizon of what Sartre called his 'phenomenological ontology' remains the unity of human-reality." In describing the structure of this human-reality, Sartrean existentialism was a "philosophical anthropology" or simply an anthropologism.[2]

In Derrida's presentation, the humanist-anthropological outlook was projected by existentialist writers even on thinkers who were relatively free of the existentialist bias: thinkers like Hegel, Husserl, and Heidegger. In the case of Hegel, a certain privileging of the *Phenomenology of Spirit* encouraged an "anthropologistic" reading of the philosopher's work that sidelined such non-humanist texts as his *Logic* and *Encyclopedia*. In the case of Husserl, the existentialist vogue fastened on the centrality of pure consciousness and subjectivity—neglecting the fact that the critique of anthropologism was "one of the inaugural motifs" of Husserl's phenomenology. As Derrida states emphatically: "The transcendental structures described after the phenomenological reduction are not those of the intrawordly being called 'man'; nor are they essentially linked to man's society, culture, language, or even to his 'soul.' " A similar misreading (or lopsided reading) characterized the reception of Heidegger's work in France, where the tendency has been to interpret "the analytic of *Dasein* in strictly anthropological terms." At this point, "The Ends of Man" waxes somewhat rhetorical, complaining about a kind of intellectual culture lag that has allowed the existentialist mentality to persist in the radically changed situation after 1968. "After the tide of humanism and anthropologism that had covered French philosophy," Derrida writes, "one might have thought that the antihumanist and anti-anthropological ebb that followed, and in which we are now, would rediscover the heritage of the systems of thought that had been disfigured." Unfortunately, "nothing of the sort" has happened. On the contrary, despite the dominant aversion to existentialism, the prevailing tendency still seems to be "to amalgamate Hegel, Husserl, and—in a more diffuse and ambiguous fashion—Heidegger with the old metaphysical humanism."[3]

The remainder of the essay means to offer a corrective to these prevalent readings or misreadings. Given the strong condemnation of humanist or anthropological misconstruals, one would have expected a novel exegesis that completely exonerates the discussed philosophers of any humanist leanings. Surprisingly and curiously, this is not—or only partly—the case. Although transgressing existentialist appropriations, the essay still detects in the works of the three thinkers traces of a metaphysical humanism—traces that block the needed radical exodus from the humanist tradition. Turning first to the author of the *Phenomenology*, Derrida finds it necessary to recognize that according to Hegel "the relations between anthropology and phenomenology are not simply external" because "the Hegelian concepts of truth, negativity, and *Aufhebung*, with all their results, prevent this from being so." Basically, the Hegelian system culminated in the notion of "spirit" that in turn was a stand-in for subjectivity and purified consciousness; in this manner, it proclaimed—and could not but proclaim—a higher-level anthropologism: "Consciousness is the *truth* of the soul, that is, precisely the truth of that which was the object of anthropology." To be sure, subjectivity in Hegel was not just an isolated ego, but rather a subject writ-large, a synonym for a perfected humanity—and to this extent testified to the unity "of God and man, of onto-theo-teleology and humanism." Although critical of Hegel's system, Husserl still followed Hegel's perfectionist teleology by presenting "humanity" as the telos of philosophy. Despite his antisystemic bent, Derrida observes, "humanity" in Husserl's work still serves as "the name of the being to which the transcendental telos . . . is announced." As in the case of Hegel (but with a different accent), transcendental phenomenology for Husserl remains committed to "the ultimate achievement of the teleology of reason that traverses history." Hence, although distancing itself strictly from any empirical or sociological anthropologism, phenomenology in Husserl's sense is "only the affirmation of a transcendental humanism."[4]

Things are more complicated in the case of Heidegger because of his radical turning away from the philosophy of subjectivity (inherited from Descartes, Kant, and Husserl). As Derrida acknowledges: "The existential analytic [that is, the analysis of *Dasein* as offered in *Being and Time*] has already overflowed the horizon of a philosophical anthropology: *Dasein* is not simply the 'man' of metaphysics." On the other hand, several of Heidegger's writings—including his *Letter on Humanism*—testify to the attraction of the "proper [*eigen*] of man," an attraction that will not cease to direct "all the itineraries of his thought." Basically, what Derrida is trying to do is to bring to light a certain ambivalence in Heidegger's work—his oscillation between humanism and antihumanism—by drawing attention to the "hold" that "the 'humanity' of man and the thinking of Being" maintain on one another. This hold or attraction is manifest already in *Being and Time* where human *Dasein* is singled out as the privileged being able to interrogate, or raise the question of, Being. In Derrida's words: "It is the proximity to itself of the questioning being which leads it to be chosen as the privileged interrogated being. The proximity to itself of the inquirer authorizes the identity of the inquirer and the inter-rogated. We who are close to ourselves, we interrogate ourselves about the meaning of Being." This emphasis on the proximity of *Dasein* and Being is a prominent feature that has inspired many "anthropologistic" interpretations of Heidegger in the past—from which Derrida demurs only partially or half-heartedly. "We can see then," he states, "that *Dasein*, though not man, is nevertheless *nothing other* than man. It is, as we shall see, a repetition of the essence of man permitting a return to what once were the metaphysical concepts of *humanitas*."[5]

As Derrida acknowledges, Heidegger's work does not merely assert the proximity of *Dasein* and Being but also their mutual distance, their unfathomable remoteness. "The *Da* of *Dasein*," he writes, "and the *Da* of *Sein* will signify as much the near as the far." Ontologically speaking, the so-called "Being of beings" signals a distance that is "as great as possible." Notwithstanding this admission, the essay returns quickly to the charge of humanism, claiming that Heidegger's entire thought is guided "by the motif of Being as presence" and "by the motif of the proximity of Being to the essence of man." Derrida at this point turns to the *Letter on Humanism* in an effort to corroborate this charge. The *Letter* famously describes thinking as the "thinking of Being" (in the dual sense of a subjective and objective genitive). Seizing on this formulation—but bracketing its internal complex-ity—Derrida briskly integrates the passage into his overall humanist interpretation, stating that "the thinking of Being, the thinking of the truth of Being" remains after all just the "thinking *of* man." What is happening generally in the *Letter on Humanism* is not so much a dis-missal or transgression but rather a "re-evaluation or revalorization of the essence and dignity of man." Another formulation that can be construed along similar lines is the passage presenting *Dasein* as a creature of "care" (*Sorge*), as the caretaker of the Being of beings. For Derrida again, the passage is revealing because: does the stress on care not imply also "a concern or care about man? Where else does 'care' tend but in the direction of bringing man back to his essence?" Still another formula invoked for the same purpose is the notion of "authenticity" (*Eigentlichkeit*), with its corollary notion of the "proper" (*eigen*), familiar already from *Being and Time*. As Derrida interprets the formula, giving it an anthropological twist: if Being is "near" to man and man is "near" to Being, then one can also say that "the near is the proper" and that "man is the proper of Being." What all this adds up to is a refurbished version of humanism, a humanism in which human beings are seen as close to themselves and their being: "The proper of man, his *Eigenheit*, his 'authenticity,' is to be related to the meaning of Being; man is to hear and interrogate it in ek-sistence, to stand straight in the proximity of its light."[6]

In opposition to half-hearted revivals or modifications of traditional metaphysics, Derrida's essay proposes or intimates a more thorough-going rupture with the past—a rupture more faithful to, and in keeping with, the anti-existentialist mood after 1968. Are we not witnessing, he asks, a deeper seismographic tremor dislodging the past: "Is not this security of the near what is trembling today, that is, the co-belonging and co-propriety of man and the name of Being, such as this co-propriety inhabits, and is inhabited by, the [metaphysical] language of the West?" For Derrida, this trembling is not generated by an internal teleology inhabiting Western thought, but "can only come from a certain outside," which puts an "end" to the internal telos. In his account, this trembling has already given rise to several profound changes or outcomes. One is the decline of existentialism and phenomenology and their replacement by theoretical frameworks focusing on "system" and "structure"—frameworks that seek to determine the possibility of significance "on the basis of a 'formal' organization which in itself has no meaning." This shift of focus has a more radically "deconstructive" effect than Heidegger's own so-called "destruction" of metaphysics that still operated in the mode of a hermeneutical questioning of the meaning and truth of Being. Leaving hermeneutical questioning behind, the structural reduction of meaning operates by means of "a kind of break with a thinking of Being which has all the characteristics of a *relève* (*Aufhebung*) of humanism" (in the sense of preservation). Another, still more important outcome of the trembling is a geopolitical dislocation, that is, its impact on the "violent relationship of the whole of the West to its other" or the non-West—with Derrida leaving no doubt that, for him, cultural or linguistic violence is "in structural solidarity" with military and economic violence.[7]

Taking together these and related repercussions of the perceived trembling, Derrida sketches two main strategies or responses that intellectuals might adopt—among which he clearly prefers the second. The first strategy is to attempt an exit from, or a "deconstruction" of, the past "without changing terrain," by simply repeating "what is implicit in the founding concepts and the original problematic." Although seemingly promising, the strategy comes at a price: for "one risks ceaselessly confirming or consolidating" that which one "allegedly deconstructs." The second strategy requires "to change terrain, in a discontinuous and irruptive fashion, by brutally placing oneself outside, and by affirming an absolute break and difference." As Derrida maintains, the first response or mode of deconstruction is "mostly that of the Heideggerian questions," whereas the second strategy is "mostly the one which dominates France today"—at least partly because of Derrida's interventions. Although admitting that the choice between the two strategies "cannot be simple or unique," the ending of the essay is by no means ambivalent or equivocal. Derrida at this point invokes the legacy of Nietzsche, a thinker portrayed as the icon of super-deconstruction, as the one rupturing all forms of proximity and traditional humanism. The essay here likens the difference between the two strategies to Nietzsche's distinction between the "higher man" and the "overman" (*Übermensch*), where the former is "abandoned to his distress," whereas the latter "awakens and leaves, without turning back to what he leaves behind." In a frequently quoted passage the essay concludes:

> He [the overman] burns his text and erases the traces of his steps. His laughter will then burst out, directed toward a return which no longer will have the form of a metaphysical repetition of humanism, nor doubtless . . . the form of a memorial or a guarding of the meaning of Being, the form of the house and of the truth of Being. He will dance, outside the house, the *aktive Vergesslichkeit*, . . . the active forgetting of Being.[8]

Beyond Eurocentrism

The exit from humanism was one of the early exercises in radical deconstruction; it also was the necessary precondition for all ensuing forms of rupture, exodus, and transgression. In subsequent years, Derrida became preoccupied with many philosophical as well as political issues—but without ever veering too far from the preferred strategy outlined in "The Ends of Man." Among the important and somewhat startling themes dealt with by Derrida at the time were the topics of friendship and Marxism. As is well known, the topic of friendship—and especially of a "politics of friendship"—has a long and venerable pedigree in Western thought, dating back to Aristotle and Cicero. For readers unfamiliar with the "Nietzschean" strategy (discussed previously), Derrida's decision to deal with the theme might thus have suggested a return of the author to this tradition and his willingness to settle for a continuation or "*relève*" of the past "without changing terrain." This assumption, however, proved to be misguided. The friendship extolled in Derrida's book-length treatment was an entirely aporetic relation—in fact, a relation of "nonrelation," an "anchoritic" relation or a community of "anchorites" far removed from each other, and hence without proximity (or shared practices). A similar surprise was awaiting readers of *Specters of Marx*. Again, readers unacquainted with the rupturing strategy might have suspected—and many did in fact suspect—a slight of hand: that is, the sly or covert return of the author to the kind of "humanist" Marxism that had been in vogue in France before 1968. This, needless to say, was not the case. Derrida's book did not so much deal with Marx or Marxism, as rather with shadowy and fugitive "specters" of Marx far from any actually lived community or "communism." In fact, the central hero of the book was not so much Marx as rather one of his genuinely solitary and "anchoritic" contemporaries: Max Stirner, author of *Der Einzige und sein Eigentum* (*The Ego and His Own*).[9]

Probably the most politically transgressive and "unsettling" text of the period was *The Other Heading*, subtitled *Reflections on Today's Europe*. Derrida in this text refers explicitly to earlier thinkers and literary figures who had reflected on the meaning and future of "Europe" with the aim of preserving the continuity of this meaning or spiritual "mission" of the Continent. Prominent among these "Europeanists" (or Europe-centered) intellectuals were Edmund Husserl and Paul Valéry. In his famous lecture on "The Crisis of European Humanity" (of 1935), Husserl had bemoaned the loss or decline of the inner trajectory or rationale that had animated Europe from the beginning. To counteract this decline or crisis the lecture pleaded for a restoration of this animating spirit and a recovery of that spiritual-transcendental trajectory "for which Europe would be at once the name and the exemplary figure." At about the same time (before World War II), Paul

Valéry portrayed the ongoing crisis afflicting Europe as a "crisis of spirit," a crisis of the spiritual meaning and telos of European culture. For Valéry, the ongoing crisis affected the very essence of European identity, the essence of Europe's cultural "capital"—a capital that, although geographically delimited, carries a universal or universalizing significance. In Derrida's words, European culture for Valéry "is in danger when this *ideal* universality, the very ideality of the universal as the production of capital, finds itself threatened." What surfaces here is a traditional European self-identification as not just a limited place but as the guardian or avant-garde of a rational–spiritual mission guiding all of humanity to its intrinsic telos: "What threatens European identity would not essentially threaten Europe but, in spirit, the universality for which Europe is responsible, of which it is the reserve, *le capital* or *la capitale.*"[10]

This fusion of local identity and universality is at the heart of Derrida's critical reflections in his text, reflections that revolve around what he calls the "capital paradox of universality." The paradox resides in a certain mixture of particularity and universality, more specifically in the self-elevation of a particular culture or society to the status of universal "exemplarity" linked with extraordinary rights and privileges. What is involved in this self-elevation is the claim to exemplary leadership, to the ability to offer "unique testimony to the human essence and to what is proper to man." In his reflections on the crisis of Europe, Valéry had described Europe as the cape, the headland or spiritual promontory of civilization. It is precisely at this point that Derrida's text signals a break, as expressed in its title *The Other Heading* (in French *L'autre cap*). As he mentions, the word "cap" or "cape" refers to the head, the promontory, the aim or telos, but also the ending or eschatology. In this sense, the title "The Other Heading" might simply suggest, "that another direction is in the offing, or that it is necessary to change destinations." This, as it turns out, does not quite capture Derrida's intent, because it falls short of the strategic requirement of "changing terrain." Instead of simply calling for a change of goal or destination, or else for the replacement of one promontory by another (say Europe by America), the title intimates a completely different meaning of "heading," something that might be rendered as "another heading" or even as "the other of the heading" (or something other than a heading). As the text states in a central passage: What the title brings to the fore is

> that there is another heading, the heading being not ours [*le nôtre*], but the other's [*l'autre*]—not only something which

we identify, calculate, and decide upon, but the *heading
of the other* before which we must respond and which we
must remember, . . . the heading of the other being perhaps
the first condition of an identity or identification that is not
an egocentrism destructive of oneself and the other. But
beyond *our heading*, it is necessary to attend not only to
the *other heading*, and especially to the *heading of the other*,
but also perhaps to the *other of the heading*, that is to say, to
a relation of identity with the other that no longer obeys
the form, the sign, or the logic of the heading, nor even
of the *anti-heading*.[11]

In countering Valéry's notion of the spiritual mission of Europe,
Derrida does not hesitate to call attention to another side of this
culture—which perhaps is an outcome of its "capital" self-elevation.
As he writes, in a statement that might be extended from Europe
to the West as a whole: is it not the same cultural context where,
"precisely in the name of self-identity," the "worst violences"—the
crimes of xenopholia, racism, anti-Semitism, religious or nationalist
fanaticism—have been and are being "unleashed, mixed up, mixed
up with each other" and even "mixed in with the breath, the respira-
tion, the very 'spirit' of the promise"? In light of these derailments
of self-identity, spiritual or otherwise, Derrida's text calls for a complete rethinking of identity, where the "heading" or direction signals
would be radically changed. Contrary to customary definitions, in a
dramatic "change of terrain," the text advances this lapidary axiom
or guidepost: "*What is proper to a culture is to not be identical to itself.
Not to not have an identity, but not to be able to identify itself; . . .* to
be able to take the form of a subject only in the non-identity to itself
or, if you prefer, only in the difference with itself." Pondering further
the notion of self-difference, the text indicates that it means not only
a difference from or with others, but also a difference from or with
oneself (*différence à soi, avec soi*), that is, a difference "at once internal"
and irreducible to being "at home with oneself." Underscoring this
point, another lapidary statement adds, "there is no self-relation, no
relation to oneself, no identification with oneself, without culture, but
a culture of oneself *as* a culture *of* the other, a culture of the double
genitive and of the difference to oneself."[12]

With regard to the meaning and character of Europe and its
presumed mission, *The Other Heading* proposes a deflation of identity
that involves not so much an erasure as a radical transformation.
"And what if Europe were this," the text asks: "the opening onto

a history for which the changing of the heading, the relation to the other heading or to the other of the heading, is experienced as always possible? An opening and a nonexclusion for which Europe would in some way be responsible?" By comparison with this openness and nonexclusion of otherness, Valéry's discussion of the "capital" exemplarity of the European "idea" appears now dated and nostalgic, in fact as a part of the "traditional discourse of modernity"—which, to be sure, cannot be entirely discarded or elided by Europeans. Derrida speaks in this context of a "double-bind," which consists in the need not to abandon what is best in the past and the simultaneous (and more urgent) need to exit from the past by "changing terrain." As he remarks in a remarkable formulation of the "double-bind" (which in some ways resembles the strategic tension in "The Ends of Man"): "It is necessary to make ourselves the guardians of an idea of Europe, of a difference of Europe, *but* of a Europe that consists precisely in not closing itself off in its own identity and in advancing itself in an exemplary way toward what it is not"—namely, "toward the other heading or the heading of the other, indeed . . . toward the other *of* the heading which would be the beyond of the modern tradition, another border structure, another shore."[13]

With this emphasis on the needed "change of terrain," the accent is shifted from the past to the future, from the actual to the possible—which, from the vantage of actuality, always appears "impossible." Derrida's text insists, in both ethical and political domains, on the need for a radical adventure, that is, the "experience and experiment of the possibility of the impossible." With regard to cultural identity this means that, if Europe wishes to live up to itself and its own "immeasurable difference 'with itself,'" it must come to terms with a certain nonactuality, namely, the "experience and experiment of the impossible." At this point, the term *adventure* changes terrain and turns into a more potent formula: the prospect of an advent, an arrival, an unexpected event "to come" (*à venir*). As Derrida writes, a Europe no longer enclosed in self-identity must be attentive not only to what is concretely present outside Europe, but also to "a gateway to the future, to the to-come [*à venir*] of the *event*," to "that which *comes* [*vient*], which comes perhaps and perhaps comes from a completely other shore." It is at this juncture that the notion of "democracy"—not previously thematized—enters the discussion, and again not in the sense of an actual political condition but of an "impossible" possibility, of an event or advent that may or may not arrive. In opposition to traditional classificatory systems and to facile self-descriptions of many regimes (especially in the West), the text places the term on an entirely different terrain, by stating that democracy "must have the structure of a promise—and thus the memory of that which carries the future, the to-come, here and now."[14]

Democracy to Come

During the later years of Derrida's life, his fascination with transgression and exodus was steadily intensified and deepened. In this respect, the work of Emmanuel Levinas exerted a powerful, and perhaps dominant influence—above all, Levinas' opposition between a radically transgressive "infinity" and a totalizing-mundane immanence, between an incalculable (im)possibility and a calculable and manageable actuality. In large measure, this influence prompted Derrida to explore with increasing intensity the domain of religious faith (especially in the Abrahamic tradition) and also the vast emerging domain of global or cosmopolitan obligations transgressing the traditional confines of state sovereignty. In the former domain, the most important publications are Derrida's *Acts of Religion* and also his conversations with Gianni Vattimo in the volume *Religion*, texts adumbrating a completely nondogmatic religiosity and a kind of (im)possible messianism (or a messianic hope without messianism). In the second domain, Derrida has made significant contributions to a reduction of global violence by advocating (together with Levinas) the establishment of "cities of refuge" and the transformation of traditional "hospitability" into a global institution ensuring intercultural tolerance and recognition. As he writes in *On Cosmopolitanism*, perhaps it is possible to retrieve the medieval notion of the "free city" (*ville franche*) in the contemporary context in such a manner that some cities would serve as places of refuge from the violence of nation-states.[15] For present purposes, I concentrate on one of Derrida's last writings titled *Rogues: Two Essays on Reason*, which is a translation of two lectures presented by the philosopher in 2002 under the summary title "*Voyous*."

In his preface to *Rogues*, titled "*Veni*" ("Come"), Derrida points immediately to the problematic character of a "democracy to come"—at all times, but especially in our age of "so-called globalization or *mondialisation*." As he notes, dramatic global events and developments, like September 11 and the upsurge of "terrorism," have called into question the status of traditional nation-states together with their presumed absolute territorial sovereignty. At the same time, these developments have given rise to a rigid bifurcation between legitimate or lawful states—whose lawfulness is disrupted only by sovereign fiat (in a "state of exception")—and so-called "rogue states" (*états voyous*) bent on violating both national and international laws (thus claiming a permanent "state of exception"). Taking up this bifurcation, the preface considers it crucial to distinguish between "sovereignty," viewed as absolute mastery, and "unconditionality" seen as an exit from mastery and human control. As opposed to sovereign power (or counter-power), unconditionality signals a "weak" or "vulnerable force," a force "without power"; predicated on an "unconditional renunciation of sovereignty," it paves the way or opens up "unconditionally to what or who *comes* and comes to affect it." Derrida at this point invokes the notion of *"khora"* from Plato's *Timaeus*, where the term means (or can be interpreted to mean) a place before any place, a spacing "before the world or cosmos or globe." Taken in this sense, he observes, *khora* "would make or give place"; it would give rise "to what is called the coming of the event." In particular, from this angle, "a call might be taken up and take hold: the call for a thinking of the event *to come*, of the democracy *to come*, of the reason *to come*."[16]

In his subsequent reflections—gathered together under the label "The Reason of the Strongest"—Derrida elaborates in detail on the difference between sovereignty and the unconditional (im)possibility of the event "to come." In these reflections, the roots of sovereignty are traced to ancient mythological stories as well as philosophical–metaphysical speculations. As Derrida writes, the "theogonic mythology of sovereignty"—exemplified in Hesiod's theogony—belongs to "a long cycle of political theology that is at once paternalistic and patriarchal and thus masculine" and that might also be called "ipsocentric" (i.e., centered in the self or self-same). In terms of Greek metaphysics, comparable impulses can be found in Aristotle's notions of *energeia* and a "prime mover" conceived as "pure actuality." From these early beginnings a line can be drawn to the writings of Jean Bodin and Hobbes and to the "modern political theology" undergirding monarchic absolutism. The line can be extended further to a certain kind of democracy, namely, the "unavowed political theology" of the "sovereignty of the people" or democratic sovereignty. Derrida in this context refers to *Democracy in America* where de Tocqueville asserted that in America "the principle of the sovereignty of the people has been adopted in practice in every way that imagination could suggest" and further claimed, "the people reign over the American political world as God rules over the universe." To this equation of the people with divine power or super-power *Rogues* opposes an entirely different view of democracy far removed from the lure of sovereign mastery. As we read: "The ipseity of the [sovereign] One, the *autos* of autonomy, symmetry, homogeneity . . . and even, finally, God" remains entirely "incompatible with, and even clashes with, another truth of the democratic, namely, the truth of the other, heterogeneity, the heteronomic and dissymmetric, disseminal multiplicity, . . . the indeterminate 'each one.' "[17]

The question which arises here inevitably is whether democracy—even a democracy to come—can exist without some kind of sovereignty, given that democracy has traditionally been closely linked with sovereign freedom of action. In Derrida's words: "There is [seemingly] no freedom without ipseity and, vice versa, no ipseity without freedom—and thus without a certain sovereignty." The issue here becomes whether freedom can be disengaged from sovereignty and self-sameness (ipseity) so that it can turn into a free play or movement, into a "freewheeling" kind of indeterminacy. What emerges into view here, *Rogues* states, is "the concept of a democracy without concept, a democracy devoid of sameness and ipseity, a democracy whose concept remains free, like a disengaged clutch, in the free play of its indetermination." Viewed from this anti-essentialist angle, democracy does not denote a substantive regime or form of government; rather, its meaning resides precisely in "this lack of the proper and the self-same." Invoking his well-known notion of *"différance"*—a term involving both deferral and referral—Derrida presents democracy as an exemplification of that notion. In terms of deferral, democracy reveals an "interminable adjournment" of its present actuality. At the same time, referral is manifest in democracy's openness to the "experience of the alterity of the other, of heterogeneity, of the singular, the not-same, the dissymmetric, the heteronomous." Here is a remarkable passage that succinctly articulates democracy's escape from customary definitions or clichés:

> Democracy is what it is only in the *différance* by which it defers itself and differs from itself. It is what it is only by spacing itself beyond being and even beyond ontological difference; it is (without being) equal and proper to itself only insofar as it is inadequate and improper, at the same time behind and ahead of itself; behind and ahead of the Sameness and Oneness of itself.[18]

As Derrida realizes, his differential notion of democracy is at odds with traditional "democratic theory" where democracy is linked with freedom conceived as "power, faculty, or the ability to act, . . . in short, to do as one pleases." In an effort to find alternative approaches, *Rogues* turns first to some writings of Jean-Luc Nancy, and especially to *The Experience of Freedom,*which locates that experience somehow outside the "autonomy of a subjectivity in charge of itself." Although appreciating the decentering gesture in Nancy's work, Derrida is troubled by a certain emphasis on "sharing" or partitioning of freedom—an emphasis that appears too close to the kind of proximity, togetherness, or "fraternocracy" that had been the target of his long-standing critique. Returning from a brief review of relevant literature, Derrida draws attention to his own writings on the topic of democracy starting around 1990, particularly to *The Other Heading* and *Sauf le Nom* (translated as *On the Name*). As indicated before, *The Other Heading* had presented "democracy to come" as an unconditional demand, as a radical promise that is "kept in memory, handed down, inherited, claimed and taken up." The sense of unconditionality was intensified in *On the Name* where the term "without" (in "without condition") referred obliquely to "the apophatic discourse of so-called negative theology" and indeed to "a *khora* or spacing before any determination" and even "before a negative theology." Transferred to the political domain, the accent on "without" entails that democracy to come operates "like the *khora* of the political." As Derrida insists, neither *khora* nor the phrase "to come" should be taken in the sense of a Kantian "regulative idea," but rather in that of an unconditional promise. In the words of *On the Name*: "The difficulty of the 'without' [*sans*] spreads into what is still called politics, morals, or law, which are just as threatened as promised by apophasis."[19]

Based on these distinctions and nuanced elaborations, Derrida finally ventures to spell out more clearly the contours of a "democracy to come," and he does so with the help of five "focal points." The first point is that the expression translates into a call for a "militant and interminable political critique," one that protests against "all naïveté and every political abuse." Above all, such critique assails any rhetoric that presents as "democratic" an actual or existing regime that, in fact, remains "inadequate to the democratic demand." Sharpening the critical edge, Derrida upholds democracy as "the only system, the only constitutional paradigm" in which, in principle, one has the right "to criticize everything publicly, including the idea of democracy, its concept, its history, and its name." Second, the phrase implies the coming of an "event" which—though evoking a notion of democracy—remains in itself "unforeseeable . . . unmasterable by any ipseity or any conventional and consensual performativity." The third point is that the expression inevitably reaches beyond the confines of nation-state sovereignty and hence intimates the creation or emergence of an "international juridico-political space," a space exemplified in the notion of global human rights. Fourth, the idea of a democracy to come aligns itself not only with the axiomatic of a "messianicity without messianism" but also with a rigorous distinction between (actual) law and (infinite) justice where the latter coincides "with disjuncture, . . . with the interruption of relation, with unbinding, with the infinite secret of the other." Finally, democracy to come—contra de Tocqueville—does not refer to an evolutionary process, a teleology unfolding in time. Rather, the phrase wavers between different registers: a descriptive or connotative register (something is coming); a preformative register (I believe, I promise its coming); and an elusive non- or transperformative register (involving the "patient *perhaps* of messianicity").[20]

A Democratic Praxis?

Having followed Derrida's transgressions and peregrinations through the years, the reader—certainly this reader—is likely to waver also between different registers of response. The primary response is prone to be one of performative affirmation, a response saluting and welcoming Derrida's spirited exodus from oppressive realities or actualities. Certainly in a time marked by totalizing ideologies and the steady entrenchment and widespread glorification of the "powers that be," his plea for a "militant and interminable political critique" corresponds to an urgent contemporary need. Likewise, his critical observations on "sovereignty"—especially nation-state sovereignty—resonate with deep-seated aspirations in our age of globalization or *"mondialisation."* In the same direction point his remarks on a new kind of cosmopolitanism, on an "international juridico-political space" making room for global human rights and the cultivation of cross-cultural "hospitality." As it seems to me, some of the most appealingly transgressive passages in *Rogues* have to do with the notion of an "unconditionality without sovereignty" and its corollaries of unconditional hospitality, gift-giving, and forgiveness. As Derrida writes in the concluding section: "Only an unconditional hospitality can give meaning and practical rationality to a concept of hospitality. . . . The incalculable unconditionality of hospitality, of the gift or of forgiveness, exceeds the calculation of conditions, just as justice exceeds law, the juridical, and the political."[21]

Difficulties arise when the text turns to the non- or transperformative register of the "to come"—and often settles on the language of antinomies (the binary oppositions between inside–outside, calculable–incalculable, actual–im-possible). Derrida's *Rogues* frequently seems to speak not only about, but also from the side or in the name of the "to come," and to do so with insistence. But how can this happen? The prophets of ancient Israel were sometimes called "criers in the wilderness or desert"—but the voice in *Rogues* seems to come from a desert beyond any desert, from a *khora* before and beyond any space or place. While appreciating the spirited élan, one seems entitled to ask: What language is adequate to this no-place, and how can one speak at all in (what Derrida calls) a "language to come"? Moreover, in this nonlanguage, how can one thematize at all the "who" or "what" of the "to come"—how, for instance, suggest reliably that it is democracy that is coming and not some tyranny or new barbarism? Noting the difficulty, Derrida seeks to guard against incoherence by appealing to the linkage of "to come" with a certain tradition of faith or (what he calls) "the inheritance of a promise."[22] Inheritance at this juncture seems to point to a certain historical sedimentation of expectancy, a sedimentation that might be able to sift the salutary "possible" from the monstrously "impossible." Yet, how legitimate is this appeal to a faith tradition—given that history has in large measure been deconstructed in an effort to ward off any notion of teleology or any derivation of the promise from the past?

Difficulties inhabit not only the transperformative, but also the performative register of Derrida's text. *Rogues* speaks repeatedly of the "urgency" of the "to come"—an urgency to which we are called to respond, and to do so urgently. The preface to the text, titled *"Veni"* (Come), clearly involves an appeal or performative solicitation. The same preface describes this appeal as "an act of messianic faith" (to be sure, "irreligious and without messianism"), and also links solicitation with greeting or salutation of the "to come." Elsewhere the text speaks of a "fidelity to come, to the to-come, to the future," or else of "the *hic et nunc* of urgency" excited by the to-come. But what kind of performance or performativity is involved in this appeal or solicitation? It is at this point, it seems to me, that Derrida's anti- or counter-humanism—delineated in "The Ends of Man"—exacts its toll. In order to preserve the pure unconditionality of the irruption, Derrida needs to detach—in quasi-Manichean fashion—the "to-come" from any human contamination, any human action or practice (beyond verbal invocation).[23] But is this sufficiently attentive? Precisely given the august status of the "to-come"—its near-messianic quality—would one not expect human beings to prepare busily for this event and thus show themselves worthy to receive it—just like any good host would before the arrival of an important guest? In my view, the prophet Isaiah had a better sense of what is needed when, in pointing to the coming kingdom, he said (Isaiah 40:3–4): "A voice cries: In the wilderness prepare the way of the Lord, make straight in the desert a highway for our God. Every valley shall be lifted up, and every mountain and hill made low."

What comes into view here is the possibility (and not just impossibility) of a post-humanist *praxis*, a *praxis* no longer tied to anthropocentrism. Without claiming self-mastery, and especially without pretending to master the coming event, human beings are still called upon to ready themselves through transformative *praxis*. Traditionally, transformative *praxis* is a synonym for the cultivation of virtues, a cultivation that—like piano playing—requires steady application and diligence. Since ancient times, ethical teachings have emphasized the practice of the so-called "cardinal virtues," a practice that over time can lead to a sort of self-overcoming, to a freedom from spurious attachments and forms of bondage, and perhaps even to a display of that unconditional hospitality and forgiveness extolled in Derrida's *Rogues*. During the Middle Ages, theologians added to traditional teachings a set of so-called "theological virtues" designed to prepare practitioners more fully for the "coming event"—while simultaneously upholding the complementarity of all virtues (in accordance with the formula of "grace completing nature").

By stipulating the radical antinomy between unconditionality and conditional human conduct, Derrida's work tends to stress—onesidedly—radical human incapacity over human "capability" to act. A post-humanist *praxis*—including democratic *praxis*—requires a correction of this imbalance. Viewed from this angle, democratic *praxis* and "democracy to come" complement each other, rather than being separated by an abyss. Just as steady practice in music precedes the great virtuoso, steady democratic *praxis* makes room and prepares the ground for the democratic event beyond mastery and control. This requires a rethinking of the notion of "action"—perhaps along the lines that Heidegger suggested in the opening lines of his *Letter on Humanism* where he noted that the essence of action is "fulfillment" (*vollbringen*), that is, to allow or enable something to unfold on its own.[24]

8

Who Are We Now?

For an "Other" Humanism

One of the most impressive features of our age is the rapid expansion of knowledge, sometimes resembling a knowledge explosion. According to reliable estimates, the volume of available knowledge about nature and the universe today doubles every ten years—compared with the slow centennial pace of earlier times. Moreover, the expansion involves not only the outer universe, but penetrates deeply into the genetic and molecular structures of all living beings, including human biology. Curiously, however, this saturation and even oversaturation with knowledge is accompanied by a sense of depletion or strandedness: the arsenal of data generated in our "information age" does not inform us about its meaning; scientific advances—however staggering—do not by themselves advance understanding or (what is often called) human "self-knowledge." Hence, the widespread experience of both cognitive growth and disorientation. In recent times, several prominent intellectuals have published books with titles like "Who Are We?" or "Who Are We Now?"—titles disclosing anguish about the status and meaning of being "human" or our "humanity" in the present world.[1] Needless to say, this anguish is heightened and fueled by our precarious global situation: the danger posed by steadily proliferating weapons of mass destruction to the very survival of human life on earth.

The new situation clearly calls for renewed reflection on the question signaled by the cited books: the question who we are as human beings or what it means to be human. In large measure, such reflection has been carried forward in the past under the rubric of "humanism." In the long Western tradition of humanism—a tradition stretching back to the Roman period—human beings have tended to be assigned a central place in the universe, a centrality not basically unsettled by the Copernican revolution and subsequent intellectual upheavals. Given their dominant or pivotal status, human beings were considered capable of inventing or designing, and even constructively constituting the (meaning of the) world. The conception persisted throughout the horrible debacles of the twentieth century and even experienced a certain renewal in the face of these debacles. However, confronted with the devastations of that century, a suspicion began to grow that maybe the trust placed in human competence was misplaced, that the overly self-confident humanism of the past was perhaps illusory or deceptive. As a result, efforts were afoot to re-imagine or reconceive the status of humanity in the world—efforts that pointed in a variety of directions: from a softening of traditional humanism to the formulation of radically trans-human and even anti-humanist perspectives.

In the present context, only a few major strands of this intellectual scenario can be lifted up for discussion. In a first step and in limiting myself to European philosophy, I review the resurgence of humanism in the mid-twentieth century, using as my chief exemplars the work of Ernst Cassirer and Jean-Paul Sartre. Next, I turn to the upsurge of counter-currents to humanism, focusing attention on some prominent post-structuralist and deconstructive formulations and also on Emmanuel Levinas' proposal of a "humanism of the other." By way of conclusion, I shall ponder the possibility of a chastised or non-anthropocentric perspective where the "emptying-out" of traditional self-confidence prepares the ground for the transformative trajectory of an "other" humanism. My chief guides at this point are Theodor Adorno, Martin Heidegger, and Raimon Panikkar.

Humanism Reaffirmed

As indicated, humanism has been a mainstay of Western culture since ancient times. To be sure, commitment to this feature has waxed and waned over the centuries; however, periods of partial eclipse have always been followed by reaffirmations or revivals—from the Carolingian renaissance of the Middle Ages to the Italian "Renaissance" of early modernity to the "classical" age of European thought and literature in the era of Enlightenment. Apart from these ebbs and flows, Western history has also repeatedly spawned counter-trends or counter-voices—but rarely of sufficient vigor to challenge the dominant outlook. Things began to change in late modernity, due to a number of factors. One was the powerful, iconoclastic counter-voice of Nietzsche whose writings contested dominant assumptions while confining humanism to the nostalgia of the "last man." Another, even stronger factor were the darkening clouds descending on Europe in the early twentieth century in the form of militarism and aggressive ideologies. As a result of these factors, a sense of crisis was beginning to sweep through Europe, sometimes engendering anguish about an impending end or "decline" of the West. Yet, even at this point, tradition strongly reasserted itself. In the early period of the Nazi era, the philosopher Edmund Husserl—in a celebrated lecture presented in Vienna in 1935—boldly reaffirmed the European and Western commitment to humanism seen as an infinite task of self-understanding. In his words: "The 'crisis of European existence.' . . . is not an obscure fate, an impenetrable destiny; rather, it becomes understandable and transparent against the background of the *teleology of European history*," a teleology involving pursuit of "the *infinite goals of [human] reason*."[2]

Husserl was not alone in countering the perceived crisis of culture with a humanist re-affirmation. Another prominent voice was Ernst Cassirer, a philosopher trained in the Kantian tradition and as such not too far removed from Husserl's "transcendental phenomenology." Moreover, as a close student of late medieval philosophy and a renowned expert on Renaissance humanism, Cassirer was intimately familiar with the persistent trajectory or teleology of European thought.[3] Less than a decade after Husserl's Vienna lecture, in the midst of the Great War, Cassirer penned a text that aptly pinpointed the most admirable aspects of that trajectory. Titled *An Essay on Man* and composed while he was teaching at Yale University, the text can also be regarded as the capstone of his own intellectual career. The conception of humanism—or the meaning of being "human"—articulated in the text resembles in many ways the Husserlian teleology; as for the latter, being human is treated not as a stable possession or compact identity but as an infinite process or progression: the process of steadily deepening self-awareness and self-understanding.

As the opening lines of the *Essay* observe: "That self-knowledge is the highest aim of philosophical inquiry appears to be generally acknowledged." Despite conflicts between different philosophical schools, "this objective remained invariable and unshaken: it proved to be the Archimedean point, the fixed and immovable center, of all thought." As Cassirer recognizes, that center piece has tended to be assailed from numerous quarters throughout history; yet, unwittingly, even the assailants needed to embrace the same Archimedean point. What this confluence demonstrates is a basic principle of human or anthropological evolution: the steady emancipation of human beings from nature. While in the earliest stages, the chief task for humanity was to react or adjust to the external world, the situation changes with the first "glimmering of human consciousness" and the onset of "introspection." "The farther we trace the development of humanity from its beginnings," we read, "the more this introvert [or introspective] view seems to come to the fore." Introspection soon invades primitive cosmology, giving it an anthropological cast; in due course, it also permeates religious life: "In all the higher forms of religious life the maxim 'know thyself' is regarded as a categorical imperative, as an ultimate moral and religious law."[4]

For Cassirer, the basic breakthrough to the stated maxim occurred in the life and thought of Socrates. Despite anticipations among some Pythagorean and Eleatic thinkers, it is in the "problem of man" that one discovers "the landmark separating Socratic from pre-Socratic thought." In the Socratic *elenchus*, all the older problems are seen in a "new light" because they are referred to a new, distinctly human center: "His philosophy—if he possessed a philosophy—is strictly anthropological." What is at a first glance curious about this philosophy is its seemingly evasive character: although discussing numerous qualities and virtues of human beings, Socrates "never ventures a definition of man." However, it is precisely this elusiveness that provides a clue and, in the end, offers a "positive insight into the Socratic conception of man." The clue hinges on the difference between humans and external nature. For, whereas physical things may be described in terms of "objective properties," human beings can be described "only in terms of [their] consciousness." Hence, "human nature"—if this phrase is still used—can only be found in an inner- or self-directed activity, intentionality, and self-understanding. Here, Cassirer comments, we have "the new, indirect answer to the question 'What is man?' " From the Socratic vantage point, "man is declared to be the creature who is constantly in search of himself—a creature who in every moment of his existence must examine and scrutinize the conditions of his existence." Given his involvement in the market place, this existential quest for Socrates is not a purely solitary venture, but occurs in dialogical exchanges: "It is . . . by this faculty of giving a response to himself and to others, that man becomes a 'responsible' being, a moral subject."[5]

The Socratic example was pursued and deepened in subsequent classical thought from Plato to the Stoics. What linked European thought during these centuries was the persistent differentiation of humanity from external nature and the focus on internal self-knowledge. Cassirer mentions a text by the Roman Emperor Marcus

Aurelius titled "To Himself" (*Ad se ipsum*) in which we read: "Neither is the end for which man lives placed in these [external] things, nor yet that which is perfective of that end, namely, the good." As Cassirer comments, underscoring the difference: "All that which befalls man from without is null and void. His essence does not depend on external circumstances; it depends exclusively on the value he gives to himself." For the Stoics, as in the case of Socrates, giving value to oneself requires inner scrutiny and self-questioning. In the relation between human beings and the outer world, it is the inner self, not the universe, that has "the leading part"; once the self has found its inner core, that core remains "unalterable and imperturbable." The same core is the untarnished source of truth and morality as well as the fountainhead of human freedom; for once "man" depends only on himself, he is essentially "free, autonomous, self-sufficing." The curious aspect of Stoicism was the linkage of anthropology and a certain metaphysical cosmology. By projecting the central core of human existence—self-reflective reason—onto the inner workings of the cosmos, human introspection and deliberate exile from the world could find a deeper resonance outside. Thus, the "greatest merit" of Stoicism, for Cassirer, resided in its ability to give to "man" at the same time "a deep feeling of his harmony with nature and of his moral independence from nature."[6]

The continuity of classical humanism was disrupted by the rise of Christianity and the ensuing Middle Ages. What Christianity shared with the older tradition, in Cassirer's account, was the focus on inner human nature; where it disagreed was in its devaluation of this core as "fallen." Hence, "the asserted absolute independence of man, which in Stoic theory was regarded as man's fundamental value, is turned in Christian theory into a fundamental vice and error." The older humanist trajectory, however, was taken up again, after nearly a millennium, in the Italian Renaissance and the dawn of Enlightenment in the thought of Descartes. At this point, the focus on introspection—now centered in the *cogito*—was converted into the ambition of human mind to know both itself and the workings of external nature. In this situation, Cassirer comments, "the question 'What is man?' is transformed and, so to speak, raised to a higher level." For, "now for the first time the scientific spirit, in the modern sense of the word, enters the lists." Hence, in (Western) modernity, inner self-knowledge is linked with refined forms of logical analysis and new methods of empirical inquiry and experimentation. For Cassirer, modern science—like introspection—transcends nature by virtue of its "infinite" questions and research agendas. As a result, a new type of human freedom comes into view. In modernity, he writes, "man no longer lives in the world as a prisoner enclosed within the narrow walls of a finite physical universe"; rather, he can "traverse the air and break through all the imaginary boundaries" established by earlier cosmologies. Hence, the human intellect "becomes aware of its own infinity through measuring its powers by the infinite universe." The preferred means of measuring human powers during the Enlightenment was mathematics—a mode of reasoning capable of restoring the older Stoic harmony between human beings and the structure of nature: "Mathematical reason is the bond between man and the universe. . . . [It] is the key to a true understanding of the cosmic and the moral order."[7]

The humanist path opened up by Descartes continued after the Enlightenment period—although often in revised or modified forms. For Cassirer, the infinite capacity of humanity to transcend nature resides not only in mathematics and logical analysis; as a late modern philosopher aware of the crucial role of language, he detects the same capacity in the construction of human culture and the formation of "symbols." What became increasingly important in late modernity, he notes, is not the mere accumulation of empirical facts but the "interpretation" of these facts—an endeavor that requires language and symbol systems. Through the invention of symbols and symbol systems, humanity in a way gains a further degree of freedom or independence, for at this point, "man" exists no longer in a merely physical world but "lives in a symbolic universe." In fact, the distance between the two worlds widens steadily, in the sense that physical reality recedes "in proportion as man's symbolic activity advances." For Cassirer, symbols and symbolization achieve the same kind of mediation achieved by Stoicism and modern mathematics: by symbolically interpreting the world, human beings deepen their self-knowledge. His *Essay* at this juncture offers a reformulation of the traditional conception of "man" as "rational animal" (*animal rationale*). Analytical reason, he observes, is a "very inadequate term" with which to comprehend "the forms of man's cultural life" in their richness and variety. Hence, instead of speaking of "*animal rationale*" one should speak of "*animal symbolicum*": "By doing so we can designate [man's] specific difference, and we can understand the new way open to man—the way of civilization."[8]

During the years Cassirer spent in exile, a new intellectual movement was emerging in Europe that in some ways was quite revolutionary and in others continued the humanist legacy. Termed *existentialism*, the movement broke with past metaphysical notions of "human nature"; however, by focusing on stripped-down human "existence" as the creative pivot of the world, the older legacy was not so much abandoned as radicalized. The leading champion of the movement was Jean-Paul Sartre, whose philosophical fame was based mainly on a study published at the end of the war, titled *Being and Nothingness: An Essay on Phenomenological Ontology.*[9] In many respects, in that study, Sartre relied on Husserl's earlier teachings, especially his conception of the constitutive role of human "consciousness" or "subjectivity." However, by attributing to Husserl's cognitive conception a strongly activist and constructivist cast, Sartre's work infused phenomenology with a dramatically new, "existentialist" pathos. What this pathos preserved from traditional humanism was above all the stress on human freedom or independence from external nature (what Sartre terms *being*)—an independence that now is seen not only as the pathway to self-knowledge but as the source of creative world-construction and even "self-making" or self-constitution. After the war, in response to numerous misunderstandings or misconstruals, Sartre was at pains to clarify the central meaning of his philosophy, placing the emphasis squarely on its congruence with the humanist trajectory (newly conceived). Eloquently written, the text simply affirmed in its title: *Existentialism is a Humanism (L'existentialisme est un humanisme).*[10]

In the very opening pages of his text, cutting through an underbrush of confusions, Sartre offers a concise definition of his conception of existentialism. What existentialists have in common, he writes, is simply the fact that "they believe that *existence* comes before *essence*—or, if you will, that we must begin from subjectivity." This means that there is no pregiven "human nature" or "essence" that determines or shapes human beings; rather, it is bare human existence that fashions or designs whatever essence or meaning humanity or human life may have—and does so on the basis of "transcendental" (or nonobjective) human freedom or subjectivity. Elaborating on this definition, and especially on the precedence of existence over essence, Sartre adds: "We mean that 'man' first of all exists, encounters himself, surges up in the world—and defines himself afterwards." Seen from the vantage of existentialism, "man" or human being is not substantively or metaphysically definable—"because to begin with he is nothing(ness). He will not be anything until later, and then he will be what he makes of himself." Underscoring this point of radical self-constitution, the text continues: "Man is nothing else

but what he makes himself. That is the first principle of existentialism; and this is what is called 'subjectivity.' " In an effort to obviate
the danger of confusing subjectivity with an isolated individualism,
Sartre—remembering Husserl and perhaps also Kant—invokes the
"transcendental" and hence universalizing quality of human consciousness. If existence precedes essence, he notes, this implies that "man"
is fashioning himself and hence is solely "responsible for what he
is." But since, in fashioning himself, he relies on a transcendental or
infinite source (subjectivity), responsibility likewise becomes infinite:
"When we say that man is responsible for himself, we do not mean
that he is responsible only for his own individuality, but that he is
responsible for all men. . . . Our responsibility thus is much greater
than supposed: for it concerns humanity as a whole."[11]

Although distancing itself from earlier "metaphysical" presupposi-
tions, Sartre's view of humanism clearly resonates with the humanist
tradition in several respects, especially two: the emphasis on human
freedom (from the external environment); and the assignment of
certain moral values to this freedom. Returning to the precedence of
existence over essence, the text declares: If this primacy is taken seriously, "one will never be able to explain one's action by reference to
a given human nature; which means: there is no determinism—man
is free, man *is* freedom." Carrying this idea forward, the text reaches
the famous, and deliberately paradoxical formulation: since we have
no metaphysics to back us up, "we are left alone, without excuse.
That is, . . . man is condemned to be free." For Sartre, to look for
"excuses" or external justification of one's behavior means to act
"inauthentically" or in "bad faith," whereas shouldering one's freedom and accepting responsibility for one's conduct means to behave
"authentically" and in morally "good faith." As he states: "Any man
who takes refuge behind the excuse of his passions, or by inventing
some deterministic doctrine, is a self-deceiver." This self-deception is
"evidently a falsehood, because it is a dissimulation of man's complete
liberty of commitment." By contrast, someone who accepts his or her
responsibility recognizing freedom as the "foundation of all values,"
is able to live with (at least a measure of) good faith: "The actions of
men of good faith have, as their ultimate significance, the quest of
freedom itself"; they are actions that "will freedom for freedom's sake"
(although always in concrete circumstances). This, Sartre concludes,
is "existential humanism" because "we remind man that there is no
legislator but himself; that he himself . . . must decide for himself and
[thus] realize himself as truly human."[12]

Counter-Humanism and Humanism of the "Other"

As mentioned previously, the dominant humanist trajectory in Western thought has periodically been challenged or interrupted by counter-trends or counter-voices. In *An Essay on Man*, Cassirer recalls one particularly eloquent counter-voice at the onset of Western Enlightenment: the French thinker Blaise Pascal. For Pascal, the traditional postulate of human self-understanding, expressed in the maxim "Know thyself," was erroneous and misleading; following the postulate in a strict sense could only lead into darkness and an abyss. As Cassirer summarizes this outlook: "Man" from this angle has "no 'nature,' no simple or homogeneous being" because he is "a strange mixture of being and non-being." Lodged at the threshold of non-being, it is pointless for humans to inquire into themselves and listen to their own voice. Rather, the demand is to silence themselves in order to hear another, higher voice—as expressed in Pascal's statement: "Know, haughty man, what a paradox you are yourself. Humble yourself, impotent reason; be silent, imbecile nature; learn that man infinitely surpasses man, and hear from our [divine] master your true condition of which you are ignorant." The master appealed to in this passage is God—but conceived as a hidden God or *Deus absconditus*. Because "man" is fashioned in the divine image, he too "cannot be other than mysterious . . . [and] remains a *homo absconditus*."[13]

Seen against the foil of Renaissance humanism, Pascal's remonstration offered a powerful corrective; however, lodged by an isolated thinker, his complaint was soon swallowed up by the rising tide of Enlightenment rationalism and the spreading creed of social progress. It took three centuries and the immense shocks of late modernity for dissenters to gain a broader and more receptive audience. Even then, however, change was initially slow and halting. As indicated earlier, the aftermath of World War II witnessed a strong reaffirmation and revindication of traditional humanism. It took several decades for this reaffirmation to be seriously challenged and nearly overturned. What emerged at this point was a widespread sense of malaise, more intense than earlier cultural critiques: a malaise which led many people to wonder whether the horrors experienced in this century were not somehow traceable to the self-confident humanism and progressivism of the past. Since humanist self-assertion had reached its apogee in French existentialism, it was also in France that the attack on humanism found it most eloquent articulation. As it happens, French counter-humanism at the time was part and parcel of a broader counter-cultural movement that, in academic contexts, sailed under the labels of "structuralism" and "post-structuralism." While structuralists, on an empirical level, debunked humanist claims by inserting human beings into networks of nonpurposive forces, post-structuralist thinkers proceeded to attack the basic philosophical or metaphysical underpinnings of humanist beliefs. The most prominent champions of this post-structuralist agenda were (the early) Jacques Derrida and Michel Foucault.

It was in 1968—the year of a major political upheaval in France—that Derrida took up the issue of humanism and endeavored to "deconstruct" its basic meaning. Deconstruction here took the form of a radical reversal: in lieu of the traditional humanist teleology—pointing toward ever greater self-knowledge, self-transparency, and freedom—Derrida shifted the accent toward another sense of "telos" as ending, vanishing point, or disappearance. His essay "The Ends of Man" (discussed from another angle in the preceding chapter) unearthed astutely the deep ambivalence inhabiting such notions as end, telos, or finality. In the very opening pages, Derrida situated his intervention concretely and historically by depicting "the thought that dominated France" in the postwar period "essentially as humanist." The most prolific and influential version of this outlook was Sartre's existentialism—which that author himself had advertised as a "humanism." What, in Derrida's view, was entirely lacking in Sartre's work, as well as the writings of other existentialists, was a sober examination of the meaning and inherent limits of he "human." Despite much philosophical erudition, the "unity of man" with its constitutive boundaries was "never examined in and of itself." More importantly, the history of the concept of man was never analyzed—as if "man" was a timeless or perennial idea: "Everything occurred as if the sign 'man' had no origin, no historical, cultural, or linguistic limit." For Derrida, the entire postwar period in France could neatly be summarized under the perennial label: "Thus defined, humanism or anthropologism, during this period, was the common ground of Christian or atheist existentialisms, of the philosophy of values (spiritual or not), of personalisms of the right or the left, [and even] of Marxism in the classical [or Western] style."[14]

After having reviewed the high tide of humanism and anthropologism that had covered French philosophy, Derrida turned his attention to the "anti-humanist and anti-anthropologist ebb that followed, and in which we are now"—but found the counter-trend often too timid or half-hearted.[15] For Derrida, what had to happen was not some slow, continuous transformation of the past but rather a resolute break with humanism. As he wrote, what is needed is a decision "to change terrain, in a discontinuous and irruptive fashion, by brutally placing oneself outside, and by affirming an absolute break and difference." At this point, moving along briskly—and ignoring the lingering "humanist" quality of a human decision to "change terrain"—Derrida's text invokes the legacy of Friedrich Nietzsche whose work, he notes, was experiencing on "increasingly insistent and increasingly rigorous" revival in France at the time. What is particularly significant in Nietzsche's legacy, and especially his *Zarathustra*, is his distinction between the "higher man"—the figure celebrated in traditional humanism—and the "overman (*Übermensch*)." It is only the latter who is able to rupture the bonds of the "human" and to venture into utterly unfamiliar terrain. Not concerned with, or being beholden to, any tradition, the overman "burns his text and erases the traces of his steps." In this manner, he enters into an arena where no definition or conception of the "human" is any longer applicable.[16]

Derrida was by no means alone at the time in taking aim at the humanist legacy. His foray against that legacy was seconded by a number of French intellectuals and, above all, by Michel Foucault. Already of few years before Derrida's text, the latter had mounted a spirited assault on the legacy in a text suffused with structuralist or post-structuralist leanings, titled *The Order of Things* (*Les mots et les choses*). As Foucault noted in the Preface of his book, something uncanny was happening at the time: a kind of sea change or change of terrain affecting all aspects of cultural–intellectual life. A major feature affected by this change was humanism or the "figure of man" that had dominated modern Western thought. "Strangely enough," we read, man "is probably no more than a kind of rift in the order of things," a rift exposing as illusory "all the chimeras of the new humanisms." A relatively recent invention and a mere "wrinkle" in the fabric of modern knowledge, it was possible to predict that "man" will "disappear again as soon as that knowledge has discovered a new form." In the conclusion of the book, the counter-humanist theme is taken up vigorously, and this time with explicit reference to the teachings of Nietzsche. "In our day," Foucault states, "and once again Nietzsche indicated the turning point from a long way off, it is not so much the absence or the death of God that is affirmed as the end of man (that narrow, imperceptible displacement, that recession in the form of identity, which are the reason why man's finitude has become his end)." This statement is followed by another passage that in many ways encapsulates the anti-humanist creed—and seems to have inspired Derrida's later text:

Man will disappear. Rather than the death of God—or rather in the wake of that death and in profound correlation with it—what Nietzsche's thought heralds is the end of his murderer; it is the explosion of man's face in laughter, and the return of masks. It is the scattering of the profound stream of time by which [man] felt himself carried along and whose pressure he suspected in the very being of things; it is the identity of the Return of the Same with the absolute dispersion of man.[17]

Critique of the humanist tradition did not always take the shape of a radical anti-humanism (whose extreme formulations were later disowned by both Derrida and Foucault). Frequently, critical dissent was couched in more subtle and circumspect language, choosing as its target the subject-centered focus of modern humanism and its tendential disregard of the "other" or *alter ego*. The most prominent example of this counter-trend is the work of Emmanuel Levinas, well known for his insistence on the "primacy of ethics" grounded, in turn, in the primacy of the other's "face" (revealing the other's unmanageable or "transcendental" selfhood). As can be seen, counter-humanism here takes the form of a transgression of Husserl's (and Sartre's) reliance on constituting subjectivity—not in the direction of a structuralist or post-structuralist "end of man," but in favor of the constitutive role of the other's subjectivity. This outlook is eloquently stated in Levinas's book *Humanism of the Other* (*Humanisme de l'autre homme*), first published a few years after the 1968 events. As Richard Cohen, in introducing the book to English-speaking readers, points out, Levinas's philosophy starts from "the superlative moral priority of the other person" and proposes "a conception of the 'humanity of the human,' the 'subjectivity of the subject,' according to which being 'for-the-other' takes precedence over . . . being for-itself." Although critical of traditional (especially Husserlian) humanism, the new approach clearly preserves—under changed auspices—the accent on humanist meaning-constitution. In Cohen's words: Meaning or significance for Levinas "emerges from the face-to-face encounter as an ethical event, that is, from the other person as moral command and the self as moral response." In this encounter, the intervention of the other "disturbs, upsets, and overwhelms the self-relation of the self"—and does so in a manner that "cuts deeper" than "cultural formations" (as outlined by Cassirer) or "ontological configurations" (as explored by structuralists and, presumably, by Heidegger).[18]

In a central chapter of his book (titled "Without Identity"), Levinas distances himself from some of the catch phrases of the period—phrases like "the end of humanism, end of metaphysics, the death of man, death of God"—describing them as "apocalyptic ideas or intellectual high-society slogans." Under the impact of such slogans as well as the upsurge of certain positivist methodologies, he notes, humanist discourse tends to be exorcised with the result that "the subject is eliminated from the order of reasons." The ultimate upshot of this elimination is that "the interiority of an ego identical to itself dissolves in a totality without folds or secrets. All that is human is outside." While distancing himself from extreme formulations, Levinas is willing to grant them a certain plausibility in the light of real-life experiences of the period—experiences liable to render humanist discourse vacuous or inane. What recent developments have taught people, he observes, is the contrast between intentions and consequences—the fact "that an action can be hampered by the technique destined to make it easy and effective; that a science born to embrace the world delivers it to disintegration; and that a politics and administration guided by the humanist ideal maintain the exploitation of man by man and war." These and similar "reversals of reasonable projects" have engendered a widespread cultural malaise and even an existential *"angst"* that is profound. In terms of the text, the malaise derives from "seeing revolutions founder in bureaucracy, and repression and totalitarian violence passing for revolution." Transposed into the traditional humanist register, these experiences disclose as fallacious "the idea of an ego that is identified in finding itself," the trajectory of a "reunion of self and self."[19]

For Levinas, acknowledging the shallowness of traditional rhetoric does not amount, however, to a complete dismissal of the humanist idea. What is needed to salvage the latter is a shift from the self-enclosure and assertiveness of the ego to the dimension of the *alter* or "other" seen as the carrier of a humanist agenda. Is it necessary, Levinas asks—critiquing a certain (narrow) mode of phenomenology—to construe the ego's subjectivity as enclosed and at home with itself? "Does not subjectivity mean precisely its incapacity to shut itself up from inside" and hence a radical openness to what lies beyond? The question then becomes as to what "lies beyond." For Levinas, this other domain cannot be found in an objective network (as defined by structualist social science) nor in a realm of "being" (conflated somehow with "nature"). Rather, openness here points to the "other's" humanity or the "humanism of the other" experienced as an incursion or demand: "Opening is the vulnerability of a skin offered in wound and outrage beyond all that can show itself, beyond any essence of being showing itself to understanding." Elaborating further on openness as vulnerability to the other and underscoring its counterpoint to active self-assertion, the text states that vulnerability means a "sensibility beneath all will, all act, all declaration, all taking stands." In fact, it designates a "radical passivity of man who elsewhere poses himself and declares his own being," and even "a passivity more passive than all passivity." What renders the self's openness "more passive" than mere passivity is that it allows itself to be vulnerable and hence is an accomplice in its own vulnerability. What we discover here, Levinas observes, is "a hard unbearable consent that animates passivity, strangely animates it in spite of itself, whereas passivity as such has neither force nor intention, neither like nor dislike." By virtue of this openness, the ego is no longer for itself but "for the other," involving substitution, responsibility, expiation—a change bringing into view a changed humanism: a "humanism of the other."[20]

Toward an "Other" Humanism

Pondering the different versions of counter-humanism, one can hardly deny the cogency of some of their arguments. Given the immense calamities produced by egocentrism and brash self-assertion—both in terms of inter-human violence and the damage inflicted on the natural environment—one is bound to be weary of humanist rhetoric and to concur with Maurice Blanchot's statement: "To nobly speak of the human in man, to exalt the humanity in man, means to arrive quickly at a discourse that is untenable and, beyond doubt, more repugnant than all the nihilist vulgarities."[21] What is intimated in Blanchot's statement is a disconcerting collusion or complicity: the fact that high-sounding rhetoric can, and often does, serve as a smokescreen covering inhuman practices and vulgarities. This fact by itself, however, does not settle the issue. It may be quite correct, as post-structuralist authors have affirmed, that there is no fixed human essence and that "man" is a welter of contingencies; but there is still a considerable stretch between this assertion and the vastly more ambitious claim of a radical negation and effective "end of man." On the contrary, precisely the lack of a determinate human "substance" may lead to an intensified effort to search for the "human"—yielding the insight that to be human means to be "underway" or be involved in a genuine quest. Seen from this angle, the presumed "end of man" is in effect nothing else but the continuous and ever renewed beginning of a journey. Although less radically formulated, Levinasian counter-humanism, in prioritizing the "other," also sidelines or distorts the sense of being underway. Although others may be instigators and even companions on a journey, they cannot dispense with the need to move along and shoulder the burdens of one's own journeying. Moreover, ethical formation cannot be a task left entirely to the "Other." Quite frequently, ethical conduct is demanded in the absence of fellow-beings and, on occasion, may require acts of resistance against others seeking to thwart one's sense of justice or fairness

What these reflections lead to is not a simple rehabilitation of traditional humanism, but a transgression that proceeds more cautiously than some of the counter-humanist strategies. What needs to be contemplated here is not so much an erasure or replacement of human selfhood as rather a debunking or deflation of anthropocentrism in favor of a released openness to others, nature, and the recessed ground of being(s). This kind of openness is surely receptive and dependent on fellow-beings—but not in the sense of an utter passivity (or heteronomy), because ethical conduct has still to be actively cultivated and nurtured. Perhaps it is better to speak here again of conduct in the "middle voice" (balancing activity and passivity) in the sense that ethical conduct has to be responsive to others while also being ready to tackle difficult challenges or tasks without prompting. Theodor Adorno, co-architect of the early Frankfurt School, has coined a formula for this "other," more recessed kind of humanism when he recommends a deflation of the subject or a *reductio hominis* in opposition to the traditional anthropocentric humanism (with its *reductio ad hominem*). The formula is found in Adorno's late work titled *Negative Dialectics*, published shortly before the events of 1968. The study takes aim at the long-standing fascination of Western thought with self-centered humanism, a centering usually coupled with the stress on individualism and autonomous "subjectivity." Although propagated as part of an ongoing process of human liberation or emancipation, this centering for Adorno has carried a steep price. In his words: as a "penalty for its self-glorification," human subjectivity has increasingly become "incarcerated in its own selfhood," condemned to gaze at fellow-beings and the world "like a knight through the casemate of a fortress." This self-confinement of human subjectivity, he adds, undermines itself by robbing it of its linkage with "truth" and the world: "The truth-quality of the self unfolds only in its relation to what it is not—and not through a self-centered assertion of its existence or givenness."[22]

Adorno's remedy for self-enclosure resides in a *reductio*, that is, a radical debunking or deflation of selfhood, not its sheer erasure (or equation with passivity). Debunking here involves an effort to break open subjectivity in the direction of "otherness" involving fellow-beings, nature, and the world—an effort guided not by the desire to control or manipulate, but by an attitude of care and a willingness to respect difference and the intrinsic integrity of diverse beings. Things or beings, Adorno states, "are reified as targets of a long-standing oppression." Their recovery requires expiatory measures, measures which, contrary to "the imperialist impulse to annex the otherness of the world," would be willing to "recognize the element of distance and strangeness even in proximate surroundings." As his text emphatically reiterates, recovery and recognition of this kind are incompatible with possessive self-enclosure: "Nothing on earth or in an emptied heaven can be salvaged through stubborn self-defense." This is followed by a passage that admirably blends activity and passivity, self-being and self-emptying, and thus captures the core of an "other" humanism: "Nothing can be saved without transformation, nothing which has not passed through the portals of its death. While preservation is the innermost impulse of human being, there is no hope outside of unconditional surrender: a surrender of both the target of salvation and the searching human mind guided by hope."[23]

In many ways, Adorno's outlook finds a parallel—although couched in a different, ontological idiom—in Heidegger's work, and especially in a text dating from his middle period: the *Letter on Humanism*. Like Adorno, Heidegger was always anxious to distance himself from the Cartesian focus on subjectivity and "thinking sub-stance" (*cogito*) and, more generally, from the anthropocentric leanings of modern Western philosophy or metaphysics. In his early *magnum opus, Being and Time,* opposition to these leanings was evident in his portrayal of human existence as "being-in-the-world," that is, a crea-ture not self-confined but enmeshed in the context of a complex life world. The crucial distinguishing trait of this creature, in Heidegger's presentation, was not a fixed substance nor an inner self-constitution but rather the capacity for "care" (*Sorge*) seen as an ongoing search for meaning and truth. Whatever anthropocentric elements were still present in this early work became the target of sustained critique and self-correction in subsequent writings. In the *Letter on Humanism*, the effort to transgress "existentialism" (in the subjective Sartrean sense) was highlighted by an emphatic recasting of the meaning of "exis-tence" itself. Relying on the etymological roots of the term, the text defined human being as an "ek-static" creature constitutively propelled beyond itself and hence capable of transgressing purely subjective, self-centered designs. As a corollary, "being-in-the-world" was sharply differentiated from a purely empirical condition and reinterpreted as a mode of self-transcendence, a "standing-out" into the open horizon of meaning. Placed into this open arena, human life could be seen as a "project"—but not in the (Sartrean) sense of human construction and self-construction. "Man" is human, the *Letter* states, "insofar as he exists, that is, insofar as he stands out into the openness of Being which has 'projected' man in the basic modality of 'care.' " Seen from this angle, "world" designates "the clearing of Being into which man reaches out by virtue of his own 'thrown' or 'projected' nature."[24]

Given its accent on openness and responsiveness to Being, Heidegger's *Letter* clearly departs from traditional Western "humanism" viewed as synonym for anthropocentrism. This departure, however, does not equal a simple negation or "end of man." As the text specifically states, critique of the traditional view has no truck with an "anti-human" impulse, and especially not with the desire to "vindicate inhumanity and debase human dignity." What is involved is not the abolition of "man" nor a blind leap into alterity but rather the formulation of a new, relational vision of human existence—a vision bringing into view a new or "other" version of humanism. "If we decide to keep the label," the *Letter* states, "the term 'humanism' signifies that human nature is indeed crucial for the truth of Being—but crucial precisely in a way where everything does not depend on 'man' alone or as such." It is at this point that Heidegger introduces his famous notion of human being as the caretaker, guardian, or "shepherd" of Being (in all its forms)—a notion radically at odds with any conception of unilateral mastery or control. As such a caretaker, human existence shoulders an enormous responsibility and is called into active service—but without ascribing to itself any particular preeminence or privilege. Differently phrased, responsiveness and surrender to Being are here coupled—in a "middle voice"—with practical engagement and self-giving. "As the ek-static project of Being," we read, "man is more than *animal rationale* precisely to the degree that he is less in comparison with man construed in terms of subjectivity. Man is not the master of reality, but rather the shepherd of Being." In a way, self-surrender and self-finding are here curiously allied; through self-transgression and the caring quest for Being, human existence also rediscovers its own nature or the point of its own being, that is, the "*humanitas* of the *homo humanus*," a humanity "in the service of the truth of Being but freed from the shackles of metaphysical humanism."[25]

Heidegger's "reduced" or relational view of human being has clear implications for ethics and political praxis. Seen as a caretaker, human existence is charged with the task of guarding and not willfully exploiting nature's bounty for the sake of economic gain. In an age of steady resource depletion and global warming, this task of preservation assumes the urgency of an ecological imperative. At least equally important as this imperative is the cultivation of caring relations with fellow human beings—relations shunning the lure of assimilation or synthesis and above all the temptation of unilateral mastery and imperial control. (As may be recalled, Heidegger's *Being and Time* had outlined the possibility of a "liberating-anticipatory solicitude" aiming to further the other's freedom without managerial intervention.) A further dimension of careful relationality is the openness to the "call" of Being and the steadfast quest for its truth—where "Being" in many ways serves as a synonym for the "divine" seen as the transcendent-immanent (un)grounding of all things. What is clear in all these relations is that care or caretaking is a challenge that cannot be shunned or simply be delegated to the "other." Contrary to some facile assumptions, ethical dispositions like hospitality and generosity to strangers are not ready-made natural endowments but require cultivation and practice, including a kind of self-cultivation and self-care (*cura sui*). Seen from this angle, caretaking bears some affinity with the Aristotelian cultivation of practical "virtues"—notwithstanding the inevitable distantiation of contemporary philosophy from Aristotelian metaphysics (rigidly construed) and from the Greek conception of '"being" (as substance).[26]

Probably the most important implication of the "other" humanism sketched here is its transformative quality: its accent on the steady quest toward truth and goodness guided by care. As we read in *Being and Time*: "Man's *perfectio*—his transformation into that which he can be in being free for his ownmost possibilities—is accomplished by 'care.' "[27] This aspect brings into view another parallel to the discussed "*reductio*": the work of Raimon Panikkar and especially his so-called "cosmotheandric" vision, involving a balanced relation between nature, human, and the divine. In several of his writings, Panikkar has approximated Heideggerian insights by placing human existence between or in the interstices of two poles: the demands of a radical alterity or "otherness" termed "heteronomy" and the pretensions of an anthropocentric self-reliance termed "autonomy." In opposition to both external and purely internal modes of self-constitution, human existence is placed by Panikkar in the role of caretaker or attentive guardian of all beings, a role labeled "ontonomy." In his words: ontonomy refers to "the realization of the [relational] *nomos* of being" on that profound level where freedom does not conflict with self-giving or self-surrender and where "unity does not thwart or impinge upon diversity." Operating basically in the "middle voice," human beings in this view must be considered neither as sovereign agents nor as passive victims of some kind of "exteriority," but rather as participants in an ongoing disclosure or epiphany of "being"—in the persistent labor of (what Panikkar calls) the *"consecratio mundi,"* that is, the ethical-spiritual transformation and sanctification of the world.[28]

As can readily be seen, transformation from this angle has a dual significance, involving both the healing and salvaging of the world and the transfiguration of the human agents of change. Viewed against this background, the "other" humanism outlined here acquires a new, quasi-eschatological connotation: by pointing to the long-range process of the "humanization" (*Menschwerdung*) of humanity or humankind. In the context of the so-called "Abrahamic" religions, this process has been announced or foretold in the famous dream of the prophet Daniel during the time of the Babylonian captivity. In recounting his dream (Daniel 7:2–27), Daniel mentions the successive appearance of four great beasts, the first looking like a lion, the second like a bear, the next like a leopard, and the fourth (most "terrible" to behold and with "great iron teeth") like a monster with multiple horns—adding the interpretation that the beasts represent four kingdoms or empires, with the last empire being most comprehensive or global seeking to "devour the whole earth, trample it down, and break it to pieces." Beastly domination, however, is not the conclusion of the Daniel's dream, for at the end of the last kingdom there arises someone "like the son of man" (*Menschensohn*) who is presented to the "Ancient of Days" and granted ever-lasting rule over "peoples, nations, and languages."

In offering his own interpretation of the dream, Pope Benedict XVI highlights the core meaning of a transformed or "other" humanism. In the image of the four great beasts, he states, Daniel depicts the succession of worldly powers or dominions, powers that arise "from below" and rely on beastly force. In the end, however, the darkness of human-political history is transformed and illuminated by the vision of the "Ancient of Days" and the glorious epiphany of the "son of man." "The beasts from the depth," Benedict writes, "are confronted with the 'man' from on high. Just as the beasts from the depth symbolize the historical empires of this world, the image of the 'son of man' (*Menschensohn*) appearing 'on the clouds of heaven' announces a new regime, a reign of *'humanitas'* (*Menschlichkeit*) sustained by genuine, divinely granted power." As he adds: "With this reign there arises the true universality, the final and silently always already yearned-for positive meaning of human history."[29] Translated into more ordinary or accessible terminology, the arrival of *"humanitas"* announces the advent of a properly human society and public regime—a regime attentive to the "promise of democracy" and the arduous path of democratization.

9

Religion, Politics, and Islam

Toward Multiple Modes of Democracy

Islam demands loyalty to God, not to thrones.

—Mohammad Iqbal

When dealing with the general topic of religion and politics, a preliminary terminological clarification is in order. As used here, the term *religion* refers to a domain transcending willful human control or appropriation. Etymologically, the term derives from the Latin *religare*, which means to connect or to reconnect. What is here reconnected? Basically, religion aims to reconnect humans with the divine or "God" where the latter means something unconditional and unconditioned, something beyond human caprice or control, something that cannot be domesticated, possessed, or marketed. Hence, religion as used here is radically different from the "idols of the markets" or what is sometimes called the "religion of the market." This does not mean that religion is not also a human striving or aspiration—precisely the aspiration to "reconnect."

The question I raise here is: can democracy be religious and, if so, how can it be religious? How can we bring religion into modern democratic politics, and how can modern democracy be reconciled with religion? In the famous formulation of Max Weber, modernity means basically a process of "disenchantment." So how can modernity be "re-enchanted" or at least permit a measure of re-enchantment without completely undermining modern democracy? In his *Political and Social Essays*, the French philosopher Paul Ricoeur addresses forthrightly the situation of the religious believer in the modern world, especially in modern secular society. Quoting from scripture (Matthew 5:13), Ricoeur insists that believers are meant to be "the salt of the earth"—a phrase militating against both world domination and world denial, that is, against the dual temptation of either controlling or rejecting worldly society. As he writes poignantly, "the salt is made for salting, the light for illuminating," and religion exists "for the sake of those outside itself," that is, for the world that faith inhabits. In Ricoeur's view, religion—including (especially) Christianity—has been for too long enamored with political power and domination, a collusion that has exerted a "demoralizing effect" on believers and nonbelievers alike, driving them to "cynicism, amoralism, and despair." However, the situation is perhaps not entirely bleak. When it emerges from this collusion, he adds, religion "will be able to give light once more to all men—no longer as a power, but as a prophetic message."[1]

As one of the great world religions, Islam faces the same challenges. Like Christianity, Islam has been sorely tempted by the lure of worldly power and public dominion; this at least is the impression given by a large number of its adherents, especially by many so-called Islamic governments and Islamist movements (often labeled or rather mislabeled "fundamentalist" in Western media). As in the case of Christianity, this lure of collusion is baffling and disconcerting—given the strong commitment of Islam to human equality and its opposition to any kind of idolatry, that is, to the substitution of any worldly images or power structures for the rule of the one transcendent God (*tawhid*). How can Muslim believers be expected to submit or surrender themselves to any worldly potentates, no matter how pious or clerically sanctioned, if their faith is defined as surrender ("*islam*") to nothing else but the eternal "light" of truth? How can they be asked to abandon their religious freedom (in the face of the divine) for the sake of contingent political loyalties to rulers who often lack even a semblance of public or collective legitimation?

As in the case of traditional Christendom, Islam's collusion with public power has often exerted (in Ricoeur's words) a "demoralizing effect" on believers and nonbelievers alike, driving many of them to "cynicism, amoralism, and despair." In this situation, it is high time for Muslims and all friends of Islam to take stock of the prevailing predicament. Concisely put: it is time, not to abandon Islam in favor of some doctrinaire secularism or laïcism (which does not have sufficient resources to resist the idols of the market), but to reinvigorate the "salt" of Islamic faith so that it can become a beacon of light both for Muslims and the world around them. Differently phrased: it is time to recuperate the genuine meaning of Islam as a summons to freedom, justice, and service to the God who, throughout the *Qur'an*, is called "all-merciful and compassionate" (*rahman-i-raheem*). The present pages are meant to contribute to such a recuperation.

Religion, Political Power, and Democracy

As it seems to me, contemporary Islam is in a state of agony, with the fortunes of recovery hanging in the balance. The point here is not to impugn the motives of political Islam or political Islamists whose strategies often seem to be dictated by mundane political and geopolitical considerations. What is at issue is rather the wisdom and sensibility of politicized religion, seeing that the yoking together of power and religion inevitably exacts a heavy toll both on the sobriety of political judgment and on the integrity of religious faith.

To speak in general terms, religion and politics are neither synonyms nor necessarily antithetical. On a theoretical level, one can distinguish a limited number of "ideal-typical" constellations involving the two terms. On the one hand, there is the paradigm of complete separation or isolation (an extreme version of the Augustinian formula of "two cities"). In this paradigm, religious faith withdraws, or is forced to withdraw, into inner privacy while politics maintains a radical indifference or agnosticism vis-à-vis scriptural teachings or spiritual meanings. As can readily be seen, both sides pay a heavy price for this mutual segregation: faith by forfeiting any relevance or influence in worldly affairs, and politics by tendentially shriveling into an empty power game. In the historical development of religion and politics, this segregationist paradigm has been relatively infrequent (its contours emerge mainly in the context of Western modernity). Much more common has been another paradigm or constellation: that of fusion or amalgamation—which may be accomplished in two ways or along two roads: either religion strives to colonize and subjugate worldly politics, thereby erecting itself into a public power (which may result in "theocracy"), or else politics colonizes religious faith by expanding itself into a totalizing, quasi-religious panacea or ideology. As history shows, both strategies have seriously tempted most religions in the past.

Turning to Islam: by common agreement some kind of fusion has tended to prevail during its "founding" period. With minor variations, public power in Islamic society during the early centuries was wielded either by charismatic leaders (the "rightly guided caliphs") or else by a combination of dynastic imperial rulers (presumably descendants of the Prophet) and a battery of clerical jurists or jurisconsults (*fuqaha*). In his account of political authority in early Islam, Ira Lapidus distinguishes between two models or (what he calls) two "golden ages": namely, an "integral" or holistic model and a more "differentiated" or symbiotic structure. In the first model, he writes, Islamic society "was integrated in all dimensions, political, social, and moral, under the aegis of Islam." The prototype of this model was the unification of Arabia under the guidance of the Prophet and his immediate successors. In the second, more differentiated model, imperial Islamic government—from the Umayyads and Abbasids to the Ottomans—was erected on the diversified structures of traditional Middle Eastern societies, thus yielding a complex, symbiotic amalgam. In this case, the original caliphate was transformed "from the charismatic succession to the religious authority of the Prophet" into a far-flung imperial regime governed both by religious norms (*shari'a*) and more adaptive political laws, or rather by a mixture of imperial-political authority and clerical jurisprudence (resembling the medieval theory of "two swords").[2]

According to Lapidus, contemporary Islamic traditionalists or "revivalists" harken back—though often unsuccessfully—to the two models of Islam's "golden ages." To this extent, Islamic revivalism or political Islamism necessarily is at odds with basic features of modern life—given that, in its core, "modernity" (at least in its Western form) aims at the differentiation, disaggregation, and radical diffusion of the unified, holistic worldviews and political structures of an earlier age. Being an integral part of modernity and its way of life, modern democracy inevitably falls under the same verdict of traditionalists: namely, as testifying to the modern abandonment of religious faith in favor of an "un-godly" secularism or nihilism. Here we have the crux of the problem of the relation between Islam and modern democracy: how can traditional holism and modern differentiation or disenchantment be reconciled? Are Islam and democracy compatible, or are they basically incompatible? There are two ways to assert their incompatibility: either one claims that democracy negates or destroys Islam, or one asserts that Islam negates democracy.

Traditional Islamists basically make the first claim: that democracy (and modernity in general) undermines faith. Their strategy is to present the transition from tradition to modernity (and postmodernity) under the simplistic image of reversal or antithesis. According to this strategy, modernity or modernization means a lapse from faith into nonfaith, from religious devotion into agnostic rationalism, and from the holistic unity of "truth" into a radical relativism denying "truth." In a similar vein, the argument is sometimes advanced that, whereas earlier ages were founded on "virtue," modernity is founded on freedom and nonvirtue (as if virtue without freedom were somehow plausible or even desirable). In the most provocative formulation, Islamists assert that modernity has replaced the reign of God (*hakimyya*) with the reign of "man" or humanity—a replacement equaling a lapse into paganism and the state of pre-Islamic "ignorance" (*jahiliyya*).

In the present context, the latter formulation is particularly significant. Under political auspices, the charge implies a reversal of public supremacy—namely, the alleged replacement of God's sovereignty with the sovereignty of the "people" (the latter equated with democracy). In large measure, this charge is at the heart of the anti-democratic sentiments espoused by many revivalists and/or militant Islamists. In discussing the "political discourse" of contemporary Islamist movements, political theorist Youssef Choueiri highlights this point as central to that discourse. Referring especially to the writings of Sayyid Qutb and al-Maududi, Choueiri underscores the holistic religious quality of "God's sovereignty," writing that the phrase affirms God's authority "in the daily life of His creatures and servants," revealing that "the universe is judged to be one single organic unity, both in its formation and movement: the unity of the universe mirrors the absolute oneness of God." Judged by the standard of this unity, modern humanity—including modern democracy—exists in a state of disarray and incoherence, that is, in "a second *jahiliyya*, more sinister in its implications than the *jahiliyya* of pre-Islamic days." Pushing this point still further, radical Islamists (in Choueiri's presentation) tend to view the entire course of Western history as "a connected series of *jahiliyyas*: Hellenism, the Roman Empire, the Middle Ages, the Renaissance, the Enlightenment, and the French Revolution" (and its democratic offshoots). As an antidote to modernity and modern democracy, Islamist thinkers typically propose a return to "God's sovereignty," that is, to a semi- or quasi-theocracy (which usually means some form of religious authority or elitism).[3]

It becomes urgent here to look at the presumed transfer of sovereignty and its underlying premises. Is such a transfer plausible or persuasive (even on strictly religious grounds)? The idea of sovereignty implies the rule of absolute will or will power untrammeled by any rational constraints or intelligible standards of justice. To ascribe such sovereignty to God means to construe God as a willful and arbitrary despot—which is hardly a pious recommendation. Several of the great Islamic philosophers (of the classical period) had already objected to this construal, complaining that it transforms God into a tyrant similar to such tyrants as Genghis Khan or Tamerlane.[4] Whatever the status of God's sovereignty may be, however, modern democracy represents by no means a simple reversal in the sense of installing the "people" as sovereign despots. On the contrary, whatever else modern democracy means, it certainly means a dispersal of power and a constant circulation of power holders. Several leading democratic theorists, including Hannah Arendt, have gone so far as to urge the removal of "sovereignty" from the vocabulary of political discourse, in order to make broader room for grassroots participation. What emerges here is a conception of democracy not as a fixed power but as an open-ended and experimental process—open-ended precisely also toward the discourse of religion.[5]

As indicated before, there is a second way to insist on the incompatibility of Islam and democracy. Whereas in the first formulation, Islam and democracy are incompatible, with the result that democracy has to be jettisoned, the second formulation draws the conclusion that, for the sake of democracy, Islam has to be jettisoned—or at least be pushed into a completely inner realm of belief. This retreat into an inner realm is often called "privatization" of religion, and is exemplified by the effort of Western Enlightenment to "privatize" Christianity. This strategy tends to be privileged by radical secularists and agnostics, but (curiously) also by some forms of mysticism or illuminationism. The Algerian-American thinker Lahouari Addi has commented on this strategy in an insightful essay titled "Islamicist Utopia and Democracy." For Addi, Islamist "utopia" is another term for public or politicized Islam—a model that is radically incompatible with modern democracy. Public Islam, in Addi's view, is a relic of the past, of an obsolete "medievalism." As he writes: "It is necessary to show how political modernity is incompatible with the public character of religion and how modernity is built on the 'depoliticization' (that is privatization) of religion."[6]

In fairness, I should add that Addi does not completely banish religion from social life. As he admits, Islam can continue to have a "moral authority" in culture and civil society (although not in politics or the state). If this path is pursued, he is moderately hopeful that Islam and democracy may be able to coexist and hence become compatible and even mutually supportive or enriching. In his words: "Such a creation of modernity by way of Arab-Islamic culture is theoretically possible, for there is no reason—everything else kept the same—why democracy should be inherently Western and absolutism [or despotism] inherently Muslim."[7] In arguing in this manner, Addi joins a number of recent and contemporary Muslim intellectuals who have suggested or advocated a new understanding of political rule, and also a new view of the relation between religion and worldly politics, and especially between Islam and modern democracy.[8]

Toward a Religious Democracy?

From the angle of political theory or philosophy, one of the crucial demands today is the shift of attention from the "state" or central governmental structures to the domain of "civil society" seen as an arena of free human initiatives. This shift of focus is a prominent ingredient in recent Western political thought that, in this respect, has derived significant lessons from eastern European experiences (particularly the atrophy of society under totalitarian state bureaucracies). The shift brings into view a possible co-existence or symbiosis of religion and democracy without fusion or identification. Such a symbiosis would be able *both* to re-energize democracy by elevating its moral and spiritual fiber (its commitment to the public good) and to enliven and purify religion by rescuing it from conformism and the embroilment in public power. In Ricoeur's words, by renouncing domination or "religious despotism," religion would be capable of regaining its basic spiritual quality and thereby to serve as the "salt of the earth" or the salt of democracy.

In order to perform this role, religious discourse has to broaden its range and accommodate a more general humanistic vocabulary: especially the vocabulary of human rights, individual freedoms, and social justice. In our time, engagement or confrontation with these issues is indeed a requisite for the relevance and viability of religion (Islamic or otherwise). Discussion of human rights, one might say, belongs today to the domain of philosophical theology (*kalam*) and philosophy in general. Although not directly or not always nurtured by religious motives (at least in the modern era), human rights discourse is today religiously unavoidable, and a religious faith oblivious to human rights—as well as to human freedom and justice—is no longer tenable in the modern world. The tendency of many religious people to accentuate duties or obligations over rights should not be construed in a binary sense, but rather as a supplement or corrective to narrowly secular "rights talk." In a positive vein, religious discourse enriched by human rights vocabulary counteracts the pretense of "inalienable" *a priori* rights, sometimes termed *divine rights,* of public or clerical elites. In a religiously nurtured or inspired democracy—no less so than in a secular regime—rulers (including religious rulers) cannot be self-appointed but need to be approved through democratic methods or at least function within a democratically transparent structure.

In a remarkable recent study titled *Islam and the Secular State,* legal theorist Abdullahi Ahmed An-Na'im has elaborated on these issues in a lucid and exemplary manner. In the opening chapter of the study, An-Na'im reflects on the relation between Islamic faith and the modern "secular state," especially in a democratic context. As he asserts forcefully: "In order to be a Muslim by conviction and free choice, which is the only way one can be a Muslim, I need a secular state." By "secular state" he means a political regime that—in a free variation of the U.S. Bill of Rights—both prohibits the public "establishment" of religion and encourages the "free exercise" of faith. A secular state, he notes, is "one that is neutral [although not indifferent or hostile] regarding religion, one that does not claim or pretend to enforce *Shari'a*—the religious law of Islam—simply because compliance with *Shari'a* cannot be coerced by fear of state institutions or faked to appease their officials." At the same time, secularism for An-Nai'm denotes a regime that "facilitates the possibility of religious piety out of honest conviction" and "promotes genuine religious observance"—an observance operative primarily in civil society rather than on the level of formal state structures. With these formulations, *Islam and the Secular State* opposes both an overt "politicization" and restrictive "privatization" of faith. The stress on secularism, we read, does not mean "the exclusion of Islam from the formulation of public policy and legislation or from public life in general." On the contrary, "the state should not attempt to enforce *Shari'a* precisely so that Muslims are able to live by their own belief in Islam as a matter of religious obligation."[9]

An-Nai'm does not hide the complicated character of his approach; in fact, a certain tensional character seems to him constitutive of the relation between political power and religious faith. In large measure, this tension characterizes the distinction between the modern "state" and "civil society." As he notes, the state—in the sense of the modern, post-Westphalian public structure—has "its proper functions," which may include adjudication among competing claims of religious and secular institutions; but it should be seen as a "neutral institution" performing chiefly "secular functions" without claiming religious authority as such. Yet, in contrast to a strict "laïcism," he acknowledges that "the religious beliefs of Muslims" (whether as public officials or private citizens) are liable to "influence their actions and political behavior"—an influence that is bound to complicate the idea of a strict "neutrality" as employed by many Western liberal thinkers. On the one hand, in conformity with liberal tenets, "people cannot truly live by their convictions" if rulers use the "extensive coercive powers of the state" to impose religious doctrines. On the other hand, contesting these tenets, the state cannot be "completely neutral"—because as a public institution it is "supposed to be influenced by the interests and concerns of its citizens." Seen in this light, the modern principle of "the religious neutrality of the state" has an ambivalent or dual connotation: while mandating that state institutions should "neither favor nor disfavor any religious doctrine or belief," the real objective of such neutrality is precisely "the freedom of individuals in their communities to accept, object to, or modify any view of religious doctrine or principle."[10]

What emerges from these arguments is a highly mediated conception of the relation between politics and religion, a conception that is at odds with both their radical separation and their fusion. The stated aim of *Islam and the Secular State* is in fact to articulate and support the "difficult mediation of the paradox of institutional separation of Islam and the state, despite the unavoidable connection between Islam and politics [on the level of civil society] in present Islamic societies." In pursuing this aim, the study challenges two erroneous views: on the one hand, "the dangerous illusion of an Islamic state that claims the right to enforce *Shari'a* principles through its own coercive powers"; and on the other hand, "the dangerous illusion that Islam can or should be kept out of the public life of the community of believers." In An-Nai'm's opinion, it is "neither necessary nor desirable" that Islam and politics should be completely separated—just as their indiscriminate fusion is likely to lead to an autocratic or totalitarian nightmare. As he notes, separating Islam and the state while maintaining the connection between religion and social life is liable to generate respect for, and widespread observance of, Islamic teachings—an observance that today requires certain democratic safeguards. Precisely in a democracy, popular will-formation must take into account the beliefs and aspirations of ordinary citizens. Basically, democratic institutions cannot succeed "without the active and determined participation of all citizens—which is unlikely if people believe them to be inconsistent with the religious beliefs and cultural norms that influence their behavior." Yet, in a democracy, such beliefs and norms cannot be directly imposed by governmental fiat, but require mediated seasoning in the domain of civil society. In An-Nai'm's words, the motivations of ordinary citizens which are "partly influenced by their religious beliefs and cultural conditioning" must be suffused with "their appreciation of and commitment to the values of constitutionalism and human rights," including the rights of religious minorities and nonbelievers.[11]

With its subtle formulations and insights, *Islam and the Secular State* makes an important contribution to the deepening and transformation of prevalent contemporary conceptions of democracy—above all the "liberal" conception predicated on nothing but the pursuit and aggregation of individual interests (narrowly construed). Countering the reduction of politics to an economic calculus, the text in fact intimates the notion of an ethically and religiously sustained democratic life—a vision not far removed from the political thought of Alexis de Tocqueville, John Dewey, and many other Western thinkers. As one might add, An-Nai'm's voice is by no means alone in the confines of contemporary Islamic thought; a vision similar to his has been propounded somewhat earlier by the renowned Iranian philosopher Abdulkarim Soroush. Like An-Nai'm, Soroush strongly insists on the need to extricate religious faith from the coercive stranglehold of the government or the state. Surveying the history of Muslim societies, he bemoans the submissiveness of Muslims to political coercion, a submission due to "a political culture deeply influenced by centuries of tyranny." In traditional Islamic theology (*kalam*), he notes, God was portrayed as "an absolute bearer of rights and free of all duties toward human beings"; accordingly, kings and political rulers were viewed in the same light, as "God-like potentates with unlimited powers." This view—both politically and religiously obnoxious—has been challenged by modern democracy with its emphasis of human freedom and political agency. As a result of this challenge, human beings have been potentially liberated both as citizens and as believers, that is, enabled to perform political agency as well as cultivate freely their faith. In Soroush's words, freedom is a necessary requisite for the genuine cultivation of ethical and religious beliefs; it is,he says, "one of the components of justice," and the seeker of freedom is "in pursuit of justice" just as the seeker of justice "cannot help but pursue freedom as well."[12]

With this statement, Soroush intimates a democratic regime that is attentive and not indifferent toward ethics and religious beliefs—although the latter are no longer imposed by coercive power but freely nurtured in civil society. In Soroush's account, modern democracy is not simply aligned with arbitrary freedom but with the freedom to strive for justice and truth—targets that tend to be "extinguished" by despotism and autocratic regimes. For from being equivalent to the pursuit of narrow self-interest, democracy emerges here as a searching or "zetetic" enterprise, that is, as a transformative and constantly self-transforming regime in the direction of justice and the "good life." With this accent on transformation, Soroush (like An-

Nai'm) takes a stand against a version of "liberal democracy" which professes utter indifference or "neutrality" toward ethical and religious concerns. Some liberal thinkers, he observes, consider arguments in this domain "unverifiable and unfalsifiable," and hence pointless. As it happens, however, this kind of liberalism is by no means identical with democracy, or at least far from exhausting its meaning: "Equating liberalism and democracy signifies, at once, great ignorance of the former and grave injustice toward the latter." For Soroush, democratic regimes cannot be sustained without ethical and/or religious commitments, including respect for "the rights of others, justice, sympathy, and mutual trust." In this respect, democracy owes a "great debt" to genuine religious faith, and the latter can be seen as "the best guarantor of democracy." As one should note well, however, religious faith in the context of democracy cannot be coercive or uniform, but must be open to the diversity of faiths as well as the outlook of nonbelievers. Hence, for both political and religious reasons, Soroush's mode of democracy embraces pluralism: "The faithful community is more like a wild grove than a manufactured garden."[13]

The arguments of An-Nai'm and Soroush bring something else clearly into view: the likely diversity of possible democratic regimes. In discussions of modernity and modernization, it has become customary in recent years to acknowledge the possibility of diverse paths of modernization and hence of differentiated or "multiple" modernities in different parts of the world.[14] A similar acknowledgment is called for in the case of modern democracy. Given the fact that democratic life is nurtured by the motivations and aspirations of ordinary citizens, and that these aspirations in turn reflect the religious beliefs and cultural customs of people, it follows that democracies cannot be the same everywhere but are bound to vary in accordance with beliefs and customs prevalent in different societies or regions.[15] Thus, it is plausible to speak (as some writers have done) of "democracy with Confucian characteristics" or else of "democracy with Buddhist characteristics." There is no compelling reason to deny the possibility of the emergence of democracies with chiefly "Islamic characteristics" (in fact An-Nai'm's book discusses a number of cases fitting or approximating this description, such as the democracies in Turkey and Indonesia). To this one might add that none of the existing Western democracies are identical with regard to their social fabric and animating "spirit of laws." To be sure, such differentiation cannot be limitless if regimes are to qualify as "democratic." Hence, some benchmarks or constitutional safeguards have clearly to be observed. Among these benchmarks are the absence of coercive autocratic structures, the freedom of association and religious practices, and the respect for the plurality of beliefs and disbeliefs. Perhaps most important, however, is the "love of equality" extolled by Montesquieu as the distinguishing trademark of democracy.

A Modest Proposal

By way of conclusion, I may be allowed to venture a proposal designed to exemplify both the limit and the broad range of possible variations in a democracy. The proposal concerns specifically the Islamic Republic of Iran. As I understand the constitutional structure of Iran, there are presently two tiers of institutions that operate in tension and possible conflict with each other: a "democratic" component consisting of an elected parliament (Majlis) and an elected president; and a more or less "theocratic" component consisting of the "Council of Guardians" or "Trusteeship of Jurists" (*velayat-i-faqih*) whose members are unelected religious authorities. Hence, there is a structure juxtaposing democracy and theocracy in an unmediated fashion. The radical difference between these two components is liable to pull the country in opposite directions, with potential harm to its welfare and stability.[16]

As an antidote to this structural conflict, I suggest a way of building a bridge and reconciling the two components: namely, by transforming the "Council of Guardians" into an upper chamber after the model of the British House of Lords. Britain is recognized as a leading example of modern Western democracy; and yet, its House of Lords is not an elected body and includes, next to hereditary peers, leading figures of the Anglican Church. If this model were adopted in Iran, the Council as an upper chamber could be given equal legislative powers with the Majlis; or else it could be given a merely delaying and advisory power (as is the case in the House of Lords today). Whichever power would be allocated, the Council reconstituted as an upper chamber would greatly contribute to the visibility and transparency of the governmental process. The restructuring would help to reconcile the presently opposed components of the constitution, and would thereby strengthen the legitimacy of the entire government. This, in turn, would lead to a more open and peaceful development of the country—something that both Iranians and friends of Iran can only welcome and applaud.

I am under no illusions regarding the difficulties or prospects of implementing this "modest" proposal. My intent here is simply to trigger some discussion, leaving it to the wisdom and discretion of competent authorities and specialists to determine its concrete fate. I do believe, however, that the proposal is not outside of the line of political prudence as cultivated by both Western and Islamic traditions. It may also be that the proposal is particularly in line with the Shia tradition of religious faith where religious political power is deliberately deferred (as a tribute to the "hidden" Imam)[17]—a tradition that is not too far removed from Jewish messianic hope and the Christian expectation of the "coming kingdom."

10

Beyond Minimal Democracy

Voices from East and West

Heraclitus notwithstanding, history is not just random flux. Apart from its great or memorable events, every historical period also pays tribute to certain guideposts or guiding ideas—what skeptics call its *idola fori* or idols of the marketplace. Looking at our contemporary age, it is not difficult to pinpoint a guiding, and probably *the* guiding idea endorsed almost universally by people around the world: that of "liberal democracy." Although originating in Western societies, the idea today is circulating as an orienting loadstar among people in Africa, the Middle East as well as South and East Asia. As can readily be seen, the guidepost is actually a composite phrase combining the two terms *liberal* and *democracy*. Yet, despite the possibility of differentiation, the two terms in recent times have been basically conflated or amalgamated—with the result that, in the view of both ordinary people and leading intellectuals, the "democratic" component has become redundant or been absorbed without a rest in the dominant "liberal" idea. This conflation is particularly evident in, and traceable to, modern economics (with its own idols of the "market"). In large measure, the ongoing process of globalization is fueled by the idea of "neo-liberalism"—a version of the liberal tradition that insists on "downsizing" political (including democratic) oversight for the sake of promoting individual or corporate "free enterprise."

This preponderance of liberal or neo-liberal agendas is by no means fortuitous. Taking a broad view, the entire trajectory of modern Western history can be seen as a movement of progressive human liberation, above all liberation from clerical and autocratic modes of control. This trajectory was present already in the work of Thomas Hobbes, in his rupture with classical and medieval conceptions of community. The movement was carried forward by John Locke with

his accent on the persistence of "natural rights"—especially the right
to equal liberty—in the confines of an established commonwealth.
The latter emphasis was deepened and fleshed out by later liberal
thinkers, like John Stuart Mill and Benjamin Constant—whose arguments in favor of minimal government (*laissez-faire*) were by then
powerfully buttressed by the rise of capitalism and modern market
economics. Small wonder that, in view of this long-standing trajectory,
individual freedom became at last a catchword or shibboleth. As we
know, the Western world calls itself, somewhat boastfully, the "Free
World," and America celebrates itself as the "land of the free." As a
corollary of this development, democracy as a political regime has
come to be equated with an arena of free individual choice—that is,
with liberal or libertarian democracy. But how plausible is this outcome? Has freedom in the modern world completely replaced such
traditional categories as virtue and the "good life"—with the result
that Aristotle's distinction between just and unjust regimes would be
leveled into that between free and unfree forms of life?

In the following, I pursue this line of thought. First, I briefly
recapitulate arguments (mentioned in the opening chapter), favoring
liberal democracy in the sense of a minimal or minimalist democracy.
Subsequently, I examine efforts to correct this liberal conception,
turning first to the South Asian and next to the East Asian context.
By way of conclusion, I review the relation between liberalism and
democracy, invoking chiefly arguments of such American thinkers as
Walter Lippmann and John Dewey.

Minimal Liberal Democracy

As previously indicated, liberalism has a long history in the course
of which it has assumed many different shapes and shadings. During
the early period, the time of Hobbes and Locke, liberalism—in the
sense of the defense of "natural" individual rights—served precariously as an adjunct or supplement to monarchical and even absolutist
regimes. In the post-revolutionary era, liberalism became affiliated
with various republican or democratic regimes—but in such a manner that the latter would progressively be trumped by the former
(a development in which, as stated, the rise of capitalism played a
major role). In the opinion of nineteenth-century liberals, the role
of government—including democratic government—was meant to
be minimal: seen chiefly as protectors of private property, political
regimes were said to govern best when governing least. The dismal

experiences of the twentieth century with populist and totalitarian governments have reinforced the liberal preference for political or public minimalism—despite occasional concessions to "welfare" programs during times of economic hardship. As a result of these experiences and developments, the notion of individual freedom has come to be equated preponderantly with "negative liberty" (to use Isaiah Berlin's phrase) or the freedom to be left alone—with only limited allowance made for active or "positive freedom" (mainly on the level of voting rights and lobbying). In his study of John Dewey (who opposed this entire trend), Raymond Boisvert has sketched the stereotype of the minimalist liberal: "an individual with no roots and little connectedness to community; . . . a highly competitive individual fixated on narrow purposes whose practice is marked by expedience rather than conventional ethics."[1]

On a sophisticated level, aspects of democratic minimalism can be found even in the writings of theorists or intellectuals otherwise strongly committed to democratic politics. As stated in the opening chapter, an example is Robert Dahl's celebrated text *A Preface to Democratic Theory* (first published in 1956). In the very introduction to his study, Dahl delineates two basic approaches in this field: a "maximizing" theory (relying either on ethical principles or formal axioms) and a purely "descriptive-empirical" and to that extent minimalizing approach. Traditional political theory, he notes, has tended to be "maximizing" by emphasizing "internal checks"—such as conscience and ethical dispositions—to restrain possible excesses of governmental power. This approach, however, has gone out of fashion since the revolutionary period and, in America, since the writings of James Madison. From Madison's perspective, the traditional ethical approach was simply no longer viable given the increasingly competitive and interest-based character of modern politics.[2] Another example of a democratic theorist leaning in the minimalist direction is Giovanni Sartori, well known for his text *The Theory of Democracy Revisited*. Like Dahl's study, Sartori's text distinguishes at the outset between a "prescriptive" or normative conception and a "descriptive" or empirical conception—with the latter version involving greatly reduced demands on democratic politics. In his view, to introduce normative expectations is likely to overburden the democratic regime such as to render it unviable. In view of the alleged danger associated with public ethics, Sartori prefers to employ "minimalist" language and to leave phrases like "political morality, social morality, professional ethics" aside. Democracy or "democratic machinery" coincides for him—and many other empirical theorists—with voting behavior, pursuit of individual interests through pressure groups and political parties, and public policymaking on the basis of these interests.[3]

An even more resolutely minimalist approach is propagated by a perspective that, in recent times, has increasingly gained prominence in the social sciences: rational choice theory. This outlook basically transfers neo-classical economic assumptions to social and political life. As can readily be seen, what is jeopardized or called into question by this model is not only public ethics, but also politics, particularly democratic politics, as such. For, even when seen as a minimally shared regime, democracy is bound to be a burden or hindrance for the ambitions of an unrestrained economic agenda. No one has articulated this burden more forcefully than William Riker, a founder of this model, in his book *Liberalism Against Populism* (1982). As Riker states at the outset: "The theory of social [or rational] choice is a theory about the way the tastes, preferences, or values of individual persons are amalgamated and summarized into the choice of a collective group or society." Because these preferences are not ethically ranked, the primary focus is on something measurable or quantifiable: in economics monetary profit, in politics "the theory of voting" that is the core of liberal (or libertarian) democracy, barring any interference with voting preferences. Like Dahl, Riker distinguishes between a normative-ethical and an empirical or "analytical" conception of politics—placing rational choice clearly in the second category.[4]

Again like Dahl, although with modified accents, Riker delineates two different genealogies of modern democracy: a "liberal or Madisonian" type and a "populist or Rousseauistic" type. In the liberal (or libertarian) version, he notes, "the function of voting is to control officials, and *nothing else*." By contrast, "populists"—presumably following Rousseau—desire a more active, participatory role of the people and a polities that creates "a moral and collective body" endowed with "life and will," especially the (in)famous "general will." At this point, Riker endorses whole-heartedly Isaiah Berlin's notion of "negative liberty" and his indictment that "positive liberty, which appears initially innocuous, is the root of tyranny" or oppression. Tellingly, Riker also alludes to some ideological background—not unaffected by the geopolitics of the Cold War. "No government," he asserts, "that has eliminated economic freedom has been able to attain or keep democracy." On the other hand, "economic liberty is also an end in itself because capitalism is the driving force for the increased efficiency and technological innovation that has produced in two centuries both a vast increase in the wealth of capitalist nations and a doubling of the average life span of their citizens."[5]

Beyond Minimalism: Voices From South Asia

In large measure, liberal democracy—in the sense of a minimalist, libertarian regime (or nonregime)—tends to occupy center stage in recent Western social and political thought. As it is important to note, however, this has not always been the case. During important phases of Western political development, minimalist liberal democracy has been criticized or contested by able thinkers and public intellectuals. One such phase was the American colonial period when the Puritan John Winthrop proposed the formation of an ethical-communitarian republic in Massachusetts Bay. Another, post-revolutionary phase was the era of "Jacksonian democracy" when the ideal of an egalitarian republic was pitted against the *laissez-faire* ambitions of the emerging manufacturing elite (epitomized by the Bank of America). On a theoretical or philosophical plane, however, the most important development was the rise of "pragmatism" in the late nineteenth century, and especially John Dewey's eloquent defense of "radical" democracy as an antidote to *laissez-faire* liberalism. In Boisvert's words: for Dewey "democracy as an ideal for community life is not a mere provision for a minimal state that simply leaves citizens alone. Such an individualistic ideal is inimical to the kind of *associated* living which is democratic." To quote Dewey himself: "The clear consciousness of a communal life, in all its implications, constitutes the idea of democracy."[6]

For present purposes, given the contemporary global expansion of liberal (or neo-liberal) democracy, I turn my attention to non-Western intellectual contexts. An important context of this kind is South Asia and particularly India, the home of the Mahatma Gandhi. As is well known, Gandhi was not only an astute politician or public leader but also a thinker or intellectual with deep insight into public affairs, including the requisites of democracy. On the latter issue he has pronounced himself repeatedly, but perhaps most forcefully and pithily in his early book of 1909 titled *Hind Swaraj* (*Indian Home Rule*). In this text, Gandhi takes to task forms of democracy found in Western countries that are often upheld as shining models to the rest of the world. Concentrating his attention particularly on the British model, he delineates a long list of shortcomings or defects, ranging from the venality of parliament, or its subservience to vested interests, to the fluctuating whims of public opinion under the impact of power-hungry politicians or businessmen. Surveying these and a host of related blemishes, Gandhi does not hesitate to trace the malaise to a central underlying cause: the unrestrained pursuit of self-interest and self-indulgence, at the cost of shared ethical commitments to the public good. To be sure, as he acknowledges, modern life—even life in corrupt democracies—has brought greater freedom for many people in different strata of society; this advance, however, is marred and nearly eclipsed by prevailing abuses. In terms of *Hind Swaraj*, the main problem is the sway of self-centered materialism, the fact that people in the modern West "make bodily welfare the [sole] object of life."[7]

The remedy proposed in *Hind Swaraj* for this state of affairs is precisely self-rule or "*swaraj*"—which does not mean selfish rule or promotion of self-centered ambitions, but rather the ability to rein in such ambitions for the benefit of the common good, that is, the good of all people. As Gandhi points out, egocentrism or individual self-seeking is contrary not only to ethical and spiritual "rightness" (one sense of *dharma*) but also to the teachings of practically all the great religions of the world—including (next to Hinduism) Christianity, Islam, Judaism, and Zoroastrianism (he might have added Buddhism). What all these religions try to teach us, he writes, is "that we should remain passive [or reticent] about worldly pursuits and active about godly [or ethical] pursuits, that we should set a limit to our worldly ambitions, and that our religious [or *dharmic*] ambitions should be illimitable." Despite differences of accent or detail, all religions and ethical-spiritual paths can thus be seen as "different roads converging to the same point." In Gandhi's terse formulation: "Civilization is that mode of conduct which points out to human beings the path of duty. Performance of ethical duty . . . means to attain mastery over our mind and our passions. In so doing, we come to know ourselves." Even more importantly: in so doing, we come to rule ourselves both as individuals and as people. The clear implication of this view is a new understanding of democracy: in the sense not of the pursuit of individual or collective self-interest but of a transformative popular self-rule (i.e., rule of people over themselves) or *swaraj*: "It is *swaraj* when we learn to rule ourselves."[8]

Although composed relatively early in his life (and during an arduous sea voyage from London to South Africa), the basic tenets of *Hind Swaraj* remained firm guideposts during Gandhi's mature years. Although willing to revise minor details, he never disavowed his early text; in fact, he reconfirmed its central argument on repeated occasions in subsequent years. A few examples should suffice to document this continuity. In his "Constructive Program" submitted to the Indian National Congress in 1941, Gandhi strongly reaffirmed his commitment to *swaraj*, explaining the meaning of the term as denoting "complete independence through truth [*satya*] and nonviolence [*ahimsa*]" and "without distinction of race, color or creed." A letter written to Jawaharlal Nehru a few years later made explicit reference to the text of 1909, stating: "I have said that I still stand by the system of government envisaged in *Hind Swaraj*." In retrospect, what appeared to Gandhi as the central lesson of his book was the emphasis on ethical self-rule and self-restraint, on a conception of individual and public agency performed within the limits of rightness or truth (*satya*) and nonviolent generosity toward others. The most dramatic and direct application of the idea of *swaraj* came in his "Quit India" speech delivered in Bombay in 1942. In that speech, Gandhi—now the leader of a nationwide *satyagraha* (civil resistance relying on "truth power")—contrasted his vision of Indian self-rule with the kind of freedom and political rulership found in Britain and the Western world, saying:

> I do not regard England, or for that matter America, as free countries. They are free after their own fashion: free to hold in bondage the colored races of the earth. . . . According to my own interpretation of that freedom, I am constrained to say: they are strangers to that freedom which their [own] poets and teachers have described.[9]

Profiled against dominant Western approaches, Gandhi's idea of *swaraj* discloses a conception of democracy—an ethical conception—sharply at variance with interest-based models of liberal or libertarian democracy. Despite his fondness for Western writers like Ruskin, Thoreau, and Tolstoy, Gandhi was not a radical individualist (in the modern "liberal" sense) ready to separate a vast arena of private freedom from a narrowly circumscribed, perhaps minimalist, public-democratic domain. Faithful to older philosophical traditions (both in India and the West), he preferred to stress a qualitative distinction between modes of human and political conduct—a distinction that cannot readily collapsed into modern private–public or internal–external polarities. Without blandly fusing individual and society or subordinating one to the other, his thought was able to hold the two elements in fruitful, perhaps tensional balance. This aspect is clearly shown in another letter Gandhi wrote to Nehru in 1945. Picking up Nehru's suggestion regarding the importance of human and social development, he fully agreed that it was crucial to "bring about man's highest intellectual, economic, political and moral development," that is, the "flourishing" of all human abilities. The basic issue was how to accomplish this goal. For Gandhi this was impossible without thorough attention to rightness (*dharma*) and without social engagement and responsibility. Echoing Aristotle, and countering the modern Western focus on self-centered individualism carried over from an atomistic "state of nature" into society, he wrote: "Man is not born to live in isolation but is essentially a social animal independent *and* interdependent. No one can or should ride on another's back." A similar view was expressed in an interview in summer 1946 in which Gandhi stated that, although the individual does count in important ways, this "does not exclude dependence and willing help from neighbors or from the world. It will be a free and voluntary play of mutual forces."[10]

In speaking of interconnectedness and the "play of mutual forces" Gandhi displays an affinity with the spirit of Jamesian and Deweyan pragmatism. But the parallel can be carried further. Like William James and Dewey, and perhaps even more emphatically, Gandhi was an ethical and spiritual pragmatist, in the great tradition of Indian spirituality. As is well known, the most important source of inspiration for Gandhi throughout his life was the *Bhagavad Gita*, a text that delineates several paths (or *yogas*) guiding toward liberation and blessedness (in the sense of flourishing). Among these paths, Gandhi deliberately chose the path of action or *praxis* (*karma yoga*) demanding continuous ethical engagement in the affairs of the world. Again like Dewey, he did not assume that human beings are free and equal by nature (or in an original "state of nature"); rather freedom and equality for him were achievements requiring steady practice—a practice involving not only change of outward conditions but primarily self-transformation. In Gandhi's own words, freedom is not an instant boon, but is "attained only by constant heart-churn" or self-giving in service to others. As Ramashray Roy explains, in his thoughtful book *Self and Society*, *karma yoga* for Gandhi was not just a form of activism or worldly busy-ness, but rather a soteriological path or a process of sanctification that sees performance of action as sacred duty: "This sacred duty lies in exerting oneself to the benefit of others, that is, service."[11] Viewed from this angle, achievement of self-rule or *swaraj* involves self-transcendence and a diligent training in the ways of freedom. In a manner akin to Deweyan political thought, pursuit of liberating paths (or *yogas*) demands steady practice and habituation, facilitated by sound education. In a more directly Aristotelian view, such practice revolves around the nurturing of a set of virtues—which Gandhi reformulated under the rubric of ethical and spiritual "vows" (*yamas*).

Comparing Gandhian *swaraj* with dominant forms of modern Western thought, the differences care stark and obvious. What needs to be noted right away is the distance of *swaraj* from prevalent modern conceptions of freedom: those of "negative" and "positive" liberty. In this binary scheme, negative liberty basically designates the freedom to be left alone (i.e, liberalism's retreat into private self-satisfaction), whereas positive liberty denotes the unhampered pursuit of collective goals—a pursuit sometimes shading over into social engineering on behalf of ideological panaceas. As can readily be seen, neither of these options shows kinship with Gandhian *swaraj*. Even when highly spiritualized, negative liberty still bears traces of individual self-centeredness, whereas the positive type—in stressing worldly activism—seems ignorant of self-restraint, releasement, and nonattachment to the fruits of action. This distance is clearly pinpointed by Ramashray Roy. As he observers, negative liberty insists on social aloofness, on the retreat into a private realm often coinciding with selfishness or the wanton "satisfaction of desires." On the other hand, while emphasizing social and political engagement, positive liberty sidesteps the task of self-curtailment and self-transcendence by extolling the benefits of collectively chosen goals. For Roy, it was "Ghandi's genius" to have squarely faced this dilemma and have shown an exit from this binary dilemma. The central point of Gandhian *swaraj*, he notes, was the emphasis on self-rule as a transformative process—whereby people are able to rule not so much over others than over themselves.[12]

The arguments regarding freedom or liberty can readily be transferred to the basic meaning of democracy. The difference between Gandhian *swaraj* and the liberal-minimalist conception of democracy has been ably highlighted by the Gandhi-scholar Ronald Terchek, especially in his essay titled "Gandhi and Democratic Theory." Right at the outset Terchek states the crux of the matter: that democracy for Gandhi was not merely "procedural" or minimal but "substantive" in the sense of being grounded in a nonoppressive way of life. He cites Gandhi himself to the effect that, under democracy, "the weakest should have the same opportunity as the strongest. And this can never happen except through [political, social, and psychological] nonviolence."[13] Basically, for the Mahatma, democracy is a regime not organized or imposed "from the top down" (or from the state down) but one nurtured "from the bottom up." This explains his emphasis on village life and village self-government (through councils or *panchayats*) as well as on economic decentralization and local industries.

In Terchek's presentation, Gandhi believed that the means of production (at least of the basic necessaries of life) should remain ultimately in the hands of the people—and not be relinquished or alienated to corporate elites. In contrast to the rampant competition unleashed

by the capitalist market, he stressed the need to cultivate coopera-
tive dispositions so that the brute "struggle for survival" would be
transmuted into a "struggle for mutual service" or "mutual existence."
Such dispositions, in turn, presuppose the fostering of mutual respect
and the practice of such civic virtues as interpersonal and intergroup
tolerance or recognition. As Terchek observes, paraphrasing Gandhi's
own arguments: "Tolerance implies a mutual regard for others; and
if it is missing, the [bottom-up] dialogue of the democratic process is
diminished, if not destroyed." Gandhi in India, he adds perceptively,
"like Dewey in America, saw dialogue as necessary to both individual
growth and to the democratic prospect. Indeed, democracy received
one of its primary justifications from Dewey because it promoted
tolerance and fostered development."[14]

The central point of Terchek's essay is the differentiation of the
Gandhian approach from (what he calls) "the dominant model of
democracy today," which relies on the unhampered pursuit of self-
interest and, politically, on competitive elections where voters choose
delegates maximally committed to promoting their interest. From
the latter (liberal-minimalist) perspective, interests are individually
generated and by no means in a "pre-established harmony." Among
a larger group of people, pursuit of self-interest is liable to lead to
strife or conflict—whose settlement is secured either through shallow
compromise or the intervention of sovereign power. For Gandhi, such
settlement is defective under democratic auspices. As Terchek shows,
democratic life for him required "both freedom and interdepenence"
and the two could only be sustained through ethical dispositions cultivated over time. Moreover, on both the individual and group levels,
it was necessary to distinguish genuine needs from private "interests"
that are often artificially created by the media (and privilege "greed"
over need). Apart from stressing some Deweyan affinities, Terchek
also links Gandhi's thought with aspects of the "civic republican"
tradition from Cicero to the present. In his words: civic republicans
believed "that freedom could be secured only if people restrained
themselves. . . . Accordingly, they attempted to disperse power, insti-
tutionalize cooperation, emphasize service, and promote widespread
participation" in the political process. Differently phrased, for republicans as well as Gandhi, democracy was predicated on self-rule (in
the sense of *swaraj*) and a nondomineering type of public agency—an
agency captured by the Gandhian labels of nonviolence (*ahimsa*) and
"truth-force" (*satyagraha*).[15]

An argument along similar lines has been presented by the Indian
political theorist Thomas Pantham, in his article "Beyond Liberal

Democracy: Thinking with Mahatma Gandhi." As Pantham points out, Gandhi repeatedly criticized the liberal democratic model—its "objectification and technocratization of the political" (in the state) and its concomitant "alienation of the people's political rights" (by reducing such rights to private interests). The alternative he put forward was that of *swaraj* that, in addition to self-rule, can also be translated as "participatory democracy" where the gulf between "subject and object," between ruler and ruled is erased. For Gandhi, modern liberal thought was based largely on a "one-dimensional conception" of human beings as self-contained and self-seeking creatures whose pursuit of selfish ends could only be tamed by power and nonmoral force. It was impossible in his view to escape "the inherent contradictions" of this model "without abandoning the liberal-individualistic conception of humanity and the atomistic, amoral conception of its interests." The escape route he proposed was reliance on "truth-doing" (*satyagraha*) and nonviolence (*ahimsa*) as "the most important moral norms"—norms that are "not cloistered virtues" but to be discovered and formed through "the ordinary activities of life" in the social, economic, and political spheres. Once these norms are widely cultivated and taken to heart, a different version of democracy comes into view, one in which freedom and interdependence are closely linked. To quote a statement by Gandhi, written in 1946 and carrying distinct Deweyan (and Aristotelian) echoes:

> I value individual freedom, but you must not forget that man is essentially a social being. He has risen to the present status by learning to adjust his individualism to the requirements of social progress. Unrestricted individualism is the law of the beast of the jungle. We have learnt to strike the mean between individual freedom and social restraint.[16]

Beyond Minimalism: Voices From East Asia

When turning from India to East Asia, similar reservations regarding liberal democracy can readily be found. The critique of radical individualism proceeds there mainly (although not exclusively) on Confucian premises, a philosophy well known for its emphasis on human relationships. Given the essential relatedness of human beings, freedom for Confucians cannot mean either internal retreat or external manipulation and domination. This point is eloquently made by the Chinese-American scholar Tu Weiming. As he observes, Confucianism basically opposes the binary scheme of negative and positive liberty, that is, the construal of freedom in terms of either private self-withdrawal or domineering self-enhancement. "It rejects," he writes, "both an introspective affirmation of the self as an isolable and complacent ego *and* an unrestrained attachment to the external world for the sake of a limitless expansion of one's manipulative power." In lieu of these alternatives, the Confucian "way" or "*tao*"—akin to Gandhian *swaraj*—involves an "unceasing process of self-transformation as a communal act," and thus a linkage of ethics and social engagement whose seasoning effect "can ultimately free us from the constrictions of the privatized ego." As can readily be seen, human freedom from this angle is limited or circumscribed not by the state or external procedures but by the ability of ethical transformation, that is, the ability of people to rule themselves rather than ruling others.[17]

In addition to social engagement and connectedness, Confucianism also fosters the relatedness between human beings and nature as well as the "mutuality between man and Heaven." Ultimately, Tu Weiming notes, the Confucian trajectory points to the human reconciliation with "Heaven, Earth, and the myriad things"—with clearly spiritual or religious connotations. In an instructive manner, he also points to the Confucian stress on exemplification, that is, the need not merely to hold fine theories but to exemplify them in daily conduct. Despite his deep modesty, Confucius himself can be seen, and was seen, as an "exemplar" or "exemplary person" (*chün-tzu*) who taught the "way" not through abstract doctrines but through the testimony of responsible daily living. At this point, the affinity with Deweyan philosophy comes clearly into view—a fact that is perhaps not surprising given Dewey's extended visit to China after World War I.[18] As in the case of Gandhian *swaraj*, leading a responsible life in society involves self-restraint and the abandonment of domineering impulses. In Confucius's own words, humaneness or to be properly human (*jen*) means "to conquer oneself (*k'e-chi*) and to return to propriety (*fu-li*)." As Tu Weiming comments, however, the notion of "conquering oneself" should not be misconstrued in the sense of self-erasure in favor of heteronomous forces. The Confucian idea, he writes, does not mean "that one should engage in a bitter struggle" of conquest; rather the concept of *k'e-chi* is "closely linked to the concept of self-cultivation (*hsiu-shen*)" or self-transformation and hence to the task of responsible and responsive social agency.[19]

More difficult to assess is the relation of Confucian thought to modern democracy seen as popular self-rule and self-government. In large measure, the difficulty arises from the fact that, in contrast to the Gandhian legacy, traditional Confucianism is silent on democracy and the political implications of human agency. This silence is often taken as evidence of the utter incompatibility of Confucian teachings and democratic regimes. In the words of the China-scholar Ni Peinim: "The dominant view today still holds that Confucianism and democracy are like water and fire, totally incompatible and antagonistic to each other." According to this view, the former is "authoritarian, repressive, and typically associated with totalitarian policies, uniformity of ideology, social hierarchy, and discrimination against women"—while democracy is "the very opposite."[20] In a similar vein, Wm. Theodore deBary has pointed out that, during much of the twentieth century, Confucianism "was made to stand for all that was backward and benighted in China: it bore all the burden of the past, charged with innumerable sins of the old order." When in 1989—he adds—the "Goddess of Democracy" was publicly displayed in Tian-anmen Square, the display was a revolt not only against Communist repression but also against the older Confucian tradition.[21] In this context, traditional Confucian sayings like "The common people are the root or foundation of society" (from the *Shujing*) are widely regarded as pious placebos devoid of concrete political connotations.

At this point, it becomes important to ask what precisely is at issue. Does the claimed incompatibility prevail between Confucianism and democracy *tout court*, or between the former and a certain kind of liberalism or liberal democracy? In the latter case, the meaning of "liberal" and "liberalism" becomes decisive. Do these terms refer to the ethical kind of liberalism that can be traced from Montesquieu and Hegel all the way to Dewey's definition of democracy as an ethical community? Or do we mean the self-seeking, *laissez-faire* liberalism that ultimately reduces social life to an atomistic state of nature? In the former case—making room for creative adjustments—it seems quite possible to envisage a harmony between Confucianism and modern democracy. In the latter case, harmony or compatibility is clearly excluded—but only because self-centered liberalism is at variance with democracy as such (or only allows for minimalist democracy). The need for a creative adjustment or rethinking of traditional teachings is today acknowledged by many Confucian scholars, especially by such "New Confucians" as Tu Weiming and Liu Shu-hsien. As the latter has aptly stated: "We have to reject the tradition in order to reaffirm the ideal of the tradition."[22] However, such a rethinking of Confucian teachings also requires, as a complementary move, a rethinking of prevalent modern Western ideas—away from the egocentric preferences of democratic minimalism in the direction of a responsible democratic *ethos*. As it appears to me, such a double rethinking is admirably manifest in the writings of the China-scholar Henry Rosemont Jr.

In several of his texts, Rosemont has eloquently castigated the notion of an egocentric individualism patterned on capitalist economics. As he writes at one point (in a passage with patent Deweyan echoes): "For most of the world's peoples, there are no disembodied minds, nor autonomous individuals; human relationships govern and structure most of our lives, to the point that unless there are at least two human beings, there can be no human being." As one should note, however, this critique of egocentrism does not induce Rosemont to reject democracy as such. As he states in one of his more well-known writings, *The Chinese Mirror*, what he is proposing or suggesting is not a return to autocracy but rather "a somewhat different philosophical view of democracy"—a view more in line with an ethical conception of both liberalism and democracy.[23] The concrete contours of this alternative view are spelled out by Rosemont in another text that intriguingly joins Confucian "relationism" with the pragmatic account of a shared way of life. From this alternative perspective, he states, democracy—including an ethically liberal democracy—might be described as a regime in which every member has the right and duty "to participate in public affairs" and "to take the public welfare of all the other members of society as one's own." As one can see, democracy here is elevated to the height of the vision of a Montesquieu, de Tocqueville, and Dewey. To conclude with another passage from *The Chinese Mirror*, even more distinctly Deweyan in orientation: in a properly constituted democratic community, "the desired would not be equated with the desirable, and democratic participation—being a citizen—would involve engaging in collective dialogue about the appropriate means for achieving agreed-upon ends."[24]

Concluding Remarks

In the preceding pages, I have delineated critiques of liberal-minimalist democracy, focusing on Gandhian and Confucian teachings. These critical voices could readily be expanded or multiplied. One of the noteworthy developments in Asia in recent decades has been the upsurge of a "new" kind of Buddhism, an outlook that shifts the earlier accent on monastic retreat in the direction of a more worldly engagement and participation. Here again, the twin pitfalls of negative and positive liberty are bypassed (at least in intent). While transgressing the bounds of a purely internal liberation, the turn to engagement carefully steers clear of public manipulation or the pursuit of social blueprints, thus maintaining the central Buddhist focus on "self-emptying" (*sunyata*) and self-transcendence (toward others).[25] Under very different auspices and in a different idiom, tendencies pointing in a similar direction can also be found in strands of contemporary Islamic thought (as shown in the preceding chapter). In this context, the traditional biblical injunction to "pursue justice" above everything else still serves as a powerful incentive to foster an ethically vibrant public life. However, contrary to "fundamentalist" misconstruals, this incentive does not automatically translate into theocracy or clerical despotism. As indicated before, the idea of a basic compatibility of Islam and democracy has been defended in recent times by a number of able intellectuals, from Muhammad Iqbal to Abdulaziz Sachedina and Abdulkarim Soroush. In Soroush's words: "No blessing is more precious for mankind than the free choice of the way of the prophets. . . . But in the absence of this state of grace, nothing is better for humankind than [democratic] freedom. Because all free societies, whether religious or nonreligious, are properly humane."[26]

To be sure, the critique of public minimalism is not restricted to non-Western contexts. On the contrary, some of the most eloquent critical voices have been precisely Western and, in fact, American. Just a few years ago, the American political theorist Michael Sandel issued a plea for a renewed "public philosophy" that would reconnect ethics and politics. What stands in the way of such a renewal, in his account, is the predominance of, what he calls, the "voluntarist conception of freedom," that is, the *laissez-faire* ideology of untrammeled self-seeking, which dispenses with the "difficult task" of cultivating civic dispositions. As an antidote to this ideology, Sandel pleads in favor of a "formative politics" concerned with the formation of ethical civic attitudes and practices; for (he says) "to share in self-rule requires that citizens possess, or come to acquire, certain civic virtues."[27] In issuing this plea, of course, Sandel stands on the shoulders of a series of earlier American thinkers, including the journalist and public intellectual Walter Lippmann. Some seventy years ago, Lippmann had denounced the spreading cult of egocentric will power in economics and politics. As he noted in *The Good Society*, Western modernity had derailed when it moved to equate freedom with individual self-seeking. In opposition to this equation—the "doctrine of *laissez-faire*, let her rip, and the devil take the hindmost"—Lippmann invoked an older tradition of ethical liberalism congruent with public obligations. Borrowing a leaf from Aristotle as well as American pragmatism, his text observed: "There must be [in democracy] an habitual, confirmed, and well-nigh intuitive dislike of arbitrariness. . . . There must be a strong desire to be just. [And] there must be a growing capacity to be just."[28]

However, the strongest American voice against the derailment into *laissez-faire* minimalism was John Dewey. As I have stated repeatedly, Dewey was relentless in critiquing a reckless individualism and in upholding social "relationism" and the need for civic bonds. As one should note well, his animus was directed not against liberalism as such, but against a minimalist version incompatible with democratic self-rule. Likewise, his target was not individual liberty (or individual selfhood) per se, but only its imprisonment in the Cartesian fortress of the "ego cogito." In the words of Raymond Boisvert: Whereas old-style individualism connotes "both isolation and self-interestedness," "individuality" in the revised Deweyan sense identifies "the distinctive manner in which someone participates in communal life"; it recognizes "the irreducibility of community and the multiple perspectives associated with it."[29] Such individuality and the multiple perspectives to which it gives rise are not opposed to, but actually constitutive of democratic life. Above all, what needs to be remembered is that, for Dewey, democracy is not a finished state, but an ongoing process of democratizing pointing toward rich untapped horizons. Democracy, he states at one point, is "an end that has not been adequately realized in any country at any time. It is radical because it requires great change in existing social institutions, economic, legal and cultural." To this might be added his observation that, under democratic auspices, "the supreme test of all political institutions and industrial arrangements shall be the contribution they make to the all-round growth [or better: flourishing] of every member of society."[30]

Returning to the theme of self-rule or *swaraj*, it is clear that growth or flourishing cannot mean simply the enlargement of power or managerial control. Rather, to be ethically tenable, democratic self-rule has to involve a practice of self-restraint and self-transformation (even self-emptying) capable of instilling the habit of nonviolence (*ahimsa*) and generous openness toward others. As Dewey once remarked, in a very Gandhian spirit: "To take as far as possible every conflict which arises . . . out of the atmosphere and medium of force, of violence as a means of settlement, into that of discussion and of intelligence is to treat those who disagree—even profoundly—with us as those from whom we may learn and, in so far, as friends."[31] This disposition toward nonviolence, however, does not come easy. For Dewey, as we know, such a disposition or civic habit is not a ready-made "natural" endowment, but a human potentiality requiring continuous struggle and life-long educational cultivation.

Seen in this light, democracy clearly remains a "promise"—but not an empty pipedream nor a mere project of civil engineering. Construed as an ongoing process of democratization, democracy involves a striving toward human flourishing on both an individual and social level. Transposed into the idiom of Heidegger's philosophy, human *praxis*—in the basic sense of "letting be"—produces no extrinsic objects but an intrinsic good: the achievement or fulfillment of our (promised) humanity.

Appendix A

Democracy Without Banisters

Reading Claude Lefort

Because of his vast erudition and intricate subtlety, reading Claude Lefort is a difficult undertaking. Bernard Flynn has come to our rescue with his book *The Philosophy of Claude Lefort: Interpreting the Political*.[1] For English-speaking students of political philosophy, this is an eminently welcome book. Lefort is one of the most innovative and insightful philosophers and political thinkers of the last half century—but a thinker largely ignored or even sidelined in America. Bernard Flynn is highly qualified to remedy this deficit. A long-term friend of the French thinker, Flynn has attentively followed the evolution of Lefort's thought, devoting to it a series of probing articles. Flynn's own scholarly focus has been on Continental thought and especially on phenomenology after Edmund Husserl—a focus prominently displayed in his earlier study *Political Philosophy at the Closure of Metaphysics*.[2]

In the introduction to his new book, Flynn presents the French philosopher as preeminently concerned with the ambivalent character of modernity—and also with the difficult linkage between theory and practice. "From its very beginning," he notes (xiii), Lefort's work "has set for itself the task of interpreting the political life of modern society" and especially the task of discerning the political "form" or distinctive "regime" of modern democracy. In contrast to devotees of "pure" theory or abstract metaphysics, he has allowed his theorizing to be informed by his own lived condition (or his embeddedness in the "life world"). In fact, Flynn adds (xviii–xix), Lefort's political philosophy is "born from a reflection on political experience and a consideration of the *forms* of political life." In particular, his thinking about modern democracy is not a rehearsal of abstract ideas but rather an attempt to evoke "an *experience* of democracy," more specifically "a *lived experience* of the dissolution of the [metaphysical] markers of certainty that characterized the *ancien regime*."

In Flynn's view, Lefort's practical-experiential mode of theorizing distinguishes him from a number of thinkers by whom he was for a long time overshadowed—including Jean-Paul Sartre's radical subjectivism, Jacques Derrida's "worldless textualism," Emmanuel Levinas' transcendentalism, and Habermasian rationalism. To be sure, his own distinctive perspective emerged only slowly through trial and error. As a young man during World War II, Lefort joined one of the French currents of Trotskyism. After the war, together with Cornelius Castoriadis, he founded a group called *Socialisme ou Barbarie*, which championed nonrepressive socialist politics against the barbarism of the immediate past. The most decisive influence on Lefort's outlook, however, came from two of his teachers: Maurice Merleau-Ponty and Raymond Aron. The former's post-metaphysical phenomenology pointed him in the direction of "intertwining"—beyond the binaries of rationalism and empiricism, foundationalism and relativism. Aron's influence bequeathed to him the commitment to a nondogmatic or nonideological liberalism—and also a strong aversion to any kind of coercive and "totalitarian" rule. Largely under he impact of these converging influences, Lefort was inspired to develop his modern–postmodern phenomenology of democracy where the latter is seen as both a distinct political experience and a novel political "regime" on a par with the regimes of classical philosophy. Following the same trajectory, he also was led to discern the novelty and hideous quality of modern "totalitarianism" as a political paradigm distinct from traditional tyranny. In Flynn's words (xxi): "Arguably Lefort is one of the few political philosophers—together with Hannah Arendt, Raymond Aron and a small number of others—who have elaborated a plausible interpretation of the totalitarian phenomenon" by pinpointing some of its nontraditional features.

The introduction clearly indicates the correlation between the conceptions of democracy and totalitarianism in Lefort's thought. In the latter's view, modern democracy was ushered in by a series of political revolutions that overturned the basic premises of traditional society, especially the idea of the king or ruler as the visible embodiment of the "body politics." In the premodern *ancien regime*, Flynn comments, "the king's body played the role of mediator between the sensible and the supersensible, that is, the point of intersection between the visible and the invisible"; to this extent, the king *"incarnated* society's identity" (xxiv–xxvi). Against this background, modernity for Lefort signals "the disincarnation of society," that is, the emergence of a condition where no figure can embody society's unity and thereby symbolically link it with a "supersensible world." What is important to notice here is that disincarnation leaves a trace: although the "figure of the king" may be effaced, the "place" that he occupied remains—as an "empty place." Interpreting this change with the help of Merleau-Ponty, Flynn observes that the "empty place" in modern democracy "testifies to society's nonclosure on itself, which is to say, its nonidentity with itself"; differently stated, it "blocks society's 'immanence' in a manner similar to Merleau-Ponty's notion of the body's immanence with itself which is always 'short-circuited' at the last moment." What modern totalitarianism introduces, by contrast, is a reversal of this openness or nonidentity. Basically, for Lefort, totalitarianism is "a response to the modern experience of the void"—a response that seeks "to fill the empty place of power." Viewed in this light, the totalitarian project (in both its Fascist and Stalinist garb) constitutes "a counterrevolution against democracy": more specifically an attempt to fill the empty place "with a *materialization* of 'the people'—a people no longer in conflict with itself but rather a *People-as-One.*"

Somewhat surprisingly, the book opens with three chapters devoted to a detailed reading of the writings of Machiavelli as seen from Lefort's perspective. As it happens, the work of Machiavelli looms large in several of Lefort's early writings, especially his *Le travail de l'oeuvre: Machiavel* (1972). What attracted Lefort to this work was clearly not its reputed "Machiavellianism" but rather its sensitivity for political divergence. In many ways, the Florentine appeared to him as a herald or precursor of typically "modern" developments: particularly the "disincarnation" of the body politic and the nonidentity of society with itself. In Flynn's words, the significance of Machiavelli for Lefort resided chiefly in the former's insistence "that society is *always and everywhere* torn by inner conflict" and that the elimination of conflict "is not only impossible but also undesirable" (xxii). In contrast to Marxist teachings, conflict in Machiavelli's view did not revolve around an economic class struggle, but had a strictly political character, involving the opposition between the desires "to oppress" and "not to be oppressed." Turning to Machiavelli's most famous text, and emphasizing the phenomenological and even ontological dimensions of Lefort's reading, Flynn adds that, in *The Prince*, politics is constituted "across the play of desires, masking a fundamental void, a noncoincidence of the body politic with itself" (8–10). In this manner, the text inaugurates "a new ontology and a new political philosophy" that "destabilizes" traditional meanings; far from simply underwriting a "Machiavellian" project, the work in fact "adumbrates a fundamental critique" of that project, a critique which views power "not as a positive object, a sort of thing-in-itself, but rather as a relationship of poles in conflict." Taken in this sense, *The Prince* (for Lefort) discloses Machiavelli as "the quintessential thinker of modernity," where modernity is neither "the period dominated by the thought of a sovereign subjectivity" nor a simply "classificatory term" but a synonym for the dissolution of traditional "markers of certainty."

It is impossible in this brief review to attend to all the points raised in Lefort's (and Flynn's) discussion of *The Prince* and *The Discourses*. Instead, I turn to the more general topic of Lefort's "practice of interpretation." In Flynn's account, Lefort's practice in this regard is clearly distinguished both from Derridean deconstruction annd Habermasian rational discourse. As he points out (65–66)—using the language of Heidegger and Merleau-Ponty—Machiavelli's *oeuvre* for Lefort was not simply a text or discourse but had the character of an "event" or "advent"—where that term points to an occurrence of "being," a mode of "'there is' (*il y a*) in which we are irreducibly inscribed." Interpreting such an advent requires a worldly engagement, an attempt to "think in the space which it opens to the thought of others." In contrast to the "authorless" anonymity favored by some postmodernists, Lefort's practice of reading preserves the relevance of the author—not as an intentional subject (*mens auctoris*) but as someone opening up a world through his "work" (*travail*). In opposition to the Habermasian focus on rational validity, Lefort attends to the Merleau-Pontyan "intertwining" of sense and nonsense, reason and nonreason, thus steering a course between ideal finality and randomness. Lefort, Flynn comments (70–71), finds in the work of Machiavelli an intersection of "knowledge and nonknowledge," a crossing avoiding both "the 'high altitude' thinking of the philosopher king" and "the temporalizing empiricism of the *pseudo*-sages of Florence." In this manner, his writings exhibit neither a "definitive final meaning" nor a "drifting in a sea of interpretations." Given this stress on the nonfinality of meaning, Flynn finds a certain parallel or "convergence" (72) between Lefort's practice and Gadamerian hermeneutics—even though the former is much more ready than Gadamer to employ psychoanalytic vocabulary (especially Lacan's triad of the "symbolic," the "imaginary," and the "real").

The core of the book's argument is found in Parts Two and Three, dealing respectively with Lefort's conceptions of premodernity and modernity. As previously indicated, premodern society for Lefort was typically a form of life whose meaning was securely anchored elsewhere, a regime whose symbolic structure was "fixed to nature or

to a supersensible world, *another place*" (100), while remaining aloof
of history. Although medieval Christianity adhered to an eschatologi-
cal vision, this vision was not part of a historical process; at least for
mainstream theology, "the signs of providence were not legible within
history" (107). Following Ernst Kantorowicz, Lefort's conception of
premodernity stresses the role of the king's "two bodies" (empirical
and sacred) as representing symbolically society's unity. This unity
was shattered by modernity and especially by the succession of modern revolutions. Lefort accepts Alexis de Tocqueville's notion of "the
democratic revolution" whose significance resided in the fact that it
"snapped the foundations of the *distinctions* between men in society,"
distinctions which in earlier times had been "anchored in nature"
and/or "sanctified by myth or religion" (120). While undercutting
these human distinctions, modernity ushers in novel gaps between
appearance and reality, between "imaginary" interpretations and real
conditions. Lefort is fond in this context to invoke psychoanalytic
terminology. In Flynn's words (125), he is "adamant on the point
that *within* premodern society it is not possible to distinguish the
symbolic, the imaginary, and the real; perhaps we could even say
that premodernity *is* the condition in which this distinction is impossible." Differently phrased, in premodernity "the religious foundation
of power, law, and knowledge is an *imaginary* interpretation of the
symbolic," whereas *within* modernity "this imaginary interpretation becomes visible as such" (148–149). With this change comes the
distinction between representative "figure" and symbolic "place," a
distinction that is not a reversal: for, "although the *figure* of premodern transcendence is effaced, the *place* of this transcendence remains
as an *empty place.*"

For Lefort, the onset of modernity signals a loss and a gain: it
entails a loss of unity and security, but harbors the gain of openness
and radical questioning. In opposition to some "unrestrained" anti-
modernists, Lefort sees the chief gain of modern democracy in "the
institution of an interrogation that will call the Law and all authority
into question." This gain, Flynn comments (150), "is what we call
freedom" seen as "the very condition of the political and of politics."
The danger lying at the heart of modernity is the temptation of regres-
sion: the temptation to fill up the open space created by democracy
with a new type of "incarnation" or definitive unity, especially the
imaginary phantasy of the "People-as-One." Yielding to this temptation is the hallmark of "totalitarianism"—the theme of the concluding
part of the book. Paraphrasing Lefort, Flynn (213) pinpoints the gist
of totalitarianism again in the imaginary self-identity of the people,

in the "representation of the people-as-one." Whereas self-identity rules out internal strife, radical division emerges between "the inside" and "the outside," between "the people and its enemies." In contrast to purely ideological or "imaginary" treatments of totalitarianism, Lefort places the accent on the "symbolic" dimension of the regime, insisting (241) that totalitarianism is not the "instantiation of an idea, neither the idea of a classless society nor the Fascist idea of a master race," but rather involves a "mutation of the symbolic structure of democracy," namely, "a flight from the *empty place* that democracy entails." By way of conclusion, Flynn points to one of Lefort's later writings (*La complication*, 1999), which reflected on the implications of totalitarianism for the "constitution of a world space." As that text notes (268), the formation of such a space would entail "a total mastery of human relations under the sign of the One," thus conjuring up not an "interdependence of states" or societies but a complete "*unification of the globe.*"

Flynn is to be congratulated for presenting a well-crafted, lucidly written introduction to this important political thinker. Actually, his book contains a number of additional features that I bypassed for the sake of brevity. Among there features is the discussion of the relation between "modernity and law"—where Lefort stresses the rule-governed character of democracy even in the absence of an ultimate anchor—and the relation between "modernity and rights"—where Lefort emphasizes the political and symbolic (rather than purely moral) character of rights. Valuable are also Flynn's comparisons between Lefort and other prominent political thinkers, like Leo Strauss and Hannah Arendt. With regard to the character of modernity, Arendt saw the distinguishing trait in the "rise of the social" and the eclipse of politics by "labor" and "work," while Strauss located the basic change in the demise of classical "natural right" and the upsurge of history and political "science." Although appreciating some of his insights, Lefort (152–158) takes exception to several of Strauss's arguments: including the confusion of history with historicism, the tendency to equate critique with relativism, and the unwillingness to recognize modern democracy as a distinctive political "regime." Regarding Arendt, the differences are more nuanced and have to do mainly with their respective conceptions of totalitarianism. For Arendt, totalitarianism was basically a product, or at least a byproduct, of modernity's accent on the "social" and the incessant movement of labor's life cycle. For Lefort, by contrast, the same phenomenon signals a perversion of modernity's disincarnation of social unity. In Flynn's account (xxviii–xxix), Lefort diverges from Arendt mainly on two points: first, the strain in her thought "which suggests that totalitarianism is 'the denouement of modernity'"; and second, the exaggerated role attributed to motion or mobility that underestimates "the stabilizing role of the One in the totalitarian regime."

Despite its merits, the book is not free of flaws and at some points invites critical afterthoughts. Some purely technical flaws must be attributed to the editor at the press: Schleiermacher appears as "Schreimacher" (124); and Rorty's book *Achieving Our Country* is repeatedly cited as *Achieving Our Century* (xix, xxix). Other questions, however, can be addressed to the author. In the discussion of Machiavelli, one misses a sustained comparison of Lefort's "practice of reading" with the interpretations offered, for example, in Strauss's *Thoughts on Machiavelli* and John Pocock's *The Machiavellian Moment*. On many other occasions, one misses a certain critical engagement with Lefort's work. In the comparison between Arendt and Lefort on the issue of totalitarianism, Flynn clearly sides with the French thinker. However, one might wonder—with Arendt—whether the upsurge of totalitarianism is not attributable, at least in part, to certain tendencies inherent in modernity, including subjectivism, voluntarism, and rampant will to power (today manifest on the global level). More generally, questions can be raised concerning Lefort's equation of modernity with radical disincarnation and of democracy's legitimacy with an "empty place." Surely, between the "people-as-one" and the "people-as-no one" there is a vast spectrum of possibilities; above all, modern democracy still is sustained by "people" (even if ontologically nonidentical) nurtured by certain historical experiences and animated by ethical and political aspirations. This cultural and "civil society" dimension cannot be irrelevant, and actually seems crucial, to the legitimacy of democratic regimes. In this domain, I feel, Lefort tends to give undue precedence to Aron's liberalism over Merleau-Ponty's notion of the "flesh" of the political; in addition, certain linguistic teachings (deriving from Saussure and Lacan) sometimes trump his hermeneutical sensibilities. Without neglecting the liberal strand, one may wish to upgrade phenomenology in this equation in order to "humanize" the emptiness of democracy and salvage a measure of democratic legitimacy.

Appendix B

The Return of the Political

On Chantal Mouffe

Political philosophy has often been declared moribund if not entirely defunct; but its obituaries have always been premature. Undeniably, intellectual trends in late modernity have not been favorable to its enterprise. In the wake of Hegel and Marx, the upsurge of positivism or scientism mounted a fierce challenge to political reflection (and philosophy as such), forcing it into repeated attempts at self-legitimation. Still, the political upheavals of our century—two world wars followed by the contest of superpowers—were unlikely to let political thinking and argumentation come to rest. More recently, a new situation has emerged. The end of the Cold War and the demise of "really existing" socialism have ushered in a new era of ideological convergence, an era which has been greeted by many as the "end of history" or else as the end of politics or political contestation. It is this claim of a presumed global convergence that is the chief target of the book by Chantal Mouffe titled *The Return of the Political*.[1] Against both a complacent liberal consensualism and a fashionable reduction of politics to neo-liberalism or liberal market economics, her book emphatically asserts the contemporary need for "the return of the political."

The book's plea is part and parcel of the author's long-standing engagement. As editor of important theoretical texts (*Gramsci and Marxist Theory* and *Dimensions of Radical Democracy*) and as co-author with Ernesto Laclau of *Hegemony and Socialist Strategy*,[2] Mouffe has for some time been involved in the difficult task of articulating a viable theoretical agenda of Leftist politics in our time, an agenda which can no longer rely on the grand "meta-narratives" of the past nor on the "foundational" role of the traditional proletariat. *The Return of the Political* assembles and sharply profiles the major strands of Mouffe's thought in this domain, establishing her as a leading spokesperson of contemporary oppositional politics—more specifically, a politics which recasts elements of both liberal and socialist teachings in the mold of a "radical and plural democracy." In articulating her "radical and plural" agenda, Mouffe proceeds cautiously and with full attention to the rich complexity and profound transmutations characterizing twentieth-century philosophical and political reflection. Over long stretches, her book provides a competent and discerning introduction to the intense intellectual "conversation" of our time, an introduction that spotlights both prominent "voices" and salient or disputed issues in this conversation. In the domain of European thought, the discussion ranges from Machiavelli and Hegel via Carl Schmitt to Norberto Bobbio, Jürgen Habermas and Hans-Georg Gadamer as well as Derrida and Michel Foucault. In the Anglo-American terrain, Mouffe's chief interlocutors are John Rawls, Michael Oakeshott, Quentin Skinner, Michael Walzer, and Joseph Raz (with some brief side glances at Charles Taylor and Hannah Arendt).

In her treatment of this intellectual context, Mouffe does not confine herself to a descriptive account, but always is careful to situate or position herself vis-à-vis other voices. This positioning includes a number of distinctive moves that help to throw into relief the notion of radical pluralism. One such move has to do with the relation between modernity and postmodernity—terms whose prevalent meanings the book contests and seeks to redefine. On repeated occasions, Mouffe critiques and polemicizes against the Habermasian notion according to which modernity is marked by an epistemological rationalism and the premise of a constitutive subjectivity (or individualism). As she writes (7, 11), we have to "break" with this conception of modernity, with this focus on "rationalism, individualism and universalism," and instead perceive modernity as linked with a practical-political change: namely, "the advent of the democratic revolution." This move implies not so much the rejection of rationality, individuality or universality per se, but rather affirms that these categories are "necessarily plural, discursively constructed, and entangled in power relations." Seen from this angle, postmodernity is simply a continuation and radicalization of the democratic revolution; following Claude Lefort, what one means by postmodernity in philosophy is "a recognition of the impossibility of any ultimate foundation or final legitimation" of political power. While subscribing to this radicalization, Mouffe also distances herself from a postmodern flirtation with fragmentation and disunity (occasionally found in Jean-François Lyotard and Foucault). Radical pluralism, in her view, must be distinguished from "the postmodern conception of the fragmentation of the social which refuses to grant the fragments any kind of relational identity." Her own perspective, she adds, "consistently rejects any kind of essentialism—either of the totality or of the elements—and affirms that neither the totality nor the fragments possess any kind of fixed identity, prior to the contingent and pragmatic form of their articulation."

Closely related to this move is the differentiation of plural democracy from customary forms of both liberalism and communitarianism. For Mouffe, the chief defect of traditional liberalism resides in its focus on private self-interest (especially in utilitarian liberalism) as well as its assumption of public consensus (in its rationalist variant). Over long stretches, the book offers a running critique of rationalist or Rawlsian liberalism and its offshoots in contemporary political thought (relevant chapter headings here read "American Liberalism and its Communitarian Critics," "Rawls: Political Philosophy without Politics," and "Politics and the Limits of Liberalism"). Together with the accent on an a-social individualism Mouffe castigates liberalism's pretense of public impartiality as well as its (partial or full) endorsement of a content-less proceduralism and the basic "neutrality of the state" vis-à-vis substantive political differences. In this respect, her book supports Carl Schmitt's argument regarding the "incapacity of liberalism to think of the political," an argument that holds that liberal thought is confined to the "polarity between ethics and economics" and hence offers "no genuine liberal politics but only a liberal critique of politics" in the name of individual liberty (33).

While thus denouncing liberalism's shortcomings, Mouffe is unwilling to join many of its detractors, especially those proceeding under "communitarian" auspices (like Michael Sandel and, perhaps, Alasdair MacIntyre). What communitarianism neglects is precisely the modern "advent of the democratic revolution" together with its recent postmodern repercussions—repercussions that profoundly trouble or disturb the idea of a homogeneous public realm. "Contrary to what some communitarians propose," she writes (62), "a modern democratic political community cannot be organized around a single substantive idea of the common good. The recovery of a strong participatory idea of citizenship should not be made at the cost of sacrificing individual liberty." Following in Oakeshott's footsteps, Mouffe finds modern democracy akin not to a medieval *"universitas"* pursuing a common aim, but rather to a *"societas"* held together only by a shared "public concern" or a common "practice of civility"—a practice forming the heart of what Oakeskott calls *"respublica."* To belong to a modern democratic community, we read (67), "what is required is that we accept a specific language of civil intercourse, the *respublica*. These rules prescribe norms of conduct to be subscribed to in seeking self-chosen satisfactions and in performing self-chosen actions."

This notion of *respublica* appears in may ways congruent with the tradition of "civic republicanism"—a tradition inaugurated by Machiavelli and Harrington, and recuperated recently by John Pocock and Quentin Skinner. In several passages of the book, Mouffe seems favorably inclined toward this tradition, which she credits with the attempt to reconcile personal liberty with the exercise of civic virtues. Skinner, in particular, is singled out (63) for showing that there is "no fundamental necessary incompatibility between the classical republican conception of citizenship and modern democracy" and that to preserve individual liberty "we must cultivate civic virtues and devote ourselves to the common good." In other passages, however, civic republicanism is placed alongside the communitarian camp and hence found wanting for being insufficiently attentive to democratic pluralism. According to Mouffe (20–21), the proliferation of public spaces in contemporary democracy makes it imperative that we "abandon the idea of a unique constitutive space of the constitution of the political, which is particular to both liberalism and civic republicanism." If the liberal conception of the atomistic or "unencumbered" self is deficient, the alternative presented by civic republicanism (and communitarianism) is unsatisfactory as well: for, "it is not a question of moving from a 'unitary unencumbered self' to a 'unitary situated self'; the problem is with the very idea of the unitary subject." For Mouffe, what needs to be grasped is that the subject (or citizen) is not unitary but plural and the bearer of multiple identities: "Hence the importance of the postmodern critique for developing a political philosophy aimed at making possible a new form of individuality that would be truly plural and democratic."

A brief review can only offer selective glimpses of this multifaceted and eloquently argued text. Thus, I have to bypass (among other things) Mouffe's nuanced critical engagement with Norberto Bobbio as well as her subtle discussion of contemporary feminist thought (from Carole Gilligan and Carole Pateman to Judith Butler). My own intellectual leanings concur in large part with Mouffe's overall theoretical agenda—a fact that complicates, but surely does not impede, critical commentary. What I intend to do here is simply to raise some questions or point to unresolved issues (without pretending to hold more adequate "solutions" in store). One question concerns the status of civic republicanism and its relation to radical democracy. As indicated, Mouffe chides communitarian readings of the former tradition for their excessive attachment to compact unity or homogeneity (of both individuals and societies). Contrary to communitarian teachings, she insists (62), modern democracy cannot be organized around a "substantive idea of the common good." At the same time, departing from liberalism, she is unwilling to surrender public life entirely to the vagaries of private self-interest. Relying on the republican tradition (as reformulated by Skinner and Lefort), she invokes here the notion of a public space (or public spaces) seen as the arena of political action and discourse. As mentioned before, engagement in a modern democratic community for Mouffe requires that we accept "a specific language of civil intercourse, the *respublica*," a language that prescribes basic norms of conduct for all members. At this point (67), her text introduces a subtle and intriguing distinction—which probably needs (and certainly deserves) further clarification: "This modern form of political community is held together not by a substantive idea of the common good but by a common bond, a public concern."

The notion of a shared public concern also carries over into Mouffe's discussion of democratic "citizenship" construed as a common identification with the *respublica*. Such citizenship, she observes (69), involves a "common political identity of persons" who—though engaged in diverse purposive enterprises—accept submission to "the rules prescribed by the *respublica* in seeking their satisfactions and in performing their actions." As one should note, the concept of public rules here is not simply synonymous with liberal proceduralism or value-neutrality. Instead, Mouffe connects *respublica* with a "set of ethico-political values," that is, with a dimension of public ethics (or *Sittlichkeit*) as differentiated from private-individual morals or morality. To recapture a public space, she asserts (65), we need to reaffirm the "lost connection between ethics and politics"—although this must be done without sacrificing the "gains of the democratic revolution," that is, without abandoning the modern separation of morality and politics. This reaffirmation is surely one of the most captivating and challenging features of her book—one calling again for further development and elucidation. Arguing against Rawlsian liberalism (31–32), Mouffe asserts the need to distinguish between the "common moral good" and the "common political good," where the latter is more democratically open-ended; buttressing this point, she even invokes the classical concept of a "regime" (or *politeia*) which, she says, is defined "by the political good that it puts to work." This concept clearly puts pressure on the Rawlsian priority of the right over the good and, more generally, on the liberal aloofness from public ethics. For, although liberal democracy may be "agnostic in terms of morality," it surely "is not—and cannot be—agnostic concerning the political good" (which in a democracy is summarized by the principles of liberty and equality).

The question that surfaces here, among others, is how the notion of a shared political good can be squared with the postmodern pluralism of subject positions, or to turn things around: how postmodernism can make room for the cultivation of civic virtues (or a "civic conscience," p. 36) and hence for the postulate of public accountability or responsibility. At issue here is a delicate and tensional balance—as Mouffe recognizes when she writes that civic conscience must not "necessarily be consensus" or sacrifice diversity to unity. At least occasionally, it seems to me, this balance is titled in favor of a liberal consensualism (along Rawlsian lines). This tilting is evident already in the discussion of "individualism," which Mouffe—rightly, I believe—treats as a cornerstone of modern liberalism. Arguing against Rawls as well as Bobbio, she asserts (97) that "the framework of individualism must be relinquished," although without lapsing into holism or organicism. What radical democracy requires is the attempt to "theorize the individual, not as a monad, an 'unencumbered' self that exists prior to and independently of society, but rather as a site constituted by an ensemble of 'subject positions,' inscribed in a multiplicity of social relations, the member of many communities and participant in a plurality of collective forms of identification." Somewhat later, however, this postmodern accent is jeopardized when Mouffe (now against Schmitt) vindicates the legacy of "liberal individualism" and even equates it with "pluralism," stating (120) that by pluralism "I mean the recognition of individual freedom, that freedom which John Stuart Mill defends in his essay *On Liberty* as the only freedom worthy of the name." At this juncture, pluralism seems to merge with the contours of a regime that, at other points, is criticized for its neglect of pluralism and diversity (or its relegation of the latter to the private domain).

To some extent, the tilting against pluralism has to do with the constitutive principles of modern democracy per se (liberal, radical, or otherwise): the principles of liberty and equality. Accentuating the aspect of equality, Mouffe's text often centerstages the so-called "logic of equivalence," a logic that, in her view, provides the necessary common denominator for democratic citizenship. As she writes, seconding Laclau (77), radical democracy requires "a chain of equivalence among the different democratic struggles so as to create an equivalent articulation between the demands of women, blacks, workers, gays and others." Pushing this aspect further, her book at crucial points endorses a kind of "difference blindness" which, in many ways, resembles the liberal universalism espoused by Rawls and others. With particular reference to gender difference, Mouffe argues (82) that "the limitations of the modern conception of citizenship should be remedied, not by making sexual difference politically relevant to its definition, but by constructing a new conception of citizenship where sexual difference would become effectively irrelevant." Mouffe's basic thesis (directed against Pateman and others) is in effect that "in the domain of politics, and as far as citizenship is concerned, sexual difference should not be a valid distinction." In the same context, (85–86), Mouffe also polemicizes against Iris Young's notion of "group differentiated citizenship," accusing her (I think, unfairly) of holding an "essentialist notion of groups"—and this despite an earlier endorsement of rights that "can only be exercised collectively" and that are "no longer rights that can be universalized" (13, 19). Curiously, these arguments against difference are said ultimately not to "preclude the construction of multiple forms of unity and common action" (87).

Pluralism's fragile status in the text is compounded by Mouffe's acceptance of the modern "state"—an acceptance traceable in part to Schmitt's influence. A section devoted to "The Limits of Pluralism" states explicitly (131) that Schmitt was right to insist on "the specificity of the political association," that is, on the primacy of the state over society. Concern with pluralism, we read, should not mislead us into believing "that our participation in the state as a political community is on the same level as our other forms of social integration." As Schmitt has shown (in *The Crisis of Parliamentary Democracy* and elsewhere), "antagonistic principles of legitimacy cannot coexist within the same political association"; hence, "there cannot be pluralism at that level without the political reality of the state automatically disappearing." Mouffe also follows Schmitt in viewing the state as the result of a series of divisions and neutralizations, especially the divisions between public and private spheres and between state and religion. Because these divisions are constitutive of the modern state, she writes (132), one cannot "call these distinctions into question in the name of pluralism. Hence, the problem posed by the integration of a religion like Islam, which does not accept these distinctions." Somewhat emphatically (and bypassing the example of Anglicanism, among others), the text here insists on "the relegation of religion to the private sphere, which we now have to make Muslims accept." Notwithstanding these passages, the text elsewhere (151) issues a plea to "make room for the pluralism of cultures, collective forms of life and regimes, as well as for the pluralism of subjects, individual choices and conceptions of the good."

As it happens, these "limits" of pluralism are offset in the book by a tilting of the balance in the opposite direction: the transformation of diversity into rigid separation and division. While contracting pluralism within the confines of a given political regime, Mouffe—again following Schmitt—sharpens the difference between regimes and between political orientations into a radical confrontation along friend–enemy lines. As the writes approvingly (111, 113), for Schmitt "the political is concerned with the relations of friend and enemy; it deals with the creation of a 'we' opposed to a 'them'; it is the realm of 'decision' not free discussion." In opposition to liberal (especially Rawlsian) consensualism, she finds it "useful to remember with Carl Schmitt that the defining feature of politics is struggle." This emphasis on struggle colors her conception of "the political," and hence also of its proclaimed "return." "For Schmitt," we read (123), "the criterion of the political, its *differentia specifica*, is the friend–enemy relation; this involves the creation of a 'we' which stands in opposition to a 'them.' . . . The political always has to do with conflicts and antagonisms." Schmitt's teachings provide a corrective not only to liberal consensus, but also to Oakeshott's notions of *societas* and *respublica*. Oakeshott's basic shortcoming, we are told (68–69), lies in his "flawed idea of politics," an idea that—in center staging a shared language of civility—is "only adequate for one aspect of politics: the point of view of the 'we,' the friend's side." Yet, as Schmitt has "rightly pointed out, the criterion of the political is the friend/enemy relation." Hence, what is "completely missing" in Oakeshott is "division and antagonism, that is, the aspect of the enemy." Borrowing (although perhaps misleadingly) from recent postmodern or deconstructive literature, Mouffe links antagonism with the inside–outside distinction, and especially with the notion of a "constitutive outside." While politics, she adds, aims at "constructing a political community," a fully inclusive community can never be realized "since there will permanently be a 'constitutive outside,' an exterior to the community that makes its existence possible."

Although valuable as an antidote to liberal complacency, this stress on conflict seems to me troublesome and not quite tenable. Simply put: Schmitt (in my view) leads Mouffe here astray. In my own reading, Schmitt was basically a Hobbesian thinker—although one who construed Hobbes counterliberally (along de Maistre's and/or quasi-Nietzschean lines). Proceeding from this vantage, Schmitt was on the whole ignorant of Hegelian dialectics, and especially of the notion of dialectical mediation—according to which opposing elements are opposed precisely in virtue of their relationship. A similar

point might be made about the postmodern inside–outside distinction—which I interpret not as the contrast between compact internal
and external domains, but as the inevitable mutual embroilment and
contamination of inside and outside. Seemingly esoteric, these comments have a bearing an contemporary politics. As it seems to me,
the basic challenge for "radical and plural" democracy consists in the
task to recognize the difference of individuals and groups, without
either externalizing them as enemies or else internalizing or assimilat-
ing them to sameness.

Mouffe is not unaware of this task—which leads her occasionally
to stray from Schmitt's doctrine. As she writes at one point (4), given
the inevitability of political antagonisms, "what needs to be envisaged
is how it is possible *under those conditions* to create and maintain a
pluralistic democratic order. Such an order is based on a distinction
between 'enemy' and 'adversary'"—a distinction which entails that "the
opponent should be considered not as an enemy to be destroyed, but
as an adversary whose existence is legitimate and must be tolerated."
Unfortunately, this statement is nearly cancelled by other portions of
the book, especially by a passage (127) that castigates any attempted
move of pluralism beyond the friend–enemy division as a "dangerous
liberal illusion." Between the two passages my own sympathies are
clearly with the former (provided we are also allowed to learn from
"adversaries"). Regardless of such critical qualms, however, Mouffe's
book must surely be credited with stirring up crucially important
theoretical questions and thus with contributing, even if indirectly, to
the much-needed "return of the political" in our time.

Appendix C

Exiting Liberal Democracy?

Bell and Confucian Thought

Some twenty years ago, with the demise of the Soviet Union, the so-called "Cold War" came to an end, terminating four decades of intense global rivalry. This ending, no doubt, had profound repercussions, ushering in radically new geopolitical alignments together with a new phase of economic globalization. Behind or despite these transformations, however, one can also detect a curious kind of ideological persistence: in many Western societies, and especially in the United States, the liberal individualism cultivated as stark antidote to Soviet collectivism remained in place unchanged and was even strengthened and elevated into a global ideological panacea. Under the auspices of "neo-liberalism," individual and corporate profit-seeking was steadily unleashed while older social and political restrictions on profit-seeking were marginalized or "downsized." As a result of both the Cold War and subsequent developments, it became customary virtually to equate democracy with "liberal democracy" or a system prioritizing individual rights—completely neglectful of the long-standing tension between the latter and democracy seen as a shared political regime. That this equation is by no means cogent or self-evident, even in the United States, is demonstrated by the work of such prominent American intellectuals as John Dewey and Walter Lippmann. For both, the glorification of self-seeking or atomistic individualism was a derailment or corruption of democracy. For Dewey, in particular, democracy constituted an ethical association or community where private self-seeking is necessarily curbed.[1]

In light of this background one can only welcome Daniel Bell's recent book, *Beyond Liberal Democracy*, a text that exposes some of the glaring defects or short-comings of liberal individualism as practiced in Western societies today.[2] Without ignoring some of the benefits of individual freedom, the book seeks to correct or remedy these shortcomings through recourse to older Asian teachings, especially the teachings of Confucius and Mencius. In a way, the front cover captures the animus pervading the text: it shows a picture of the Statue of Liberty holding up a copy of the *Analects* of Confucius. What aggravates or antagonizes Bell is not the Western "liberal" model as such but the missionary zeal with which this model tends to be exported today by Western, especially American, intellectuals and policymakers. His opening chapter makes reference to the American legal theorist Ronald Dworkin who, during a lecture tour in China in 2002, exhorted Chinese audiences to embrace Western liberal-individualistic values in preference to older indigenous traditions. As Bell comments wryly: "His less-than-modest demeanor and hectoring tone did not help. The deeper problem, however, is that [he] made no serious attempt to learn about Chinese philosophy, to identify aspects worth defending and learning from, and to relate his own ideas to those of Chinese political traditions such as Confucianism and Legalism" (3–4). What renders the "hectoring tone" even more odd and even absurd is the fact that the same theorist more recently has cast doubt on the very possibility of liberal democracy in the United States—never mind the rest of the world.[3]

Regardless of the possibility or impossibility of exportation, the meaning of "liberal democracy" in the text is not left in doubt. According to the introductory chapter, the "main hallmarks" of liberal democracy are basically three, comprising "human rights, democracy, and capitalism" (9). As Bell adds at a later point (333): "I define liberal democracy as being composed of three main pillars—human rights, democracy, and capitalism—that have originated and been developed in Western countries." The chief aim of the text is to delineate "alternative models" of these pillars "that may be more appropriate—more feasible and desirable—for East Asian societies." In conformity with this aim, the book is divided into three major parts, dealing respectively with human rights, democracy, and capitalism "for an East Asian context." The first section concentrates on such issues as the relevance of "Asian values" for human rights, the activities of international human rights nongovermental organizations, and comments by Mencius on just and unjust war. The second part turns to such problems as the merits and demerits of "active citizenship," the possibility of a "democracy with Confucian characteristics" (which, we are told, involves "taking elitism seriously"), the effect of democracy on minority groups, and the system of education in Singapore. The last part offers discussions of Confucian "constraints on property rights," East Asian provisions for social welfare, the treatment of migrant workers in East Asia, and more generally the pros and cons of Confucian teachings in both "ideal" and "real" settings in the contemporary world.

The book offers valuable insights in each of the three focal areas. In addressing the issue of human rights, Bell deals sensibly with the "Asian values" conundrum that often has generated more heat than light; somewhat unexpectedly, he delineates Mencius's view on warfare, pointing out that—although not strictly a pacifist—the Confucian sage strongly opposed wars of conquest, holding that "states can defend themselves if the ruler is supported by the people" (10). Surely a good maxim for all times and places! The section on democracy compares the state-centered citizenship in Western societies with the more local and communal loyalties in East Asia; it also contains important comments on the need for civic education in our multicultural world, noting (13) that "one of the teaching methods designed to improve democratic education is public recognition of the intellectual contributions of different groups, including those historically marginalized." Again, a good maxim valuable in many contexts. Probably the most intriguing idea advanced in the democracy section is the notion of a bicameral mode of representation, with the popularly elected "lower house" being supplemented by a "meritocratic" upper chamber. In a time dominated by neo-liberal *laissez-faire* capitalism, readers will appreciate learning about East Asian attempts to curb rampant individual and corporate greed. In Bell's words, "Confucians defended constraints on the free market in the name of more fundamental values" (15–16). Among the constraints imposed by Confucian policymakers to secure people's basic "material welfare" was the so-called "well-field system" designed by Mencius, a system allowing farmers to make productive use of their land while ensuring that enough food is supplied to the nonfarming population. Among other constraining features was the principle that ownership rights should be vested in the family rather than the individual, an arrangement that encouraged filial piety and the care of elderly parents by their offspring. Although permitting regulation of the economy by a strong interventionist state, East Asian capitalism, past and present, is said to rely heavily on social networks to "grease the wheels" of economic transactions.

From the angle of political theory or philosophy, Bell's text displays a number of qualities that are urgently needed but also in short supply in our era of civilizational clashes. Among these qualities are a certain humility or tentativeness and a complete absence of "hectoring." Repeatedly, Bell stresses the importance of cultural sensitivity, the need to be familiar with one's own as well as to be open to "other" cultural traditions. This "culturally sensitive approach," he writes, "allows for the possibility that deeply held values provide the motivational resources to influence certain outcomes" (18). Closely connected with this cultural sensitivity is the need to rely not only on abstract generalities but on concrete local knowledge. As he states (65, echoing Abdullahi An-Na'im): "It is more likely that the struggle to promote human rights can be won if it is fought in ways that build on, rather than challenge, local cultural traditions."[4] Although deviating from a bland universalism equaling uniformity, such attention to local knowledge and cultural particularities does not at all amount to an endorsement of "relativism" in the sense of parochial self-enclosure. For Bell, different particularities can and should engage in mutual scrutiny and critique, with the result that "different cultural values can at best justify different priorities given to rights in cases of conflict" (62). One of the most valuable aspects of the text, in my view, is the deliberate attempt to connect or reconnect theory and practice, philosophical reflection and practical engagement. As Bell writes, in a passage implicitly harking back to Deweyan pragmatism: "I work at the intersection of theory and practice. I have a particular context in mind when I am arguing for something, and I try not to lose sight of the question of effectiveness" (325).

Notwithstanding these and many other qualities, the book is not as even or even-handed as one might wish. By *even-handed* I have in mind especially the front cover: the Statue of Liberty holding in her hand the *Analects*. Quite often one has the impression of a mismatch between the latter and the hand—despite the basic attractiveness of the image. What the image suggests, at least to me, is the notion of an ethical democracy, a democracy sustained by Confucian virtues, or perhaps by a mixture of Confucian, Aristotelian, and contemporary pluralist or multicultural virtues. This is a notion I find on the whole appealing (and have defended in this volume). However, this does not quite seem the direction in which Bell's text is moving. As indicated, the book's title is *Beyond Liberal Democracy*; but one frequently gets the impression that the move is not just beyond "liberal democracy" but beyond democracy *tout court* (leaving as a remnant only what Bell calls "minimal democracy"; 14, 151). Apart from the hankering for elitism (to which I turn later), the impression is sustained by the very definition of "liberal democracy" in the book. As previously stated, the term for Bell means a combination of three elements: human rights, democracy, and capitalism—with all three pillars marked by *laissez-faire* individualism. Hence, in the definition, and in the title of the book, "democracy" is already swallowed up by liberal individualism. Bell does not seem to know, or least seems reluctant to explicate, that there are and have been different meanings of "democracy" not congruent with liberal individualism: among them "social" democracy, popular or populist democracy—and also the kind of ethical democracy extolled by Montesquieu and Dewey. As mentioned before, it seems to be largely the pervasive effect of the Cold War that has blotted these alternatives out of the public imagination. Clearly, any one of these alternatives would have a different relation with the *Analects* and hence a different fit with the Statue of Liberty's hand.[5]

The front cover involves another unevenness or incongruity that touches the book's basic intent. According to its subtitle, the text offers "political thinking for an East Asian context." Each one of the three major parts of the book adds the clause "for an East Asian context" to its heading. The clause speaks well for Bell's modesty or humility and his distaste for missionary posturing. However, not all comparisons are missionary endeavors. There is also the possibility—which lies at the core of comparative studies—that comparison is done for the sake of mutual learning where all parties are able to raise questions while being questioned in turn. Clearly, such mutual questioning (which can be, and has been, called a "dialogue of cultures") cannot be arbitrarily restricted in terms of content or geographical scope—without necessarily being conducive to universal consensus or uniformity. Bell frequently wavers or seems reluctant to concede this point; by tailoring his agreement to "an East Asian context," in any event, he courts the danger of obliterating the cover's Statue of Liberty in favor of a narrowly confined Asian parochialism. At least some of the statements in his book point in that direction. As we read in the concluding chapter (336): "My book is meant for an 'East Asian' context"; its main point is "to provide ideas for people thinking about how to improve East Asian societies" and hence, hopefully, "East Asians will read it." Because it is written in English, "Westerners" may also wish to read it; but the reason given for this expectation—that they "have the power to shape events in East Asia"—oddly contradicts the book's antimissionary bent. At another point (83), seemingly reinforcing Asian parochialism, Bell questions the value of "cross-cultural dialogue" stating that it "will lead to either empty platitudes or politically controversial conclusions likely to be rejected by affected constituents."[6]

Fortunately, parochialism is not the book's prevailing tenor. Referring specifically to Mencius's teachings, Bell acknowledges at one point (251–252) that "the 'founding fathers' of Confucianism defended ideals and practices that were held to be universalizable; they did not view Confucianism as being necessarily confined to a particular group such as the Chinese." At another juncture (63), remembering the central Confucian virtue of "humaneness" or "benevolence," he states that "values similar to aspects of Western conceptions of human rights can also be found in the Confucian tradition; the notion of *ren* (variously translated as benevolence, humanity, or love), for example, expresses the value of impartial concern to relieve human suffering." Such concern, he adds, shows that "Confucianism allows for duties or rights that belong to human persons *simpliciter*, independent of their roles" (or geographical location).[7] To be sure, just as in the case of Western traditions, the "universalizable" character of Confucian teachings does not entail a missionary or imperialist trajectory; but it does imply that "Westerners" can learn from Confucian teachings just as East Asians can learn and benefit from Western ideas about human rights and democracy. In some of the book's more inspiring passages, the value of mutual learning—and hence also the worth of comparative study—is recognized and underscored. Thus, in reflecting on education in contemporary pluralist societies, Bell comments (217) that "multicultural education should draw on the traditions of all ethnic groups in society"; such an inclusive curriculum "has the advantage of encouraging mutual learning and understanding, and thus strengthening the links between the various ethnic groups in society." To this one can add a passage from the concluding chapter that states: "In present-day East Asian societies, 'Western' categories [like human rights and democracy] have also become part of everyday political discourse"; hence, "the scholar of contemporary East Asian political thinking can't help being a comparativist" (326).

Comments of this kind make it all the more puzzling that democracy is presented as uncongenial to, or not "learnable" by East Asians. As indicated earlier, the phrase "beyond liberal democracy" often points beyond democracy *tout court*. Here Bell's elitist penchant comes to the fore, with largely disorienting results. As he writes somewhat condescendingly at one point (150–151): Most people in East Asia "have devoted their time and energy to family and other 'local' obligations, with political decision making left to an educated, public-spirited elite"; hence, the ideal regime in East Asia is one "that reconciles minimal democracy with elite politics"—where the term "minimal" denotes an arrangement "not much more demanding than visiting the voting booth every few years." For Bell, elite politics basically means a system of "meritocracy" where leaders are chosen by means of literary and educational tests (patterned in part on the civil service examinations of imperial China). No doubt, there is a great need for people with talent, expertise, and integrity in modern governments—a need recognized at least since John Stuart Mill. The question is how this demand can be reconciled with democratic aspirations. Bell's proposed meritocracy faces several issues on this score. For one thing, who can devise an equitable set of examinations that will not degenerate into a social caste system? Next, once chosen, how and to whom will the "meritocrats" be held accountable? These questions penetrate into the proposed bicameral structure where one chamber is popularly elected while the upper chamber (the *Xianshiyan*) is based on merit. Although presented as an ideally balanced structure (between people and elite), the insistence on "minimal democracy" (with people only voting every few years but otherwise inactive) tilts or undermines the balance in favor of elite rule.[8]

To Bell's credit, meritocracy is decidedly not synonymous with rule by a power-hungry, autocratic, and self-serving elite; ideally construed again, its function is one of service and educational guidance. As he notes (153), a basic assumption of Confucian ethics, undergirding meritocracy, is that "the highest human good lies in public service"; accordingly, Confucius in the *Analects* speaks of "teaching the people." This assumption, however, implies that the people engaged in public service are imbued with the self-transcending virtues of Confucian ethics (rather than being slaves of their ambitions). The assumption of the *Analects* also implies that the people are indeed "teachable," that is, that they understand the difference between ethical service and domination and thus can differentiate between benign teachers and vile autocrats (and express this distinction, if need be, in political action). This ability, in turn, means that democracy (in more than a minimal sense) cannot be out of their reach, providing proper education. Unfortunately, Bell's comments on education are not always helpful. As he reports (211–215), in a cross-cultural course offered in Singapore he emphasized mainly "politics without morality," choosing as his main exemplar the Chinese "legalist" thinker Han Fei Zi. Generally speaking, *Beyond Liberal Democracy* often displays a disconcerting fascination with Legalism or Chinese "realpolitik" (despite the recorded atrocities inflicted by Legalists on Confucian scholars). This aspect is related to Bell's assertion that East Asian political discourse involves basically an interaction between Legalism and Confucianism, and his repeatedly stated preference for a "Legalistic Confucianism" (19, 258–259).

As against this preference, seeing that the West is already fully saturated with power politics, I find it advisable to uphold the idea of the "Three Teachings" in East Asia: Confucianism, Daoism, and Buddhism.[9] In this formula, East Asian thought is marked by an admirable multicultural blend: with Confucians affirming a strong public ethics which, at the same time, is tempered by the playful an-archy of Daoists and the Buddhist reminder of the contingency or "emptiness" of all supposedly stable worldly structures. With this blending of traditions, East Asia clearly has much to teach the rest of the world.[10]

Notes

Preface

1. Jean Bethke Elshtain, *Democracy on Trial* (New York: Basic Books, 1995), pp. xii, 12. See also Ronald Dworkin, *Is Democracy Possible Here? Principles for a New Political Debate* (Princeton, NJ: Princeton University Press, 2006), and Alan Keenan, *Democracy in Question: Democratic Openness in a Time of Political Closure* (Stanford, CA: Stanford University Press, 2003).

2. Dworkin, *Is Democracy Possible Here?*, 1.

3. Romand Coles, *Beyond Gated Politics: Reflections on the Possibility of Democracy* (Minneapolis, MN: University of Minnesota Press, 2005), 263.

4. For a critique of the "spectator theory of knowledge" see John Dewey, "The Quest for Certainty" (1929), in *John Dewey: The Later Works, 1925–1953*, ed. Jo Ann Boydston (Cardondale, IL: Southern Illinois University, 1983), vol. 4:19. At another point, Dewey eloquently exposed the consequence of the turn to "pure" knowledge and epistemology: "Knowledge divided against itself [i.e., divorced from practice] . . . has played its part in generating enslavement of men, women and children in factories in which they are animated machines to tend inanimate machines. It has maintained sordid slums, flurried and discontented careers, grinding poverty and luxurious wealth, brutal exploitation of nature and man in times of peace and high explosives and noxious gases in times of war." See "The Public and Its Problems" (1927), in *John Dewey: The Later Works*, ed. Jo Ann Boydston (Carbondale, IL: Southern Illinois University, 1981), vol. 2:346.

5. See William E. Connolly, *Pluralism* (Durham, NC: Duke University Press, 2005), 48, 64; also his *The Ethos of Pluralization* (Minneapolis: University of Minnesota Press, 1995). For an anticipation of this kind of pluralism see Dewey, "The Public and Its Problems," 326–327.

Chapter 1

1. Theodor W. Adorno, *Negative Dialektik* (Frankfurt: Suhrkamp, 1966), 51–52. Trans E. B. Ashton as *Negative Dialectics* (New York: Seabury Press, 1973).

2. On Leibniz see Hans Heinz Holz, *Leibniz* (Stuttgart: Kohlhammer Verlag, 1958); John Dewey, "Leibniz's New Essays Concerning the Human Understanding (1888)," in *John Dewey: The Early Works, 1882–1898*, vol. 1, ed. George E. Axtelle et al. (Carbondale, IL: Southern Illinois University Press, 1969), 253–435; also my "The Natural Theology of the Chinese: Leibniz and Confucianism," in *In Search of the Good Life: A Pedagogy for Troubled Times* (Lexington, KY: The University Press of Kentucky, 2007), 80–94.

3. See Montesquieu, *The Spirit of Laws*, ed. David W. Carrithers (Berkeley: University of California Press, 1977), 132–33.

4. *The Spirit of Laws*, 118, 130. The reason why education is particularly important in democracy is clearly spelled out (130): "The fear of despotic governments rises naturally of itself amidst threats and punishments; the honor of monarchies is favored by the passions, and favors them in its turn. But virtue is a self-renunciation which is always arduous and painful. . . . This love [of equality] is peculiar to democracies. In these alone the government is entrusted to private citizens. Now government is like everything else: to preserve it, we must love it." In my view, it is important to distinguish between Montesquieu and Rousseau. There are three basic differences. First, following modern "voluntarism," Rousseau builds his theory on "will" (general will, will of all), whereas Montesquieu relies on the more classical notions of spirit, heart, and soul. Second, Rousseau fellows Hobbesian teachings regarding social contract and the notion of popular "sovereignty"—a notion not very prominent in Montesquieu. Finally, Rousseau's general will can be unified or collectivized in Jacobin fashion; by contrast, Montesquieu's spirit allows for great diversity held together only by the gentle bond of affection.

5. See G. W. F. Hegel, *Philosophy of Right*, trans. T. M. Knox (Oxford: Oxford University Press, 1967), 16 (par. 3), 161 (par. 261), 177–78 (par. 273).

6. Alexis de Tocqueville, *Democracy in America*, ed. Phillips Bradley, vol. 1 (New York: Vintage Books, 1945), 3, 6–8. Despite the great renown rightly enjoyed by the author, it seems to me important to point out certain theoretical shortfalls. Thus, his discussion of "sovereignty of the people" (57–60) still seems strongly indebted to Hobbes and does not sufficiently question the idea of "sovereignty." Similarly, his discussion of "equality" (48–56) seems to deal mainly with quantitative egalitarianism, whereas his comments on "love of equality" (vol. 2, 99–103) fall far below Montesquieu's insights on this topic.

7. See Dewey, "Creative Democracy—The Task Before US" (1939) in *John Dewey, The Later Works, 1925–1953*, vol. 14, ed. Jo Ann Boydston (Carbondale, IL: Southern Illinois University Press, 1988), 226; and "Democracy and Education" (1916), in *John Dewey: The Middle Works, 1899–1924*, vol. 9, ed. Jo Ann Boydston (Carbondale, IL: Southern Illinois University Press, 1980), 93.

8. John Dewey, "The Public and Its Problems" (1927), in *John Dewey: The Later Works, 1925–1953*, vol. 2 (Carbondale, IL: Southern Illinois University, 1981), 325. As he adds pointedly (326): "There is no sanctity in universal suffrage, frequent elections, majority rule, congressional and cabinet government."

9. Robert A. Dahl, *A Preface to Democratic Theory* (Chicago: University of Chicago Press, 1956), 2, 18–19. With regard to pre-revolutionary "virtue" he refers to Clinton Rossiter, *Seedtime of the Republic* (New York: Harcourt, Brace & Co., 1952), 429–32. Apart from Madison, the minimalist cenception of democracy finds precursors in some of the writings of Max Weber and Joseph Schumpter.

10. Dahl, *A Preface to Democratic Theory*, 22, 82–83. The index to the study contains no entry for education.

11. Giovanni Sartori, *The Theory of Democracy Revisited* (Chatham, NJ: Chatham House Publ., 1987), vol. 1, 12–13, 17–18, 241–42. Although leaning toward proceduralism, Sartori clearly keeps his distance from "rational choice theory," which was becoming popular at the time of his writing (243): "The citizen of present-day democracies is told by all quarters that he should be 'rational,' meaning by this that he should perceive and calculate rationally his own interest and that his political behavior should be, if rational, exactly like his individual economic behavior. Can a truly ethic-minded person accept this? What has an image of man that portrays him—not in fact, but normatively—as a well-calculating egoist to do with ethics?" A strong proceduralist leaning is also present in the work of Jürgen Habermas; see, e.g., his "Struggles for Recognition in the Democratic Constitutional State," in Amy Gutman, ed., *Multiculturalism: Examining the Politics of Recognition* (Princeton, NJ: Princeton University Press, 1994), 107–48. What is called "deliberative democratic theory" (partly influenced by Habermas) tends to waver between proceduralism and a more robust Hegelian conception of ethical recognition.

12. *The Theory of Democracy Revisited*, vol. 2, 476–77. Sartori often refers polemically to C. B. Macpherson, *The Real World of Democracy* (Oxford: Clarendon Press, 1966).

13. William H. Riker, *Liberalism Against Populism: A Confrontation Between the Theory of Democracy and the Theory of Social Choice* (Prospect Heights, IL: Waveland Press, 1982), 1–3.

14. *Liberalism Against Populism*, 7, 9–12, 246. To drive home the contrast he adds (252): "Populism puts democracy [read: liberalism or liberal democracy] at risk. . . . The maintenance of [liberal] democracy requires therefore the minimization of the risk in populism."

15. Jean-François Lyotard, *The Postmodern Condition: A Report on Knowledge*, trans. Geoff Bennington and Brian Massumi (Minneapolis: University of Minnesota Press, 1984), xxii–xxv. Compare also his *The Postmodern Explained*, trans. Julian Pefanis and Morgan Tomas (Minneapolis, MN: University of Minnesota Press, 1992).

16. Stephen K. White, *Political Theory and Postmodernism* (Cambridge, UK: Cambridge University Press, 1991), x, 1–2, 72. To avoid the danger of a self-defeating "hypermodernism" Wayne Gabardi opts for the term "critical postmodernism." Somewhat confusingly, however, he also uses "postmodern" to designate a very dubious political development: the rise of a "postmodern,

neo-liberal, techno-oligarchy." See his *Negotiating Postmodernism* (Minneapolis: University of Minnesota Press, 2001), xix–xxi, xxii. Compare also my "Modernity in the Crossfire: Comments on the Postmodern Turn," in John Paul Jones III, Wolfgang Natter and Theodore R. Schatzki, eds., *Postmodern Contentions: Epochs, Politics, Space* (New York: Guilford Press, 1993), 17–38.

17. See Martin Heidegger, "What is Metaphysics?" in David F. Krell, ed., *Martin Heidegger: Basic Writings* (New York: Harper & Row, 1977), 95–112. As Heidegger writes there (105): Nothing is "neither the annihilation of beings nor does it spring from a negation. . . . The essence of the originally nihilating nothing lies in this, that it brings human *Dasein* for the first time before beings as such."

18. See Claude Lefort, *Democracy and Political Theory*, trans. David Macey (Minneapolis: University of Minnesota Press, 1988), 9–12, 217–26. The distinction between the visible and the invisible refers back to Lefort's friend, Maurice Merleau-Ponty and his *The Visible and the Invisible, followed by Working Notes*, ed. Claude Lefort, trans. Alphonso Lingis (Evanston, IL: Northwestern University Press, 1968). For a fuller discussion of Lefort see my "Post-Metaphysics and Democracy," *Political Theory*, vol. 21 (1993), 101–27; a revised version of the essay, under the title "Post-Metaphysical Politics: Heidegger and Democracy," appears in my *The Other Heidegger* (Ithaca, NY: Cornell University Press, 1993), 77–105. See also below, Appendix A: "Democracy Without Banisters: Reading Claude Lefort."

19. See Ernesto-Laclau and Chantal Mouffe, *Hegemony and Socialist Strategy: Towards a Radical Democratic Politics*, trans. Winston Moore and Paul Cammack (London: Verso, 1985), 51–62, 122–33. Compare also Laclau, *New Reflections on the Revolution of Our Time* (London: Verso, 1990); Mouffe, *The Return of the Political* (London: Verso, 1993) and *The Democratic Paradox* (London: Verso, 2000); and below, Appendix B: "The Return of the Political: On Chantal Mouffe."

20. See Jacques Derrida, *Rogues: Two Essays on Reason*, trans. Pascale-Anne Brault and Michael Naas (Stanford, CA: Stanford University Press, 2005), 23, 36–38.

21. See Masao Abe, *Zen and Western Thought*, ed. William R. LaFleur (Honolulu: University of Hawaii Press, 1985), 252–56. Compare also my "*Sunyata* East and West," in *Beyond Orientalism: Essays on Cross-Cultural Encounter* (Albany, NY: State University of New York Press, 1996), 175–99; and on recent Asian thought Appendix C below, "Exiting Liberal Democracy: Bell and Confucian Ethics."

Chapter 2

1. Hyppolite's lecture was held on February 16, 1947, in the *Institut d'Etudes Germaniques*. Hyppolite had earlier composed a French translation, titled *Phénoménologie de l'esprit*, and achieved fame with his *Genèse et structure de la Phénoménologie de l'esprit* (Paris: Aubier, 1946), translated into English

by Samuel Cherniak and John Heckman as *Genesis and Structure of the Phenomenology of Spirit* (Evanston, IL: Northwestern University Press, 1974). Hyppolite's work was preceded and in part stimulated by lectures on Hegel presented by Alexandre Kojève's at the *Ecole des Hautes Etudes* from 1933 to 1939, lectures that formed the basis of Kojève's *Introduction to the Reading of Hegel* (French 1947), ed. Allan Bloom, trans. James Nichols, Jr. (New York: Basic Books, 1969).

2. Maurice Merleau-Ponty, "Hegel's Existentialism," in *Sense and Non-Sense*, trans. Hubert L. and Patricia A. Dreyfus (Evanston, IL: Northwestern University Press, 1964), 64. See also Merleau-Ponty, "Philosophy and Non-Philosophy Since Hegel" (1961), trans. Hugh J. Silverman, in Silverman, ed., *Philosophy and Non-Philosophy Since Merleau-Ponty* (London & New York: Routledge, 1988), 9–83; and Sonia Kruks, "Merleau-Ponty, Hegel, and the Dialectic," *Journal of the British Society for Phenomenology*, vol. 7 (1976), 96–110.

3. G. W. F. Hegel, *The Phenomenology of Mind*, trans. J. B. Baillie (New York: Harper & Row, 1967), 69. My translation does not always follow Baillie's text, but takes its cues also from the German version: *Phänomenologie des Geistes*, 2nd ed., ed. Eva Moldenhauer and Karl M. Michel (Frankfurt: Suhrkamp, 1975), 13.

4. *The Phenomenology of Mind*, 80–81, 85–86, 88; *Phänomenologie des Geistes*, 22–23, 28, 31. The "circle" discussed by Hegel bears a certain similarity of the so-called "hermeneutical circle," but differs from the latter by its presumed completeness or "absoluteness."

5. *The Phenomenology of Mind*, 89–90, 96; *Phänomenologie des Geistes*, 31–32, 38.

6. *The Phenomenology of Mind*, 93, 96; *Phänomenologie des Geistes*, 36, 39.

7. *The Phenomenology of Mind*, 94; *Phänomenologie des Geistes*, 36–37.

8. Hegel, "Jenaer Realphilosophie (1805/06)," in *Frühe politische Systeme*, ed. Gerhard Göhler (Frankfurt: Ullstein, 1974), 265–9.

9. "Jenaer Realphilosophie," 251–2, 267–9.

10. "Jenaer Realphilosophie," 252, 260–3.

11. Hegel, *Philosophie des Rechts (Die Vorlesung von 1819–1820)*, ed. Dieter Henrich (Frankfurt: Suhrkamp, 1983), 48, 50–52, 55.

12. Hegel, *Grundlinien der Philosophie des Rechts* (Frankfurt: Suhrkamp, 1976), par. 181–7, 338–44; *Hegel's Philosophy of Right*, trans. T. M. Knox (Oxford, UK: Oxford University Press, 1967), 122–5, 266–7.

13. *Grundlinien der Philosophie des Rechts*, par. 260–2, 406–10; *Hegel's Philosophy of Right*, 160–2, 280. Hegel in this context pays tribute to Montesquieu for having developed the "philosophical notion of always treating the part in its relation to the whole."

14. Martin Heidegger, *Hegel*, Part 1: *Die Negativität, Eine Auseinandersetzung mit Hegel aus dem Ansatz der Negativität* (1938/39, 1941), ed. Ingrid Schüssler (*Gesamtausgabe*, vol. 68; Frankfurt: Klostermann, 1993), 6. The same volume contains as Part 2: *Erläuterung der "Einleitung" zu Hegels "Phänomenologie des*

Geistes" (1942). Already a decade earlier (in 1930/31), Heidegger had presented a lecture course on the *Phenomenology*. See his *Hegel's Phänomenologie des Geistes* (*Gesamtausgabe*, vol. 32), ed. Ingtraud Görland (Frankfurt: Klostermann, 1980); *Hegel's Phenomenology of Spirit*, trans. Parvis Emad and Kenneth Maly (Bloomington, IN: Indiana University Press, 1988).

15. Hegel, *The Phenomenology of Mind*, 80, 82, 93, 118; *Phänomenologie des Geistes*, 23, 25, 36, 57.

16. Heidegger, *Hegel*, Part 1, 13–14. Compare in this context Diana Coole, *Negativity and Politics: Dionysus and Dialectics from Kant to Poststructuralism* (London & New York: Routledge, 2000).

17. Heidegger, *Sein und Zeit*, 11th ed. (Tübingen: Niemeyer, 1967), par. 1, 3, par. 82, 433–4; *Being and Time: A Translation of Sein und Zeit*, trans. John Macquarrie and Edward Robinson (New York: Harper & Row, 1962), 22, 484.

18. Heidegger, "Was ist Metaphysik?" in *Wegmarken* (Frankfurt: Klostermann, 1967), 12; "What is Metaphysics?" in *Martin Heidegger: Basic Writings*, ed. David F. Krell (New York: Harper & Row, 1977), 106.

19. Heidegger, *Hegel*, Part 1, 15–17, 47–48.

20. Theodor W. Adorno, *Negative Dialektik* (Frankfurt: Suhrkamp, 1966), 36, 73, 177–9; *Negative Dialectics*, trans. E. B. Ashton (New York: Seabury Press, 1973), 27–28, 67, 177–9. (In the above and subsequent citations I have altered this translation for purposes of clarity.)

21. Adorno, *Negative Dialektik*, 22, 157, 159, 312–5; *Negative Dialectics*, 12–13, 156–9, 319–21.

22. Merleau-Ponty, *Sense and Non-Sense*, 64–65.

23. Heidegger, "Hegel's Begriff der Erfahrung" (1942–43), in *Holzwege* (Frankfurt: Klostermann, 1963), pp 170–1, 173, 186; *Hegel's Concept of Experience*, trans. J. Glenn Gray and Fred I. Wieck (New York: Harper & Row, 1970), 119–21, 126, 146. (In the above, I have altered the translation slightly for purposes of clarity.)

24. Hegel, "System der Sittlichkeit," in *Frühe politische Systeme*, ed. Göhler, 26–29, 59–76; for an English version (not entirely followed here) see Hegel, *System of Ethical Life (1802/3) and First Philosophy of Spirit*, ed. and trans. H. S. Harris and T. M. Knox (Albany, NY: State University of New York Press, 1979), 111–2, 142–56.

25. Hegel, *Grundlinien der Philosophie des Rechts*, par. 142, 146–51, 292, 294–301; *Hegel's Philosophy of Right*, 105–8.

26. Adorno, *Minima Moralia: Reflexionen aus dem beschädigten Leben* (Frankfurt: Suhrkamp, 1951), 8–9; *Minima Moralia: Reflections from Damaged Life*, trans. E.F.N. Jephcott (London: Verso, 1978), 16–17.

27. Heidegger, *Über den Humanisms* (1946; Frankfurt: Klostermann, 1968), 41, 43; "Letter on Humanism," in *Martin Heidegger: Basic Writings*, ed. Krell, 234–5, 237. The English translation is by Frank A. Capuzzi in collaboration with J. Glenn Gray. (In the above citations I have altered this translation slightly for purposes of clarity. The translation mistakenly renders the term "the hale" [*das Heile*] as "healing.") In telling fashion, Hans-Georg Gadamer

has explored the connection of Heidegger's *ethos* with Aristotelian practical philosophy. See, e.g., his "On the Possibility of a Philosophical Ethics" and "The Ethics of Value and Practical Philosophy" in Gadamer, *Hermeneutics, Religion, and Ethics*, trans. Joel Weinsheimer (New Haven, CT: Yale University Press, 1999), 18–36, 103–18. On Heidegger and Aristotle compare also Walter A. Brogan, *Heidegger and Aristotle: The Twofoldness of Being* (Albany: NY: State University of New York Press, 2005) and Lawrence J. Hatab, *Ethics and Finitude* (Lanham, MD: Rowman & Littlefield Publ., 2000).

28. Merleau-Ponty, *Humanism and Terror*, trans. John O'Neill (Boston, MA: Beacon Press, 1969), xiv.

29. William E. Connolly, *Pluralism* (Durham, NC: Duke University Press, 2005), 48, 65. Aristotelian (and perhaps Hegelian) overtones are clearly evident in Connolly's statement: "An ethic is not derived in the way a conclusion is drawn from a set of premises, nor is it systematic in the way that, say, the Kantian philosophy is said to be. An ethical sensibility becomes *infused* into the interests, identities, and connections that help to constitute you" (94). A quasi-Heideggerian idiom surfaces in the section "Pluralism and Care for the World" where we read: "In a pluralistic universe, care for the world emerges from the multiplication of [available] circuits" (90).

30. Connolly, *Pluralism*, 159.

31. Hans-Georg Gadamer, "Hegel's Philosophy and Its Aftereffects until Today" (1972), in his *Reason in the Age of Science*, trans. Frederick G. Lawrence (Cambridge, MA: MIT Press, 1981), 37. The essay obviously was written long before Francis Fukuyama, *The End of History and the Last Man* (New York: The Free Press, 1992). Compare in this context also Richard J. Bernstein, "Why Hegel Now?" in his *Philosophical Profiles: Essays in a Pragmatic Mode* (Philadelphia: University of Pennsylvania Press, 1986), 141–75.

32. Merleau-Ponty, *Signs*, trans. Richard C. McCleary (Evanston, IL: Northwestern University Press, 1964), 139. "Western philosophy," he continues, "can learn from [other cultures] to rediscover the relationship to being and initial option which gave it birth, and to estimate the possibilities we have shut ourselves off from in becoming 'Westerners' and perhaps reopen them."

Chapter 3

1. For these developments see, e.g., the section "From Hegel to Marx" in Robert Tucker, *Philosophy and Myth in Karl Marx* (Cambridge, UK: Cambridge University Press, 1961), 73–120.

2. John Dewey, "How We Think" (1909), in *John Dewey: The Middle Works, 1899–1924*, vol. 6, ed. Jo Ann Boydston (Carbondale, IL: Southern Illinois University Press, 1978), 185, 190–91.

3. "How We Think," 288, 295–96.

4. "How We Think," 301, 318, 329, 332, 336, 346.

5. Richard Rorty, an avowed Deweyan, goes even a step further by stating: "Granted that Dewey never stopped talking about 'scientific method,'

I submit that he never had anything very useful to say about it. Those who think I am overstating my case here, should, I think, tell us what this thing called 'method' . . . is supposed to be." See Rorty, "Response to Gouinlock," in *Rorty and Pragmatism: The Philosopher Responds to His Critics*, ed. Herman Saatkamp, Jr. (Nashville, TN: Vanderbilt University Press, 1995), 94. For helpful comments on Dewey's notion of "inquiry" we James Scott Johnston, *Inquiry and Education: John Dewey and the Quest for Democracy* (Albany, NY: State University of New York Press, 2006), 15–60; and Larry A. Hickman, "Dewey's Theory of Inquiry," in Hickman, ed., *Reading Dewey: Interpretation for a Postmodern Generation* (Bloomington, IN: Indiana University Press, 1998), 166–86.

6. Dewey, "The Need for a Recovery of Philosophy," in *John Dewey: The Middle Works, 1899–1924*, vol. 10, ed. Jo Ann Boydston (Carbondale, IL: Southern Illinois University Press, 1980), 17. The critique of rationalism is directed chiefly against Descartes' bifurcation of mind and matter, "*res cogitans*" and "*res extensa*." In a modified sense, the critique extends to the Kantian separation of *a priori* categories and *a posteriori* phenomena. In Kantianism, we read, "a reason which transcends experience must provide synthesis" for "a sensory manifold being all of which is really empirical in experience" (13).

7. "The Need for a Recovery of Philosophy," 18, 23, 39, 41–42. For a fuller development of this view see John Dewey and Arthur Bentley, "Knowing and the Known," in *John Dewey: The Later Works, 1925–1952*, vol. 16, ed. Jo Ann Boydston (Carbondale, IL: Southern Illinois University Press, 1989), 1–294.

8. Dewey, "The Need for a Recovery of Philosophy," 44–45, 48. The concluding paragraph contains a dark observation whose relevance clearly extends from his period to our time: "We tend to combine a loose and ineffective optimism with assent to the doctrine to take who can take: a deification of power. All peoples at all times have been narrowly realistic in practice and have then employed idealizations [ideologies] to cover up in sentiment and theory their brutalities. But never, perhaps, has the tendency been so dangerous and so tempting as with ourselves" (48)

9. Dewey, "Has Philosophy a Future?" in *John Dewey: The Later Works, 1925–1953*, vol. 16, ed. Jo Ann Boydston (Carbondale, IL: Southern Illinois University Press, 1989), 358–60. Among detached or backward-looking perspectives the essay included the exclusive study of "past systems," a study whose scholarship is "often admirable" but that tends to reduce philosophy to history. At least implicitly, the charge of aloofness extended also to current fashions of logical positivism, analytical philosophy, and semiotics. "Another movement active and even assertive within its own chosen but narrow limits," we read, "identifies philosophy exclusively with the search for forms simply as forms; it engages in an attempt to discover forms that are comprehensive only because they are so abstract as to have no connection with any specific subject matter whatever, human or otherwise. This movement, in spite of or rather because of its devotion to the acquisition of merely technical skill, results in forms that are useful only in producing more forms of the same empty type" (361).

10. "Has Philosophy a Future?," 362–63.

11. "Has Philosophy a Future?," 365, 368. Compare also the essay "Philosophy's Future in Our Scientific Age" in the same volume, where we read (376–77): "Search for the kind of understanding that was lacking in Athens, Socrates termed *philosophy*, the love of wisdom. . . . The similarity of our present situation to that in which Socrates propounded the need for philosophy . . . should, it seems to me, be reasonably obvious. . . . Those philosophers who are now subjected to criticism from their fellow-professionals on the ground that concern with the needs, troubles, and problems of man is not 'philosophical,' may, if they feel it necessary, draw support and courage from the fact that they are following, however imperfectly, in the path initiated by the man to whom is due the very term *philosophy*." Of course, Dewey might also have appealed to Aristotle's "practical" philosophy.

12. Dewey, "My Pedagogic Creed," in *John Dewey: The Early Works, 1882–1898*, vol. 5, ed. Jo Ann Boydston (Carbondale, IL: Southern Illinois University Press, 1972), 84.

13. "My Pedagogic Creed," 85–86, 93. Affirming a broadly humanist orientation, Dewey adds: "I believe, finally, that the teacher is engaged, not simply in the training of individuals, but in the formation of a proper social life. I believe that every teacher should realize the dignity of his calling; that he is a social servant set apart for the maintenance of proper social order and the securing of the right social growth" (95).

14. Dewey, "Democracy and Education," in *John Dewey: The Middle Works, 1899–1924*, vol. 9, ed. Jo Ann Boydston (Carbondale, IL: Southern Illinois University Press, 1980), 301–4. (In the above I have corrected for gender bias.) In the words of Raymond D. Boisvert: "Classical liberals were wrong to conceive of freedom as something that exists antecedently and can be made manifest by the simple removal of restrictions. It is a capacity that may be developed through time and in conjunction with the aid of others. . . . Indeed, increasing 'effective' freedom often requires others (as mentors, teachers, suppliers of materials) and constraint (in the form of discipline, effort, and practice)." See his *John Dewey: Rethinking Our Time* (Albany, NY: State University of New York Press, 1998), 62. Boisvert also draws attention (66–68) to the need to distinguish between an asocial "individualism" and an "individuality" seen as "the distinctive manner in which someone participates in communal life."

15. Dewey, "Democracy and Education," 96–102, 304.

16. Dewey, "American Education and Culture" (1916), in *John Dewey: The Middle Works, 1899–1924*, vol. 10, ed. Jo Ann Boydston (Carbondale, IL: Southern Illinois University Press, 1980), 198–99.

17. Dewey, "Democracy and Education," 202–14, 258. Regarding Schiller's "play drive" compare my "Beautiful Freedom: Schiller on the Aesthetic Education of Humanity" in my *In Search of the Good Life: A Pedagogy for Troubled Times* (Lexington, KY: University of Kentucky Press, 2007), 116–37.

18. Dewey, "Art as Experience," in *John Dewey: The Later Works, 1925–1953*, vol. 10, ed. Jo Ann Boydston (Carbondale, IL: Southern Illinois University Press, 1987), 21.

19. "Art as Experience," xiii–xiv, 348, 352. Dewey quotes at this point Robert Browning: "But Art, wherein man speaks in no wise to man,/Only to mankind—Art may tell a truth/obliquely, do the deed shall breed the thought." Compare in this context Richard Shusterman, *Pragmatist Aesthetics: Living Beauty, Rethinking Art* (Oxford: Blackwell, 1992); and Thomas M. Alexander, "The Art of Life: Dewey's Aesthetics," in Hickman, ed., *Reading Dewey*, 1–22.

20. Boisvert, *John Dewey: Rethinking Our Time*, 26.

21. Dewey is sometimes one-sidedly portrayed as an advocate of liberalism, with only minor attention to the issue of democracy. Compare, e.g., Alan Ryan, *John Dewey and the High Tide of American Liberalism* (New York: Norton, 1997); Daniel Savage, *John Dewey's Liberalism: Individual, Community, and Self-Development* (Carbondale, IL: Southern Illinois University Press, 2001). Regarding the notion of "negative liberty" see Isaiah Berlin, *Four Essays on Liberty* (London: Oxford University Press, 1977).

22. Dewey, "Philosophy and Democracy" (1919), in Larry A. Hickman and Thomas M. Alexander, eds., *The Essential Dewey*, vol. 1: *Pragmatism, Education, Democracy* (Bloomington, IN: Indiana University Press, 1998), 76–77.

23. "Philosophy and Democracy," 76–78.

24. Dewey, "The Ethics of Democracy," in *John Dewey: The Early Works, 1882–1898*, vol. 1, ed. George E. Axtelle et al. (Carbondale, IL: Southern Illinois University, 1969), 229–31.

25. "The Ethics of Democracy," 233, 236–40. The concluding paragraph of the essay contains one of Dewey's most inspiring passages (248–49): "Democracy and the one, the ultimate, ethical ideal of humanity are to my mind synonyms. The idea of democracy, the ideas of liberty, equality, and fraternity, represent a society in which the distinction between the spiritual and the secular has ceased, and as in Greek theory, as in the Christian theory of the Kingdom of God, the church and the state, the divine and the human organization of society are one." Regarding the emphasis on universal "relationism," it is probably no coincidence that the volume containing the essay on "The Ethics of Democracy" also features Dewey's lengthy treatise on "Leibniz's *New Essays* Concerning the Human Understanding," 253–435.

26. Dewey, "Democracy and Education," 93.

27. Dewey, "Democracy is Radical," in *John Dewey: The Later Works, 1925–1953*, vol. 11, ed. Jo Ann Boydston (Carbondale, IL: Southern Illinois University Press, 1987), 298–99. While denouncing Communist totalitarianism, Dewey was by no means ready to present Western liberal democracy as embodiment of public virtue. As he wrote, in language reminiscent of Maurice Merleau-Ponty (298): "There is intellectual hypocrisy and moral contradiction in the creed of those who uphold the need for at least a temporary dictatorship of a class as well as in the position of those who assert that the present economic system is one of freedom of initiative and of opportunity for all."

28. Dewey, "Creative Democracy—The Task Before Us," in *John Dewey: The Later Works, 1925–1953*, vol. 14, ed. Jo Ann Boydston (Carbondale, IL: Southern Illinois University, 1988), 225–30.

29. In fairness, one needs to add that there are also pockets of "communitarianism" left. However, these pockets often tend to be walled or "gated" communities, insisting on internal conformity—and not exemplars of the generous hospitality to strangers advocated by Dewey.

30. See Charles Taylor, *The Ethics of Authenticity* (Cambridge, MA: Harvard University Press, 1992), 61, 112, 118–19.

31. Hickman, "Dewey's Theory of Inquiry," 168. Compare also Steven C. Rockefeller's comments: "Some of Rorty's statements seem to involve a dualism of science and religious faith that Dewey worked to overcome.... There are [also] important differences between Dewey's experimentalism and Rorty's linguistic pragmatism." See his "Dewey's Philosophy of Religious Experience," in Hickman, ed., *Reading Dewey*, 145. For an even stronger critique of Rorty's position see Richard Bernstein, "One Step Forward, Two Steps Backward: Rorty on Liberal Democracy and Philosophy" and "Rorty's Liberal Utopia" in his *The New Constellation: The Ethico-Political Horizons of Modernity/Postmodernity* (Cambridge, MA: MIT Press, 1992), 230–57, 258–92. Apart from Bernstein, the holistic tenor of Dewey's pragmatism has been continued in recent decades especially by Richard Shusterman, *Practicing Philosophy: Pragmatism and the Philosophical Life* (New York: Routledge, 1997); and Morton White, *A Philosophy of Culture: The Scope of Holistic Pragmatism* (Princeton, NJ: Princeton University Press, 2002). In his early writings Jürgen Habermas supported what one may call a "pragmatic critical theory." However, his subsequent turn toward "rational discourse" opened a gulf between reason and action more in tune with (non- or anti-Deweyan) analytical philosophy.

32. Dewey, "Liberalism and Social Action," in *John Dewey: The Later Works, 1925–1953*, vol. 11, ed. Jo Ann Boydston (Carbondale, IL: Southern Illinois University, 1987), 44–45. Regarding the "unity of the act," compare "The Theory of Emotion," in *John Dewey: The Early Works*, vol. 4, ed. Jo Ann Boydston (Carbondale, IL: Southern Illinois University, 1971), 174. Regarding "receptive activity" see Dewey, "Having an Experience" (1934) in *John Dewey: The Later Works, 1925–1953*, vol. 10 ed. Jo Ann Boydston (Carbondale, IL: Southern Illinois University, 1987), 47–48; and Alexander, "The Art of Life: Dewey's Aesthetics," 13, 16. Another problematic feature of Dewey's thought is his emphasis on "growth" as the goal of education, inquiry, and democratic action. In this respect, I tend to agree with John Stuhr's criticism of "growth" and also with James Scott Johnston when he writes that "growth is no longer tied to the conceptual play of the imagination" today and that in this regard "we can and must throw away our [or Dewey's] theoretical ladder." See his *Inquiry and Education: John Dewey and the Quest for Democracy* (Albany, NY: State University of New York Press, 2006), 186; also compare John Stuhr, *Pragmatism, Postmodernism, and the Future of Philosophy* (New York: Routledge, 2003).

33. As they write: "If contemporary comparative philosophic activity is any indication, it might be the pragmatic philosophies associated with Peirce, James, Dewey, and Mead, and extended toward a process philosophy such as that of Alfred N. Whitehead, that can serve as the best resource for

philosophical concepts and doctrines permitting responsible access to Confucius' thought." See David L. Hall and Roger T. Ames, *Thinking Through Confucius* (Albany, NY: State University of New York Press, 1987), 15. Compare also Barry Keenan, *The Dewey Experiment in China* (Cambridge, MA: Harvard University Press, 1977).

34. Dewey, "Creative Democracy—The Task Before Us," 228.

Chapter 4

1. Martin Heidegger, *Über den Humanismus* (Frankfurt: Klostermann, 1949), 5; "Letter on Humanism," in *Martin Heidegger: Basic Writings*, ed. David F. Krell (New York: Harper & Row, 1977), 193. (I have slightly modified the translation for purposes of clarity.)

2. See Jürgen Habermas, *The Philosophical Discourse of Modernity: Twelve Lectures*, trans. Frederick Lawrence (Cambridge, MA: MIT Press, 1987), especially 148; Charles Taylor, "Engaged Agency and Background in Heidegger," in Charles B. Guignon, eds. *The Cambridge Companion to Heidegger* (Cambridge, UK: Cambridge University Press, 1993), 317–36. For additional attempts to link Heidegger and pragmatism compare, e.g., Richard Rorty, *Philosophy and the Mirror of Nature* (Princeton, NJ: Princeton University Press, 1979); Alan Ryan, *John Dewey and the High Tide of American Liberalism* (New York: Norton, 1995); and Nikolas Kompridis, *Critique and Disclosure: Critical Theory Between Past and Future* (Cambridge, MA: MIT Press, 2006), especially 112–13.

3. Heidegger, *Sein und Zeit*, 11th ed. (Tübingen: Niemeyer, 1967), par. 15, 67, par. 18, 87; *Being and Time: A Translation of Sein und Zeit*, trans. John Macquarrie & Edward Robinson (New York: Harper & Row, 1962), 95, 121. In Taylor's perceptive words: "In *Being and Time*, [Heidegger] argues that things are disclosed first as part of a world, that is, as the correlates of concerned involvement, and within a totality of such involvements. This undercuts the first and third features of the disengaged picture [atomism of input and cognitive neutrality, postulated by positivist epistemology], and hence makes the second feature [lack of relations] inoperative." See his "Engaged Agency and Background in Heidegger," 332.

4. Heidegger, *Sein und Zeit*, par. 7, 38, par. 18, 86; *Being and Time*, 62, 119.

5. Heidegger, *Einleitung in die Philosophie*, ed. Otto Saame and Ina Saame-Speidel (*Gesamtausgabe*, vol. 27; Frankfurt: Klostermann, 1996), 2–3.

6. *Einleitung in die Philosophie*, 4–5, 11. The statement that *Dasein* cannot "possess itself" (*ganz und gar nicht das Eigentum seiner selbst ist*) seems to imply a radical rejection of Max Stirner's *Der Einzige und sein Eigentum* (1845); English: *The Ego and His Own*, trans. Steven T. Byington, ed. John Carroll (New York: Harper & Row, 1971).

7. Heidegger, *Einleitung in die Philosophie*, 22–23. As one should note, *paideia* for Heidegger does not at all coincide with indoctrination or rote learn-

ing; instead, education has to rely on a reticent and subdued (*unaufdringlich*) mode of example or exemplary living (8).

8. Martin Heidegger, "Platons Lehre von der Wahrheit," in *Wegmarken* (Frankfurt: Klostermann, 1967), 123. Compare also Heidegger, *Vom Wesen der Wahrheit: Zu Platons Höhlengleichnis und Theätet*, ed. Hermann Mörchen (*Gesamtausgabe* vol. 34; Frankfurt: Klostermann, 1988).

9. "Platons Lehre von der Wahrheit," 122–23.

10. *Einleitung in die Philosophie*, 102–3.

11. *Einleitung in die Philosophie*, 173–78, 183–84. The references are to Aristotle, *Politics* 1325b16 and *Nicomachean Ethics* 1176b1, 1177a12, 1177b30. Heidegger (p. 175) underscores and endorses especially Aristotle's statement in the *Politics* that "the *telos* of human beings is *eupraxia*."

12. Heidegger, *Einleitung in die Philosophie*, 74–75, 118–19, 206–7. Perhaps in order to differentiate "transgression" and "transcendence" toward Being from the mere cognition of perennial ideas, the lecture course portrays transcending as participation in a play (*Spiel*) or world play (*Weltspiel*), a play whose "rules" are constantly being formed in the process of playing; see 311–15.

13. *Einleitung in die Philosophie*, 213–14, 220. The citation is from Plato, *Phaidros* 247b. As one should note, in invoking Plato, Heidegger does not subscribe to the kind of "two-world" theory often ascribed to Platonism. As he states (p. 210): "Ontological truth and ontic truth—corresponding to the difference between Being and beings—stand in an original relationship. What we have here are not two 'realms' which could be juxtaposed to each other; rather, the issue is the distinctive unity *and* difference of the two in their mutual belonging."

14. *Einleitung in die Philosophie*, 84–87.

15. *Einleitung in die Philosophie*, 90–92, 96, 105–7, 324–25.

16. Günter Figal, *Martin Heidegger: Phänomenologie der Freiheit*, 3rd ed. (Weinheim: Athenäum Verlag, 2000), 23, 27. Compare also Figal, *For a Philosophy of Freedom and Strife: Politics, Aesthetics, Metaphysics*, trans. Wayne Klein (Albany, NY: State University of New York Press, 1998).

17. For studies on the Aristotelian "connection" compare, e.g., Walter A. Brogan, *Heidegger and Aristotle: The Twofoldness of Being* (Albany, NY: State University of New York Press, 2005); Mark Sinclair, *Heidegger, Aristotle, and the Work of Art: Poiesis in Being* (New York: Palgrave, 2006); Chiara Agnello, *Heidegger e Aristotele: verità e linguaggio* (Geneva: Il Melangelo, 2006); Brian Elliott, *Anfang und Ende der Philosophie: Eine Untersuchung zu Heideggers Aneignung der aristotelischen Philosophie* (Berlin: Duncker & Humblot, 2002); Antonello D'Angelo, *Heidegger e Aristotele: la potenza el l'atto* (Naples: Il Mulino, 2000); Franco Volpi, "*Dasein* as *Praxis*: The Heideggerian Assimilation and Radicalization of the Practical Philosophy of Aristotle," in Christopher Macann, ed., *Critical Heidegger* (London & New York: Routledge, 1996), 27–66.

18. On this point compare, e.g., Christian Sommer, *Heidegger, Aristotle, Luther: les sources aristotéliennes et neo-testamentaires d'Etre et Temps* (Paris: Presses Universitaries de France, 2005); Ted Sadler, *Heidegger and Aristotle: The*

Question of Being (Atlantic Highlands, NY: Athlone Press, 1996). In Sadler's somewhat provocative formulation (16): "It is a guiding thesis of the present study that Heidegger's *Seinsfrage*, in its confrontation with Aristotelian metaphysics, can only be understood within a context of 'Wittenbergian' [i.e., Lutheran] propositions."

19. For a more detailed discussion of these readings see the chapter "Ontology of Freedom: Heidegger and Political Philosophy" in my *Polis and Praxis: Exercises in Contemporary Political Theory* (Cambridge, MA: MIT Press, 1984), 102–32. According to Stephen K. White, Heidegger was "condemned to a lifelong misunderstanding of action," because of his presumed "antipathy toward everydayness." See his *Political Theory and Postmodernism* (Cambridge, UK: Cambridge University Press, 1991), 35.

20. Lawrence J. Hatab, *Ethics and Finitude: Heideggerian Contributions to Moral Philosophy* (Lanham, MD: Rowman and Littlefield Publ., 2000), 51–66, 74–84, 125. Compare also Christopher P. Long, *The Ethics of Ontology: Rethinking an Aristotelian Legacy* (Albany, NY: State University of New York Press, 2004); Jean-Luc Nancy, "Heidegger's 'Originary Ethics,' " and Jean Greisch, "The 'Play of Transcendence' and the Question of Ethics," in François Raffoul and David Pettigrew, eds., *Heidegger and Practical Philosophy* (Albany, NY: State University of New York Press, 2002), 65–85 and 99–116.

21. This, in any case, is the manner in which I prefer to read Heidegger politically or to imagine a politics compatible with (what I have called) "the other Heidegger." See Fred Dallmayr, *The Other Heidegger* (Ithaca, NY: Cornell University Press, 1993). I am aware, of course, that shortly after completing the discussed writings Heidegger came under the influence of a certain Nietzscheanism (incompatible with both Aristotle and Luther) that infected and derailed his political judgment for some time.

22. I borrow the phrase "democracy to come" from Jacques Derrida, *Rogues: Two Essays on Reason*, trans. Pascale-Anne Brault and Michael Naas (Stanford, CA: Stanford University Press, 2005), 78–108. See chapter 7.

Chapter 5

1. Although a thoroughly modern woman, Arendt did not uncritically celebrate the blessings of modern "liberalism"—which has earned her the title of a "reluctant modernist." See Seyla Benhabib, *The Reluctant Modernism of Hannah Arendt* (Thousand Oaks, CA: Sage Publications, 1996). Compare also Hannah Arendt, "We Refugees," *Menorah Journal*, vol. 3 (1943), 70–79; "The Jew as Pariah: A Hidden Tradition," *Jewish Social Studies*, vol. 6 (1944), 99–122; and R. H. Feldman, ed., *The Jew as Pariah: Jewish Identity and Politics in the Modern Age* (New York: Grove Press, 1978).

2. Compare Arendt, *Crises of the Republic* (New York: Harcourt Brace Jovanovich, 1969).

3. For the distinction between positivist political thinkers ("behavioralists") and "traditionalists" compare, e.g., George A. Graham, Jr. and George W.

Carey, eds., *The Post-Behavioral Era: Perspectives on Political Science* (New York: David McKay Co., 1972); also John S. Nelson, ed., *What Should Political Theory Be Now?* (Albany, NY: State University of New York Press, 1983). Regarding "canonical" theorists stressing perennial ideas see, e.g., Glenn Tinder, *Political Thinking: The Perennial Questions*, 4th ed. (Boston: Little Brown & Co., 1986); also Leo Strauss, *What is Political Philosophy?* (Glencoe, IL: The Free Press, 1959). Concerning the focus on historical context compare, e.g., John Dunn, *The History of Political Theory, and Other Essays* (Cambridge, UK: Cambridge University Press, 1996); and Quentin Skinner, *The Foundations of Modern Political Thought* (Cambridge, UK: Cambridge University Press, 1978).

4. Arendt, "Preface," in *Between Past and Future: Six Exercises in Political Thought* (Cleveland/New York: Meridian Books, 1965), 14. In her studies, Arendt did not seek to disclose perennial truth, but she did not dismiss truth as such: "Throughout these exercises the problem of truth is kept in abeyance; the concern is solely with how to move in this gap [between past and future]—the only region where truth eventually will appear" (14).

5. See Karl Jaspers, *Reason and Existenz* (1935; New York: Noonday Press, 1955), 48–59; also Martin Heidegger, *Einleitung in die Philosophie*, ed. Otto Saame and Ina Saame-Speidel (*Gesamtausgabe*, vol. 27; Frankfurt-Main: Klostermann, 1996), especially 1–25. In the literature on Arendt, the influence of Heidegger is often overemphasized and that of Jaspers minimized. Thus, the well-known study by Dana R. Villa, *Arendt and Heidegger: The Fate of the Political* (Princeton, NJ: Princeton University Press, 1996) contains only a few scattered references to Jaspers. For a corrective see Lewis and Sandra K. Hinchman, "Existentialism Politicized: Arendt's Debt to Jaspers," in Hinchman and Hinchman, eds., *Hannah Arendt: Critical Essays* (Albany, NY: State University of New York Press, 1994), 143–78.

6. Arendt, *Between Past and Future*, 6, 8–9.

7. In this respect compare especially Heidegger, *Der Begriff der Zeit*, ed. Hartmut Tietjen (Tübingen: Niemeyer, 1989); also Heidegger, *History of the Concept of Time: Prolegomena*, trans. Theodore Kisiel (Bloomington, IN: Indiana University Press, 1985).

8. Arendt, *Between Past and Future*, 7, 9–11. Kafka's parable is titled "HE" and dates from 1920; Arendt cites from an English translation of 1946.

9. Arendt, *Between Past and Future*, 10–13 (in the above I have not corrected for gender bias). Reminiscent again of her European mentors, the preface (13) describes thinking in the gap between past and future as the "small track of non-time which the activity of thought beats within the time–space of mortal men"—a phrase that evokes the concluding lines in Heidegger's "Letter on Humanism" to the effect that "thinking lays inconspicuous furrows in language; they are still more inconspicuous than the furrows that the farmer, slow of step, draws through the field." See David F. Krell, ed., *Martin Heidegger: Basic Writings* (New York: Harper & Row, 1977), 242.

10. Arendt, "Prologue" in *The Human Condition: A Study of the Central Dilemmas Facing Modern Man* (Chicago: University of Chicago Press, 1958), 3, 6–7. Regarding Husserl, see his *The Crisis of European Sciences and Transcendental*

Phenomenology: An Introduction to Phenomenological Philosophy, trans. David Carr (Evanston, IL: Northwestern University Press, 1970), especially 269–99 ("Philosophy and the Crisis of European Humanity") and 379–83 ("The Life-World and the World of Science").

11. Arendt, *The Human Condition*, 4. Compare in this context also Hans-Georg Gadamer, *Reason in the Age of Science*, trans. Frederick G. Lawrence (Cambridge, MA: MIT Press, 1981).

12. Arendt, *The Human Condition*, 6. Compare in this context also Heidegger's comments on thinking and acting, theory and *praxis* in his "Letter on Humanism" in Krell, ed., *Martin Heidegger: Basic Writings*, 239–41.

13. Compare, e.g., Shiraz Dossa, *The Public Realm and the Public Self: The Political Theory of Hannah Arendt* (Waterloo, Ontario: Wilfrid Laurier University Press, 1989); Margaret Canovan, *The Political Thought of Hannah Arendt* (New York: Harcourt Brace Jovanovich, 1974); Melvin A. Hill, ed., *Hannah Arendt: The Recovery of the Public World* (New York: St. Martin's Press, 1979); Bhikhu Parekh, *Hannah Arendt and the Search for a New Political Philosophy* (Atlantic Highlands, NJ: Humanities Press, 1981); George Kateb, *Hannah Arendt: Politics, Conscience, Evil* (Lanham, MD: Rowman & Littlefield, 1984); Marizio Passerin d'Entrèves, *The Political Philosophy of Hannah Arendt* (London & New York: Routledge, 1994); Michael G. Gottsegen, *The Political Thought of Hannah Arendt* (Albany, NY: State University of New York Press, 1994); Craig Calhoun and John McGowan, eds., *Hannah Arendt and the Meaning of Politics* (Minneapolis, MN: University of Minnesota Press, 1997).

14. Arendt, *The Human Condition*, 230–31, 234–35. Regarding Galileo, the text refers to Pierre M. Schuhl, *Machinisme et philosophie* (Paris: Presses Universitaires de France, 1947), 28–29; and Edwin A. Burtt, *The Metaphysical Foundations of Modern Physical Science* (London: Routledge & K. Paul, 1932), 38.

15. Arendt, *The Human Condition*, 9–11.

16. *The Human Condition*, 72, 82, 99, 109. One can only speculate to which extent Arendt's concept of "work" is indebted to Heidegger's notion of things "ready-to-hand" (*zuhanden*) and/or his later formulation of the *"Gestell."*

17. Arendt, *The Human Condition*, 82–83.

18. *The Human Condition*, 45–46, 48–50.

19. *The Human Condition*, 52–53.

20. Arendt, "Lying in Politics: Reflections on the Pentagon Papers," in *Crises of the Republic*, 24. Compare also Arendt, *Eichmann in Jerusalem: A Report on the Banality of Evil* (New York: Viking Press, 1963).

21. Arendt, *Between Past and Future*, 98–99. See also her *The Origins of Totalitarianism* (New York: Harcourt Brace and Co., 1951), and Stephen J. Whitfield, *Into the Dark: Hannah Arendt and Totalitarianism* (Philadelphia: Temple University Press, 1980).

22. In the words of Maurice Merleau-Ponty: "There is a mystification in liberalism. . . . An aggressive liberalism exists which is a dogma and already an ideology of war. It can be recognized by its love of the empyrean of principles, . . . and its abstract judgments of political systems without regard for the specific conditions under which they develop. Its nature is violent,

nor does it hesitate to impose itself through violence in accordance with the old theory of the secular arm." See *Humanism and Terror*, trans. John O'Neill (Boston, MA: Beacon Press, 1969), xiii, xxiv.

23. Arendt, *Between Past and Future*, 164–65. See also *The Human Condition*, 210–11.

24. *The Human Condition*, 11, 57. As opposed to the sheer fact of birth, Heidegger has emphasized human mortality or "being-toward-death"—the reason being that anticipation of death tends to have a sobering or seasoning and, to this extent, liberating effect. For an explicit defense of mortality as over against the stress on birth see Heidegger, *Einleitung in die Philosophie* (*Gesamtausgabe* vol. 27; Frankfurt-Main: Klostermann, 1996), 124–25. The detrimental effects of the sidelining of the "social domain" were displayed with particular vehemence in her downplaying of the American Civil Rights Movement, and particularly in her comments on the events in Little Rock. See in this context Arendt, "Reflections on Little Rock" and "The Social Question" in Peter Baehr, ed., *The Portable Hannah Arendt* (New York: Penguin Books, 2000), 231–46, 247–77. In this respect, Iris Marion Young—although influenced by Arendt—has made great strides in the direction of a stronger sensitivity for societal (ethnic, religious, and gender) differences. See Young, *Justice and the Politics of Difference* (Princeton, NJ: Princeton University Press, 1990); *Intersecting Voices: Dilemmas of Gender, Political Philosophy, and Politics* (Princeton, NJ: Princeton University Press, 1997); and especially the chapter on "Social Difference as a Political Resource" in *Inclusion and Democracy* (Oxford, UK: Oxford University Press, 2000), 52–80.

25. Arendt, *The Human Condition*, 50, 159, 162–63, 173, 184. As it seems to me, these passages reveal much more the influence of Nietzsche and Jaspers than Heidegger.

26. *The Human Condition*, 25, 68. As it appears, Arendt sought to make up for her early sidelining of philosophy and contemplation in her late work *The Life of the Mind*, 2 vols. (New York: Harcourt Brace Jovanovich, 1977–1978). Compare in this context Lisa J. Disch, *Hannah Arendt and the Limits of Philosophy* (Ithaca, NY: Cornell University Press, 1994); Leah Bradshaw, *Acting and Thinking: The Political Thought of Hannah Arendt* (Toronto: University of Toronto Press, 1989); also Agnes Heller, "Hannah Arendt on the 'Vita Contemplativa,' " in Gisela T. Kaplan and Clive S. Kessler eds., *Hannah Arendt: Thinking, Judging, Freedom* (London: Allen & Unwin, 1989), 144–59.

Chapter 6

1. Ernesto Laclau and Chantal Mouffe, *Hegemony and Socialist Strategy: Towards a Radical Democratic Politics*, trans. Winston Moore and Paul Cammack (London: Verso, 1985), 1–4. In critiquing a class-based essentialism, Laclau and Mouffe locate themselves plainly in "a post-Marxist terrain," which does not imply a summary dismissal of Marxism. As they emphasize (4): "If our intellectual project in this book is post-Marxist, it is evidently also

post-*Marxist.*" Moreover, the critique of essentialism extends beyond traditional Marxism to other discursive frameworks or "normative epistemologies" (3): "Political conclusions similar to those set forth in this book could have been approximated from very different discursive formations—for example, from certain forms of Christianity, or from libertarian discourses alien to the socialist tradition—none of which could aspire to be the truth of society."

2. See Rosa Luxemburg, *Massenstreik* (Hamburg: Dubber, 1906).

3. *Hegemony and Socialist Strategy,* 7, 14, 18. See also Karl Kautsky, *The Class Struggle (Erfurt Program)* (Chicago: Kerr, 1910).

4. *Hegemony and Socialist Strategy,* 37, 40. According to the authors, Bernstein's revisionism also supported a gradualist type of reformism—but only for contingent reasons. Basically, the two strategies or approaches do not coincide (30): "Thus, in attempting to identify the precise difference between reformism and revisionism, we must stress that what is essential in a reformist practice is political quietism and the corporatist confinement of the working class." Compare Eduard Bernstein, *Evolutionary Socialism* (New York: Schocken, 1961), and Georges Sorel, *Reflections on Violence* (Glencoe, IL: The Free Press, 1950).

5. *Hegemony and Socialist Strategy,* 51, 56, 61–62.

6. *Hegemony and Socialist Strategy,* 65–67, 69, 75–77, 85–87. Compare Antonio Gramsci, *The Modern Prince, and Other Writings* (New York: International Publishers, 1957).

7. *Hegemony and Socialist Strategy,* 95, 97–98, 105, 108–12. As the study adds (113): Since "all discourse is subverted by a field of discursivity which overflows it, the transition from 'elements' to 'moments' can never be complete. The status of the 'elements' is that of floating signifiers, incapable of being wholly articulated to a discursive chain. . . . It is not the poverty of signifieds but, on the contrary, polysemy that disarticulates a discursive structure. That is what establishes the overdetermined, symbolic dimension of every social identity. Society never manages to be identical to itself, as every nodal point is constituted within an intertextuality that overflows it. *The practice of articulation, therefore, consists in the construction of nodal points which partially fix meaning: and the partial character of this fixation proceeds from the openness of the social, a result, in its turn, of the constant overflowing of every discourse by the infinitude of the field of discursivity.*"

8. *Hegemony and Socialist Strategy,* 115–17, 122–29.

9. *Hegemony and Socialist Strategy,* 132–37.

10. *Hegemony and Socialist Strategy,* 151–52, 155, 164, 166–67.

11. *Hegemony and Socialist Strategy,* 171, 176–77, 179, 182–84, 186–88. Compare also their comment (192): "The de-centering and autonomy of the different discourses and struggles, the multiplication of antagonisms and the construction of a plurality of spaces within which they can affirm themselves and develop, are the conditions *sine qua non* of the possibility that the different components of the classical ideal of socialism—which should, no doubt, be extended and reformulated—can be achieved."

12. The distance from structuralism is expressed in these comments: "When the linguistic model was introduced into the general field of human sciences, it was this effect of systematicity that predominated, so that structuralism became a anew form of essentialism: a search for the underlying structures constituting the inherent law of any possible variation. The critique of structuralism involved a break with this view of a fully constituted structural space. . . . The sign is the name of a split, of an impossible suture between signified and signifier." See *Hegemony and Socialist Strategy*, 113. The authors refer in this context explicitly to Jacques Derrida, "Structure, Sign and Play in the Discourse of the Human Sciences," in *Writing and Difference*, trans. Alan Bass (Chicago-London: University of Chicago Press, 1978), 280.

13. *Hegemony and Socialist Strategy*, 111, 122.

14. *Hegemony and Socialist Strategy*, 153, 193. As they add, the prevalence of politics also injects instability into the distinction of public and private spheres, leading to a pervasive politicization of life (181): "What has been exploded is the idea and the reality itself of a unique space of constitution of the political. What we are witnessing is a politicization far more radical than any we have known in the past, because it tends to dissolve the distinction between the public and the private, not in terms of the encroachment on the private by a unified public space, but in terms of a proliferation of radically new and different political spaces."

15. *Hegemony and Socialist Strategy*, 79, 120–21.

16. *Hegemony and Socialist Strategy*, 94–95. The repercussions of traditional rationalism are found in Hegel's theory of the "state" and especially in his conception of the bureaucracy as "universal class" (191). The assessment of Hegel relies strongly on A. Trendelenburg, *Logische Undersuchungen* (first ed. 1840; 3rd ed., Hildesheim: Olms, 1964).

17. *Hegemony and Socialist Strategy*, 129, 184. Another passage (130) phrases the two logics in the vocabulary of linguistics, associating the logic of difference with the "syntagmatic pole" of language (the sequence of continuous combinations) and the logic of equivalence with the "paradigmatic pole" (relations of substitution).

18. *Hegemony and Socialist Strategy*, 126, 129, 136. Elsewhere the danger of the two social logics is seen in their transformation from a "horizon" into a "foundation" (183).

19. *Hegemony and Socialist Strategy*, 87, 103–4.

20. *Hegemony and Socialist Strategy*, 142, 182–84. Regarding universalism compare these comments (191–92): "The discourse of radical democracy is no longer the discourse of the universal. . . . This point is decisive: there is no radical and plural democracy without renouncing the discourse of the universal and its implicit assumption of a privileged point of access to 'the truth,' which can be reached only by a limited number of subjects."

21. *Hegemony and Socialist Strategy*, 59, 69–70, 137. For a critique of the "foundational" treatment of power or domination in political life see 142. As it seems to me, Foucault's later writings point in a similar direction; compare

my "Pluralism Old and New: Foucault on Power" in *Polis and Praxis: Exercises in Contemporary Political Theory* (Cambridge, MA: MIT Press, 1984), 77–103, and my "Democracy and Postmodernism," *Human Studies*, vol. 10 (1986), 143–70.

22. *Hegemony and Socialist Strategy*, 12, 37–38, 85, 93. For a differentiation of *praxis* from Weberian categories of action theory compare my "Praxis and Experience" in *Polis and Praxis*, 47–76.

23. *Hegemony and Socialist Strategy*, 86, 110–11.

24. *Hegemony and Socialist Strategy*, 114, 142. Another passage presents the external demarcation of the two categories under the image of a "double void" (131).

25. *Hegemony and Socialist Strategy*, 12–13, 25, 34, 47, 93, 108–10, 113. Compare Martin Heidegger, "Moira," in *Vorträge and Aufsätze* (3rd ed.; Pfullingen: Neske, 1967), vol. 3, 36–38, 45–48, also *Identität and Differenz* (Pfullingen: Neske, 1957); and Jacques Derrida, *Margins of Philosophy*, trans. Alan Bass (Chicago: University of Chicago Press, 1982). For the notion of "intertwining" see Maurice Merleau-Ponty, *The Visible and the Invisible*, trans. Alphonso Lingis (Evanston, IL: Northwestern University Press, 1968), 130–55.

26. *Hegemony and Socialist Strategy*, 125–26.

27. *Hegemony and Socialist Strategy*, 128–29. Compare also Heidegger, *On Time and Being*, trans. Joan Stambaugh (New York: Harper & Row, 1972), and the observations on negativity in chapter 2

28. *Hegemony and Socialist Strategy*, 155–56.

29. *Hegemony and Socialist Strategy*, 188–89. The tensional view is also endorsed in the assertion (189) that the "project for a radical democracy" must "base itself upon the search for a point of equilibrium between a maximum advance for the democratic revolution in a broad range of spheres, and the capacity for the hegemonic direction and positive reconstruction of these spheres on the part of subordinated groups." In part the authors' ambivalence stems from a mingling of two conceptions of politics: namely, politics as "polity" (or political regime) and politics as "policy." For this distinction see Ernst Vollrath, "The 'Rational' and the 'Political': An Essay in the Semantics of Politics," *Philosophy and Social Criticism*, vol. 13 (1987), 17–29, and my "Politics and Conceptual Analysis: Comments on Vollrath," 31–37.

30. See John Dewey, "Search for the Great Community" in *The Public and Its Problems* (1927), in *John Dewey: The Later Works: 1925–1953*, ed. Jo Ann Boydston (Carbondale, IL: Southern Illinois University, 1981), vol. 2, 325–50.

Chapter 7

1. See especially Martin Heidegger, *Nietzsche*, 2 vols. (2nd ed; Pfullingen: Neske, 1961); *Beiträge zur Philosophie: Vom Ereignis*, ed. Friedrich-Wilhelm von Herrmann (*Gesamtausgabe*, vol. 65; Frankfurt-Main: Klostermann, 1989); *Besinnung*, ed. Friedrich-Wilhelm von Herrmann (Gesamtausgabe, vol. 66; Frankurt-Main: Klostermann, 1997). For Heidegger's statement that possibility

is "higher" than actuality see *Sein und Zeit* (11th ed.; Tübingen: Niemeyer, 1967), 38 (paragraph 7C).

2. Jacques Derrida, "The Ends of Man," in his *Margins of Philosophy*, trans. Alan Bass (Chicago: University of Chicago Press, 1982), 114–16. Compare in this context Jean-Paul Sartre, *Existentialism and Humanism*, trans. Philip Mairet (Brooklyn, NY: Haskell House, 1977).

3. Derrida, "The Ends of Man," 117–19.

4. "The Ends of Man," 120–23.

5. "The Ends of Man," 124, 126–27.

6. "The Ends of Man," 127–29, 132–33.

7. "The Ends of Man," 133–35.

8. "The Ends of Man," 135–36.

9. See Derrida, *Specters of Marx: The State of the Debt, the Work of Mourning, and the New International*, trans. Peggy Kamuf (New York & London: Routledge, 1994); also Max Stirner, *The Ego and His Own*, trans. Steven T. Byington (New York: Harper & Row, 1997). Compare also Derrida, *Politics of Friendship*, trans. George Collins (London: Verso, 1997); and my "Derrida and Friendship," in Eduardo A. Velásquez, ed., *Love and Friendship: Rethinking Politics and Affection in Modern Times* (Lanham, MD: Lexington Books, 2003), 548–57.

10. Derrida, *The Other Heading: Reflections on Today's Europe*, trans. Pascale-Anne Brault and Michael B. Naas (Bloomington, IN: Indiana University Press, 1992), 33–34, 65, 69. Elaborating on the notion of a spiritual vanguard Derrida adds: "Europe takes itself [and has always taken itself] to be a promontory, an advance—the avant-garde of geography and history. It advances and promotes itself as an advance, and it will never have ceased to make advances on the other: to induce, seduce, produce, and conduce, to spread out, to cultivate, to love or to violate, to love to violate, to colonize, to colonize itself" (49). Compare also Edmund Husserl, *The Crisis of European Sciences and Transcendental Phenomenology: An Introduction to Phenomenological Philosophy*, trans. David Carr (Evanston, IL: Northwestern University Press, 1970), 269–99; also Paul Valéry, "Notes on the Greatness and Decline of Europe," in *History and Politics*, trans. Denise Folliot and Jackson Mathews (New York: Bollingen, 1962), 196–201.

11. Derrida, *The Other Heading*, 14–15, 71–73 (translation slightly altered).

12. *The Other Heading*, 6, 9–10.

13. *The Other Heading*, 17, 28–29.

14. *The Other Heading*, 41, 45, 69, 78. As one should note, "future" for Derrida is not just a linear projection from the past. More importantly, future does not denote a willful project or a reckless search for novelty. As he cautions readers explicitly (18–19): "Our old memory tells us that it is *also* necessary to anticipate and guard the heading, for under the banner—which can also become a slogan—of the unanticipatable or the absolutely new, we can fear seeing a return of the phantom of the worst. . . . We must thus be suspicious of *both* repetitive memory *and* the completely other of the absolutely new; of both

anamnestic 'capitalization' *and* the amnesic exposure to what would no longer be identifiable at all." Unfortunately, the distinction between the unexpected advent and the absolutely "unanticipatable" is not further delineated (and not sufficiently maintained in other writings). For a fuller discussion of *The Other Heading*, with specific attention to this issue, see my "The Ambivalence of Europe: Western Culture and its 'Other,' " in *Dialogue Among Civilizations: Some Exemplary Voices* (New York: Palgrave Macmillan, 2002), 49–65.

15. See Derrida, *Acts of Religion*, ed. Gil Anidjar (New York & London: Routledge, 2002); Derrida and Gianni Vattimo, eds., *Religion*, trans. Samuel Weber (Stanford, CA: Stanford University Press, 1998); Derrida, *Of Hospitality*, trans. Rachel Bowlby (Stanford, CA: Stanford University Press, 2000); *On Cosmopolitanism and Forgiveness*, trans. Mark Dooley and Michael Hughes (New York: Routledge, 2001), 8–9.

16. Derrida, *Rogues: Two Essays on Reason*, trans. Pascale-Anne Brault and Michael Naas (Stanford, CA: Stanford University Press, 2005), xii–xv. Derrida in this context (xiv) also calls the appeal to unconditionality an "act of messianic faith—irreligious and without messianism." The notion of a "weak force" might be compared with Gianni Vattimo's notion of "pensiero debole," and also with Stephen K. White comments on "weak ontology." See Vattimo and Pier Aldo Rovatti, eds., *Il pensiero debole* (Milan: Feltrinelli, 1983); and White, *Sustaining Affirmation: The Strengths of Weak Ontology in Political Theory* (Princeton, NJ: Princeton University Press, 2000). Compare also John D. Caputo, *The Weakness of God: A Theology of the Event* (Bloomington, IN: Indiana University Press, 2006); and my *Small Wonder: Global Power and Its Discontents* (Lanham, MD: Rowman & Littlefield, 2005).

17. Derrida, *Rogues*, 13–17. See Alexis de Tocqueville, *Democracy in America*, trans. George Lawrence (New York: Harper & Row, 1966), 51–53. For the critique of sovereignty compare also Derrida, *Sovereignties in Question: The Poetics of Paul Celan*, eds. Thomas Dutoit and Outi Pasanen (New York: Fordham University Press, 2005). To some extent (one can speculate) this critique involves a self-critique on Derrida's part since his earlier formulation of deconstructive "justice" as an incalculable and even "mad" decision approximated the conception of a sovereign, God-like intervention in a "state of exception." See in this regard Derrida, "Force of Law: The 'Mystical Foundation of Authority,' " in Drucilla Cornell, Michel Rosenfeld, and David G. Carlson, eds., *Deconstruction and the Possibility of Justice* (New York & London: Routledge, 1992), 3–67; also my critical comments in "Justice and Violence: A Response to Jacques Derrida," *Cardozo Law Review*, vol. 13 (1991), 1237–43. However, one may wonder about the significance of the shift, since in *Rogues* (88) Derrida still links "justice" with disjuncture or "being out of joint."

18. Derrida, *Rogues*, 23, 36–38.

19. *Rogues*, 42, 44, 50, 82, 85. See also Derrida, *On the Name*, trans. John P. Leavy, Jr. (Stanford, CA: Stanford University Press, 1995), 83.

20. Derrida, *Rogues*, 88–91.

21. *Rogues*, 149.

22. *Rogues*, 71, 82.

23. *Rogues*, xiv, xv, 4, 29. The passages can be multiplied. In this respect, I concur with Romand Coles when he notes "a certain one-sidedness in many of Derrida's discussions," adding that his "overemphasis" on rupture and discontinuity "may have certain strategic uses, but it courts the danger he seeks to resist, namely, that deconstruction might become an 'abstract and dogmatic eschatology in the face of the world's evil'—weak on textured judgment and practice. . . . At issue here is whether Derrida sufficiently cultivates a dialectical relation to the traditions by which he finds himself animated" in such a way that "ateleology and teleology can engender the work of responsibility." See his *Beyond Gated Politics: Reflections for the Possibility of Democracy* (Minneapolis, MN: University of Minnesota Press, 2005), 178. Only very occasionally and hesitantly does Derrida venture beyond antinomial formulations (unconditional–conditioned, incalculable–calculable), for example, in this passage (*Rogues*, 151) referring to the "well-worn, indeed long discredited, word *reasonable*": "I would say that what is 'reasonable' is the reasoned and considered wager of a transaction between these two apparently irreconcilable exigencies of reason, between calculation and the incalculable." Unfortunately the implications of the passage are not further explored, especially in regard to human or political *praxis*.

24. Martin Heidegger, "Letter on Humanism," in David F. Krell, ed., *Martin Heidegger: Basic Writings* (New York: Harper & Row, 1977), 193 (Krell uses the term *accomplishment* for *vollbringen*). In *Rogues*, Derrida repeats and underscores the stark opposition between Heidegger's work and his own writings, by claiming (173–74, note 14) that "Heideggerian deconstruction never really opposed logocentrism or even logos" while his own "deconstruction . . . never took the objectifying form of a knowledge [logos] as 'diagnosis' and even less a 'diagnosis of diagnosis.' " However, is it really possible simply to exit from "logos"—especially if the term is taken to mean not only reason but also "word" and language?

Chapter 8

1. See, e.g., Nicholas Boyle, *Who Are We Now? Christian Humanism and the Global Market from Hegel to Heaney* (Notre Dame, IN: University of Notre Dame Press, 1998); Jean Bethke Elshtain, *Who Are We? Critical Reflections and Hopeful Possibilities* (Grand Rapids, MI: Eerdmans, 2000); Samuel P. Huntington, *Who Are We? The Challenges to America's Identity* (New York: Simon & Schuster, 2004).

2. Edmund Husserl, "Philosophy and the Crisis of European Humanity (The Vienna Lecture)," in *The Crisis of European Sciences and Transcendental Phenomenology*, trans. David Carr (Evanston, IL: Northwestern University Press, 1970), 299.

3. Compare in this respect Ernst Cassirer, *The Individual and the Cosmos in Renaissance Philosophy*, trans. Mario Domandi (New York: Harper & Row, 1964); *The Philosophy of the Enlightenment* (Boston, MA: Beacon Press, 1965);

and *The Platonic Renaissance in England,* trans. James P. Pettegrove (New York: Gordian Press, 1970).

4. See Cassirer, *An Essay on Man: An Introduction to a Philosophy of Human Culture* (New Haven, CT & London: Yale University Press, 1944), 1–3. In the following I have tried to correct for gender bias, but have found it often to be difficult and awkward.

5. *An Essay on Man,* 4–6.

6. *An Essay on Man,* 6–8. In his references to Marcus Aurelius, Cassirer uses the English version found in C. R. Haines, *The Communings with Himself of Marcus Aurelius Antoninus* (Cambridge, MA: Harvard University Press, 1916).

7. Cassirer, *An Essay on Man,* 8–9, 13–16.

8. *An Essay on Man,* 18, 25–26.

9. Jean-Paul Sartre, *Being and Nothingness: An Essay on Phenomenological Ontology,* trans. Hazel E. Barnes (New York: Philosophical Library, 1956).

10. Sartre, *L'existentialisme est un humanism* (Paris: Les Editions Nagel, 1946). I use in the following the translation by Philip Mairet titled *Existentialism and Humanism* (Brooklyn, NY: Haskell House Publ., 1948). Again, I have tried to correct for gender bias in the text, but with only limited success.

11. *Existentialism and Humanism,* 26, 28–29. Reaching back beyond Husserl and Kant to Descartes, Sartre states (p. 44): "Our point of departure is, indeed, subjectivity. . . . And at the point of departure there cannot be any other truth than this, I think therefore I am, which is the absolute truth of consciousness as it attains to itself." Yet, modifying at the same time (his understanding of) the Cartesian and Kantian approach, he adds (45): "Contrary to the philosophy of Descartes, and contrary to that of Kant, when we say 'I think' we are attaining to ourselves in the presence of the other, and we are just as certain of the other as we are of ourselves. Thus, the man who discovers himself directly in the cogito also discovers all the others, and discovers them as the condition of his own existence."

12. *Existentialism and Humanism,* 34, 51, 555–56.

13. Cassirer, *An Essay on Man,* 11–12. Cassirer quotes from Pascal's *Pensées,* trans. O. W. Wight (New York: Derby & Jackson, 1861), Chapter 10, section 1, and Chapter 12, section 5.

14. Jacques Derrida, "The Ends of Man," in *Margins of Philosophy,* trans. Alan Bass (Chicago: University of Chicago Press, 1982), 115–17. At another point (114), Derrida dates his intervention still more precisely, namely "the month of April 1968": "It will be recalled that these were the weeks of the opening of the Vietnam peace talks and of the assassination of Martin Luther King. A bit later, when I was typing this text, the universities of Paris were invaded by the forces of order."

15. Derrida, "The Ends of Man," 118–19. Actually, Derrida himself associates Heidegger's work still in some fashion with traditional humanism. His own essay, he writes (123–24, 127), attempts "to sketch out the forms of the hold which the 'humanity' of man and the thinking of Being, a certain human-

ism and the [Heideggerian] truth of Being, maintain on one another. . . . We can see then that Dasein, though not man, is nevertheless nothing other than man. It is . . . a repetition of the essence of man permitting a return to what is before the metaphysical concepts of *humanitas.*"

16. "The Ends of Man," 135–36. The conclusion of the text makes it appear as if the option between the "higher man" and "overman" was still hanging in the balance. But clearly, the thrust of the argument points in the Nietschean direction.

17. Michel Foucault, *The Order of Things: An Archaeology of the Human Sciences* (1966; New York: Random House, 1970), xxiii–xxiv, 385.

18. Richard A. Cohen, "Introduction," in *Emmanuel Levinas, Humanism of the Other,* trans. Nidra Poller (1972; Urbana, IL: University of Illinois Press, 2003), xxvi, xxx. As Cohen elaborates (xiv–xvii, xxxv), Levinas both preserves and reverses Husserl's subject-centered phenomenology. He corrects Cassirer's reliance on culture or symbolic forms, arguing that meaning transcends "cultural determination" while, at the same time, following Cassirer (and Husserl) in viewing Heidegger's "fundamental ontology" as "but another avatar of naturalism." Regarding the historical context of Levinas's book, Cohen observes (xxvi) that it is a work "engaged at close quarters with the philosophical debates of the time and the place, caught up in a reflection on the events of May 1968, the then-current intellectual Parisian vogue of structuralism, French readings of Hegel and Nietzsche, and most particularly the French fascination with Heideggerian ontology."

19. Levinas, *Humanism of the Other,* 58–60.

20. *Humanism of the Other,* 62–64. As Levinas adds (67): "So there is no need to deny humanism as long as we recognize it there where it assumes its least deceptive mode, far away from the zones of interiority of power and law, order, culture, heroic magnificence." In the same chapter (61–63), Levinas (following Husserl and Cassirer) persists in consigning Heidegger's philosophy to the level of an ontic "naturalism."

21. Maurice Blanchot, in *La Nouvelle Revue Française, No. 179* (1967), 820–21.

22. Theodor W. Adorno, *Negative Dialektik* (Frankfurt: Suhrkamp, 1966), 141, 179, 185. For an English translation (not followed here) see *Negative Dialectics,* trans. E. B. Ashton (New York: Seabury Press, 1973), pp 139, 179–80, 186–87.

23. *Negative Dialektik,* 189–90, 382; *Negative Dialectics,* 190–91, 391–92.

24. Martin Heidegger, *Über den Humanismus* (Frankfurt: Klostermann, 1949), 15–16, 35. For an English translation (not entirely followed here) see "Letter on Humanism" in *Martin Heidegger: Basic Writings,* ed. David F. Krell (New York: Harper & Row, 1977), 204–5, 229. In large measure, Heidegger's Letter is a critical response to Sartre's *Existentialism and Humanism.* See in this context Richard J. Bernstein, "Heidegger on Humanism," in his *Philosophical Profiles: Essays in a Pragmatic Mode* (Philadelphia: University of Pennsylvania Press, 1986), 197–220.

25. Heidegger, *Über den Humanismus*, 29, 31, 37–38; "Letter on Human-ism," 221–22, 224–25, 231. In a way, Heidegger's later thought, especially his notion of the "four-fold" (Geviert), can be seen as a further deepening of the relational character of human being.

26. For the revival of Aristotelian virtue theory in our time see espe-cially Alasdair MacIntyre, *After Virtue: A Study in Moral Theory*, 2nd ed. (Notre Dame, IN: University of Notre Dame Press, 1984). Regarding self-care compare, e.g., Michel Foucault, *The Care of the Self*, trans. Robert Gurley (New York: Vintage Books, 1985). For the notion of a "liberating-anticipatory solicitude" see Heidegger, *Sein and Zeit*, 11th ed. (Tübingen: Niemeyer, 1967), section 26, 122; *Being and Time: A Translation of Sein und Zeit*, trans. John Macquarrie and Edward Robinson (New York: HarperCollins, 1962), 158-9.

27. Heidegger, *Sein und Zeit*, section 42, 199; *Being and Time*, 243.

28. See Raimon Panikkar, *Worship and Secular Man* (Maryknoll, NY: Orbis Books, 1973), 28–30, 35–36, 47–52. Compare also his *The Cosmotheandric Experience*, ed. Scott Eastham (Maryknoll, NY: Orbis Books, 1993); *Humanismo y Cruz* (Madrid: Rialp, 1963); and, more recently, *Christophany: The Fullness of Man* (Maryknoll, NY: Orbis Books, 2004).

29. Joseph Ratzinger, *Benedict XVI, Jesus von Nazareth, Part I* (Freiburg: Herder, 2007), 375–76.

Chapter 9

1. Paul Ricoeur, *Political and Social Essays*, ed. David Stewart and Joseph Bien (Athens, OH: Ohio University Press, 1974), 105, 123. Compare also my "Religious Freedom: Preserving the Salt of the Earth," in *In Search of the Good Life: A Pedagogy for Troubled Times* (Lexington, KY: University Press of Kentucky, 2007), pp. 205–19.

2. Ira M. Lapidus, "The Golden Age: The Political Concepts of Islam," *The Annals of the American Academy of Political and Social Science,* vol. 524 (Novem-ber 1992), 14–16. On the important role of jurists or legal scholars (*fuqaha*) in traditional Islam compare also Tamara Sonn, "Elements of Government in Classical Islam," *Muslim Democrat*, vol. 2 (November 2000), 4–6 (published by the Center for the Study of Islam and Democracy, Washington, DC).

3. Youssef Choueiri, "The Political Discourse of Contemporary Islamist Movements," in Abdel Salam Sidahmed and Anoushiravan Ehteshami, eds., *Islamic Fundamentalism* (Boulder, CO: Westview Press, 1996), 22–23, 28–30. Regarding Qutb, see also the discussion in Roxanne L. Euben, *Enemy in the Mirror: Islamic Fundamentalism and the Limits of Modern Rationalism* (Princeton, NJ: Princeton University Press, 1999), 49–92.

4. As Oliver Leaman writes, Averroes (Ibn Rushd) criticized fideist theologians for "only being prepared to accept a concept of God that is remarkably similar to that of a very powerful human being, God with a status rather similar to that of Superman." See Leaman, *Averroes and His Philosophy* (Oxford, UK: Clarendon Press, 1988), 14.

5. For the critique of "sovereignty" see Hannah Arendt, "What is Freedom?" in *Between Past and Future* (New York: Penguin Books, 1980), 164–65; also Jean Bethke Elshtain, *New Wine and Old Bottles: International Politics and Ethical Discourse* (Notre Dame, IN: University of Notre Dame Press, 1998), especially 6–25.

6. Lahouari Addi, "Islamicist Utopia and Democracy," *The Annals of the American Academy of Political and Social Science,* vol. 524 (November 1992), 122, 124.

7. Addi, "Islamicist Utopia and Democracy," 126.

8. There is by now a plethora of studies exploring the compatibility between Islam and democracy. See, e.g., John L. Esposito and John O. Voll, *Islam and Democracy* (New York: Oxford University Press, 1996); Ali Reza Abootalebi, *Islam and Democracy: State-Society Relations in Developing Countries* (New York: Garland Publ., 2000); Larry Diamond, Marc F. Plattner, and Daniel Brumberg, ed., *Islam and Democracy in the Middle East* (Baltimore, MD: Johns Hopkins University Press, 2003); Khaled Abu El Fadl, *Islam and the Challenge of Democracy* (Princeton, NJ: Princeton University Press, 2004); Larbi Zadiki, *The Search for Arab Democracy* (New York: Columbia University Press, 2004); M. A. Muqtedar Khan, ed., *Islamic Democratic Discourse* (Lanham, MD: Lexington Books, 2006); Sayed Khatab and Gary D. Bouma, *Democracy in Islam* (New York: Routledge, 2007).

9. Abdullahi Ahmed An-Nai'm, *Islam and the Secular State: Negotiating the Future of Shari'a* (Cambridge, MA: Harvard University Press, 2008), 1–2.

10. *Islam and the Secular State,* 3–4.

11. *Islam and the Secular State,* 4–6.

12. Abdolkarim Soroush, *Reason, Freedom and Democracy in Islam,* trans. and ed. Mahmud Sadri and Ahmad Sadri (New York: Oxford University Press, 2000), 63–64, 92–99.

13. *Reason, Freedom and Democracy in Islam,* 45–46, 103–4, 136–38, 140, 152–53. Compare also Valla Vakili, *Debating Religion and Politics in Iran: The Political Thought of Abdulkarim Soroush* (New York: Council on Foreign Relations, 1996); Forough Jahanbaksh, *Islam, Democracy, and Religious Modernism in Iran, 1953–2000: From Bazargan to Soroush* (Boston: Brill, 2001); and my "Islam and Democracy: Reflections on Abdolkarim Soroush," in *Dialogue Among Civilizations: Some Exemplary Voices* (New York: Palgrave Macmillan, 2002), 167–84.

14. Compare in this regard Mike Featherstone, Scott Lash, and Roland Robertson, eds., *Global Modernities* (London: Sage Publ., 1995); Scott Lash, *Another Modernity, a Different Rationality* (Oxford, UK: Blackwell, 1999); Dilip P. Gaonkar, ed., *Alternative Modernities* (Durham, NC: Duke University Press, 2001); Charles Taylor, "Two Theories of Modernity," *Public Culture,* vol. 11 (1999), 153–73; and my "Global Modernization: Toward Different Modernities?" in *Dialogue Among Civilizations: Some Exemplary Voices* (New York: Palgrave Macmillan, 2002), 85–104.

15. Compare in this respect Larry Diamond and Marc F. Plattner, eds., *The Global Divergence of Democracies* (Baltimore, MD: Johns Hopkins University

Press, 2001); Deen K. Chatterjee, ed., *Democracy in a Global World* (Lanham, MD: Rowman and Littlefield, 2008).

16. For some background see Shahrough Akhavi, *Religion and Politics in Contemporary Iran* (Albany, NY: State University of New York Press, 1980); also Majid Tehranian, "Khomeini's Doctrine of Legitimacy," in Anthony J. Parel and Ronald C. Keith, eds., *Comparative Political Philosophy* (Lanham, MD: Lexington Press, 2003), 217–43.

17. For some instructive comments on this point compare Emad El-Din Aysha, "Foucault's Iran and Islamic Identity Politics Beyond Civilizational Clashes, External and Internal," *International Studies Perspectives*, vol. 7 (November 2006), 377–94; also Roy Mottahedeh, *The Mantle of the Prophet: Religion and Politics in Iran* (New York: Simon & Schuster, 1985).

Chapter 10

1. Raymond D. Boisvert, *John Dewey: Rethinking Our Time* (Albany, NY: State University of New York Press, 1998), 51–52. Compare also Isaiah Berlin, *Four Essays on Liberty* (London, UK: Oxford University Press, 1977); and for a critique Charles Taylor, "What's Wrong With Negative Liberty?" in Alan Ryan, ed., *The Idea of Freedom: Essays in Honor of Isaiah Berlin* (Oxford, UK: Oxford University Press, 1979), 175–93.

2. See Robert A. Dahl, *A Preface to Democratic Theory* (Chicago: University of Chicago Press, 1956), 2, 18–19. To Dahl's credit, one has to acknowledge that he stressed not only formal procedural limits but also "inherent social checks and balances." He also refers (22, 82–83) to an "underlying consensus on policy" existing "prior to politics." But the origin of this consensus is not disclosed.

3. Giovanni Sartori, *The Theory of Democracy Revisited* (Chatham, NJ: Chatham House Publ., 1987), vol. 1, 12–13, 17–18, 241–42; vol. 2, 476–77.

4. William H. Riker, *Liberalism Against Populism: A Confrontation Between the Theory of Democracy and the Theory of Social Choice* (Prospective Heights, IL: Waveland Press, 1982), 1–3.

5. *Liberalism Against Populism*, 7, 9–12, 246.

6. See Boisvert, *John Dewey*, 58. Compare also Jo Ann Boydston, ed., *John Dewey: The Later Works: 1925–1953* (Carbondale & Edwardsville, IL: Southern Illinois University Press, 1981–90), vol. 2, 328; and John Winthrop, "A Model of Christian Charity" (1630), in Robert Bellah et al., eds., *Individualism and Commitment in American Life* (New York: Harper & Row, 1987), 21–27.

7. Mohandas K. Gandhi, *Hind Swaraj and Other Writings*, ed. Anthony J. Parel (Cambridge, UK: Cambridge University Press, 1997), 30–37.

8. *Hind Swaraj*, 42–43, 67, 73.

9. These and similar statements are collected in the "Supplementary Writings" attached by Parel to his edition of *Hind Swaraj*, 149–50, 171, 185. The sources can be found in *The Collected Works of Mahatma Gandhi* (New Delhi: Government of India, 1958–1989), vol. 75, 146–47; vol. 76, 339–401; vol. 81,

319–21. By "their (own) poets and teachers" Gandhi seems to refer to some of his favorite Western authors like Thoreau, Ruskin, and Tolstoy.

10. See "Supplementary Writings" in *Hind Swaraj*, 155, 189. Taken from *The Collected Works of Mahatma Gandhi*, vol. 85, 32–33, and Jawaharlal Nehru, *A Bunch of Old Letters* (London, UK: Asia Publishing House, 1958), 512.

11. Ramashray Roy, *Self and Society: A Study in Gandhian Thought* (New Delhi: Sage Publications India, 1984), 78. A similar point is made by Bhikhu Parekh in his stellar text *Gandhi* (Oxford, UK: Oxford University Press, 1997), 75–76: "For Gandhi *swaraj* referred to a state of affairs in which individuals were morally in control of themselves and ran their lives in such a way that they needed no external coercion. . . . For Gandhi, *swaraj* thus presupposed self-discipline, self-restraint, a sense of mutual responsibility, the disposition neither to dominate nor be dominated by others, and a sense of *dharma*."

12. Roy, *Self and Society*, 63, 189–90. The possibility of a transformative freedom was actually acknowledged by Isaiah Berlin; but he confined this mode narrowly to mystical or ascetic lifestyles—a confinement aptly criticized by Roy (186–87).

13. Ronald J. Terchek, "Gandhi and Democratic Theory," in Thomas Pantham and Kenneth L. Deutsch, eds., *Political Thought in Modern India* (New Delhi: Sage, 1986), 308. The citation is from M. K. Gandhi, ed., *Non-Violence in Peace and War*, vol. 1 (Ahmedabad: Navajivan, 1948), 269.

14. Terchek, "Gandhi and Democratic Theory," 309, 312. See also Ronald Duncan, *Selected Writings of Mahatma Gandhi* (Boston, MA: Beacon Press, 1951), 78–79.

15. Terchek, "Gandhi and Democratic Theory," 317–19.

16. Thomas Pantham, "Beyond Liberal Democracy: Thinking with Mahatma Gandhi," in Pantham and Deutsch, eds., *Political Thought in Modern India*, 334, 337–39. The citations are from *Harijan* (March 31, 1946) in Gandhi, *Democracy: Real and Deceptive*, comp. R. K. Prabhu (Ahmedabad: Navajivan, 1961), 32; and *Harijan* (May 8, 1937), 98.

17. Tu Weiming, *Confucian Thought: Selfhood as Creative Transformation* (Albany, NY: State University of New York Press, 1985), 59, 76–77. Regarding transformative freedom, he adds (78), in a passage critical of modern Western liberalism: "Historically, the emergence of individualism as a motivating force in Western society may have been intertwined with highly particularized political, economic, ethical, and religious traditions. It seems reasonable that one can endorse an insight into the self as a basis for equality and liberty without accepting Locke's idea of private property, Adam Smith's and Hobbes's idea of private interest, John Stuart Mill's idea of privacy, Kierkegaard's idea of loneliness, or the early Sartre's idea of [radical] freedom."

18. *Confucian Thought*, 175.

19. See Tu Weiming, "The Creative Tension Between *Jen* and *Li*," in his *Humanity and Self-Cultivation: Essays in Confucian Thought* (Berkeley, CA: Asian Humanities Press, 1979), 6; also Confucius, *The Analects*, 12:1. Regarding the relation between Confucianism and pragmatism compare David L. Hall and Roger T. Ames, *Thinking Through Confucius* (Albany, NY: State University of

New York Press, 1987), 15: "If contemporary comparative philosophic activity is any indication, it might be the pragmatic philosophies associated with Peirce, James, Dewey, and Mead, and extended toward process philosophy such as that of A. N. Whitehead, that can serve as the best resource for philosophical concepts and doctrines permitting responsible access to Confucius' thought."

20. Ni Peinim, "Confucianism and Democracy: Water and Fire? Water and Oil? Or Water and Fish? In Defense of Henry Rosemont's View," in Marthe Chandler and Ronnie Littlejohn, eds., *Polishing the Chinese Mirror: Essays in Honor of Henry Rosemont, Jr.* (New York: Global Scholarly Publications, 2008), 90.

21. Wm. Theodore deBary, *The Trouble with Confucianism* (Cambridge, MA: Harvard University Press, 1991), 103–8.

22. Liu Shu-hsien, "From the People-as-the-Root to Democracy" (in Chinese); quoted from Ni Peinim, "Confucianism and Democracy," 99.

23. Henry Rosemont Jr., *A Chinese Mirror: Moral Reflections on Political Economy and Society* (La Salle, IL: Open Court, 1991), 93.

24. Rosemont, *A Chinese Mirror*, 93; also his "Whose Rights? Which Democracy?" in *Confucianism and Liberalism* (Beijing: Sanlian Shudian, 2001), section 5 (in Chinese). I am following here Ni Peinim's account in his "Confucianism and Democracy," 93–94.

25. See Christopher S. Queen and Sallie B. King, eds., *Engaged Buddhism: Buddhist Liberation Movements in Asia* (Albany, NY: State University of New York Press, 1996). Among the most notable "engaged" Buddhists are Thich Nhat Hanh, Buddhadasa Bhikhu, Sulak Sivaraksa, and the Dalai Lama.

26. *Reason, Freedom, and Democracy in Islam: Essential Writings of Abdolkarim Soroush*, trans. and ed. Mahmud Sadri and Ahmad Sadri (New York: Oxford University Press, 2000), 99, 103. See also Muhammad Iqbal, *The Reconstruction of Religious Thought in Islam* (Lahore: Ashraf, 1971); Abdulaziz A. Sachedina, *The Islamic Roots of Democratic Pluralism* (New York: Oxford University Press, 2001); Khaled Abou El Fadl, *Islam and the Challenge of Democracy* (Princeton, NJ: Princeton University Press, 2004); M. A. Muqtedar Khan, ed., *Islamic Democratic Discourse* (Lanham, MD: Lexington Books, 2006); Lahouari Addi, *Islam et démocratie* (Paris: Seuil, 2003); John L. Esposito, *Islam and Democracy* (New York: Oxford University Press, 1996); Timothy D. Sisk, *Islam and Democracy: Religion, Politics, and Power in the Middle East* (Washington, DC: United States Institute of Peace Press, 1992); and Richard W. Bulliet, ed., *Under Siege: Islam and Democracy* (New York: Columbia University Press, 1994).

27. Michael J. Sandel, *Public Philosophy: Essays on Morality and Politics* (Cambridge, MA: Harvard University Press, 2005), 9–11, 27, 33.

28. Walter Lippman, *The Good Society* (1936; New York: Grosset & Dunlap, 1943), 194, 237, 346–47. See also my "Introduction" to *In Search of the Good Life: A Pedagogy for Troubled Times* (Lexington, KY: University of Kentucky Press, 2007), 2–8.

29. Boisvert, *John Dewey*, 68.

30. Dewey, "Democracy is Radical" (1937), in *John Dewey: The Later Works: 1925–1953*, vol. 11, 298; and "Reconstruction in Philosophy" (1920), in *John Dewey: The Middle Works: 1899–1924*, ed. Jo Ann Boydston (Carbondale, IL: Southern Illinois University, 1981), vol. 12, 186.

31. Dewey, "Creative Democracy—The Task Before Us" (1939), in *John Dewey: The Later Works, 1925–1953*, vol. 14, 228. See also Richard J. Bernstein, "John Dewey on Democracy: The Task Before Us," in his *Philosophical Profiles: Essays in a Pragmatic Mode* (Philadelphia, PA: University of Pennsylvania Press, 1986), 260–72.

Appendix A

1. Bernard Flynn, *The Philosophy of Claude Lefort: Interpreting the Political* (Evanston, IL: Northwestern University Press, 2005).

2. Flynn, *Political Philosophy at the Closure of Metaphysics* (Atlantic Highland, NJ & New York: Humanities Press, 1992).

Appendix B

1. Chantal Mouffe, *The Return of the Political* (London, UK: Verso, 1993). Compare also her *The Democratic Paradox* (London: Verso, 2000), and *On the Political* (London: Verso, 2005). Page numbers in the above text refer to *The Return of the Political*.

2. See Mouffe, ed., *Gramsci and Marxist Theory* (Boston, MA: Routledge & Kegan Paul, 1979); Mouffe, ed., *Dimensions of Radical Democracy: Pluralism, Citizenship, Community* (London, UK: Verso, 1992; and Ernesto Laclau and Chantal Mouffe, *Hegemony, and Socialist Strategy: Towards a Radical Democratic Politics*, trans. Winston Moore and Paul Cammack (London, UK: Verso, 1985). The latter text is discussed extensively in chapter 6, this volume.

Appendix C

1. On John Dewey see chapter 3, this volume. Regarding Walter Lippmann, see especially his *The Good Society* (1936; New York: Grosset & Dunlap, 1943); also my "Introduction" to *In Search of the Good Life: A Pedagogy for Troubled Times* (Lexington, KY: University of Kentucky Press, 2007), 1–20. Compare also C. B. Macpherson, *The Real World of Democracy* (Oxford, UK: Clarendon Press, 1966) and *The Life and Times of Liberal Democracy* (Oxford: Oxford University Press, 1977).

2. Daniel A. Bell, *Beyond Liberal Democracy: Political Thinking for an East Asian Context* (Princeton, NJ: Princeton University Press, 2006). In the following, page numbers refer to this book.

3. See Ronald Dworkin, *Is Democracy Possible Here? Principles for a New Political Debate* (Princeton, NJ: Princeton University Press, 2006).

4. Compare in this context Abdullahi A. An-Na'im, ed., *Human Rights in Cross-Cultural Perspective: A Quest for Consensus* (Philadelphia, PA: University of Pennsylvania Press, 1992).

5. The text has little or nothing to say about "deliberative democracy" and only offers a few negative comments on "republicanism" or republican democracy, mainly because of its support for active citizenship. As Bell writes (150): "The republican tradition will likely seem problematic for members of modern-day liberal Western societies for whom, in Charles Taylor's words, 'the affirmation of ordinary life' has assumed greater importance. In East Asian societies with a Confucian heritage . . . the republican tradition is so far removed from people's self-understanding that it is a complete nonstarter." Somewhat grudgingly, the text concedes (150, n. 119) a certain affinity between Sun Yat-Sen and republicanism.

6. In this context (83, n. 90), Bell criticizes my work for leaning toward universal dialogue—a critique which seems to ignore my on rejection of a "spurious universality" in favor of "a more genuine universalism" respectful of differences. As Bell himself adds: "I do not mean to imply that cross-cultural dialogue and comparative theorizing should not be done (quite the opposite), but my aim would be to identify areas of justifiable moral difference" (which precisely also is my aim).

7. Compare also this statement in the closing chapter (328): "The founding fathers of Confucianism . . . believed that their theories were universalizable; they were not intended only for one culture." The point is made even more forcefully in one of Bell's more recent writings: "What makes [the works of Confucius and Mencius] classics is precisely that they provide resources for thinking about morally relevant concerns in different times and places. . . . Certain Confucian values can and should be taken seriously in Western societies." See Daniel A. Bell, ed., *Confucian Political Ethics* (Princeton, NJ: Princeton University Press, 2008), xi–xii.

8. The stress on "minimal democracy" makes Bell curiously an ally of devotees of "rational choice" (who completely dismiss ethical considerations, Confucian or otherwise). As it happens, I have myself proposed a similar bicameral arrangement, but in the case of Iran. See my "Religion, Democracy, and Iran: A Modest-Proposal," *Comparative Studies of South Asia, Africa and the Middle East*, vol. 27 (2007), 503–8, reprinted in a revised and expanded version in chapter 9, this volume.

9. In a very instructive fashion, Wm. Theodore deBary has presented traditional East Asian thought as a multicultural dialogue involving mainly Confucianism, Buddhism, and Daoism (and more recently Western liberalism and Marxism). See his *East Asian Civilizations: A Dialogue in Five Stages* (Cambridge, MA: Harvard University Press, 1988). To be sure, in our time, the traditional "Three Teachings" need to be supplemented by acknowledgement of the role of Marxism (Maoism), liberalism, and conservatism.

10. Regarding the multiple strands of democracy as seen from a global perspective, compare, e.g., D.L. Sheth and Ashis Nandy, eds., *The Multiverse of Democracy* (New Delhi: Sage Pubications, 1996), and Seyla Benhabib, ed., *Democracy and Difference: Contesting the Boundaries of the Political* (Princeton, NJ: Princeton University Press, 1996).

Index